Child Language Development:
Learning to Talk

Child Language Development: Learning to Talk

Sandra Bochner, Penny Price and Jane Jones

School of Education, Macquarie University
Sydney, Australia

with Christine A Hardman

Whurr Publishers Ltd
London

Whurr Publishers Ltd
19b Compton Terrace, London N1 2UN, England

Reprinted 1998

British Library Cataloguing in Publication Data
A catalogue record for this book is available from the
British Library.

ISBN: 1 86156 040 0

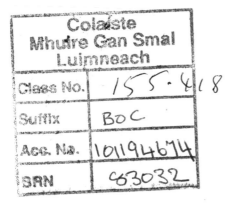
Printed and bound in the UK by Athenaeum Press Ltd,
Gateshead, Tyne & Wear

Contents

Foreword

The development of language in young children may be viewed from a variety of perspectives, ranging from the purely philosophical to the political. Current interest in the field, however, can be related to a more limited number of problem areas. These include the psychology of language development per se and its centrality in the study of cognitive processes, the roles of normal language in relation to education and socialisation, the development of early childhood education as a means of preventing later social disadvantage and the remediation of language deficiencies with pathological origins. In each of these areas, the issue of whether language development can be accelerated, enhanced or, in some cases, actually taught is of profound significance. An enormous volume of research, often undertaken on an interdisciplinary basis, has arisen from these questions and child caring and teaching strategies have been based upon its findings. This book by Sandra Bochner and her colleagues is an excellent example of how such research and development can be translated into practice.

Although an understanding of how to teach linguistic and other cognitive skills is of obvious interest to those working in the field of early childhood education, to other professionals and, of course, to parents, progress in this area has, nevertheless, a more general social significance that concerns the provision of high-quality child care. Women are increasingly involved in full- or part-time work from home rather than being restricted to the tasks of housekeeping and child rearing. Moreover, whatever its origins, single parenthood is widespread and the traditional family structure, which offers a stable background through the presence of both biological parents, is becoming less common; indeed, its desirability is often questioned. The result of these changes in social practices has been a widespread, although often unfulfilled, demand for day care of all kinds. Such a problem is by no means new of course, but the situation has changed markedly in that access to such care is almost seen as a right, irrespective of parental circumstances. In addition, it is assumed that young children should be in the care of well-trained staff, the emphasis being placed upon the quality of their daily experiences rather than upon the provision of a facility for basic child minding. Inevitably, the development of normal language and communication skills has been given high priority in the programmes provided in the different forms of child care now available for families.

Sandra Bochner, Penny Price and Jane Jones have produced this book as their contribution to our understanding of language development, its implications for child-rearing practices, and the provision of high quality care. I must say that its appearance gives me considerable pleasure. In addition to its reference to contemporary theory and research, the book reflects an impressive and, in some ways, unique set of experiences in operating early childhood language programmes. Over the last 20 years or so the authors must have spent many thousands of hours observing parent – child interaction and other forms of social interaction, and have also participated in the development and establishment of early language programmes both in Australia and in countries within the Pacific rim.

It has been interesting for me to reflect upon the origins of the approach taken in this research. In the mid-1970s there was a movement away from operant models of psycholinguistic development which, along with data from the study of grammatical forms, had been dominant for the previous two decades. This was paralleled by a similar swing towards cognitivism in general psychology. A problem was that the operant model, apart from any conceptual limitations, could neither account adequately for the complexities of normal language development, nor was it of much use in generating language programmes – except at a very rudimentary level. It came, therefore, to be supplanted by transactional models based upon the study of pragmatic forms; in other words the natural use of language in social interactions. Some reference to these changes is made in Chapter 1 which contains a useful concise account of the relevant theory and research.

The main purpose and strength of this book, however, lies in a sequential analysis of language development that allows the authors to provide a range of practical suggestions at each stage. Transactional models of language teaching focus upon the child's intentions or motivation to produce language and the use of naturally occurring social situations to elicit and elaborate upon his or her utterances and reciprocal communication such as turn-taking, in which the child is an active agent. The techniques, as depicted in this book, are flexible, capitalising on the child's love of play and willingness to practise new skills; most of the suggestions, indeed, sound like real fun! Even so, the approach calls for sound preparation in recognising the situations or 'scripts' that are likely to be productive of natural language, providing practice in a variety of settings and capitalising upon opportunities to promote more complex linguistic forms. Many such opportunities occur during play but it is recognised that some children (and parents) may have to be taught the necessary play skills.

The main substance of the book is contained in Part 2, Chapters 5–10, which first describe how to design and organise a programme, working through the beginnings of language to more complex utterances. At each of the five levels identified, the procedure involves observation and an assessment of present performance, the implementation of practical teaching suggestions and, finally, checks upon progress. Most parents, teachers and care-givers will find much to interest and inform them in these sections of the book. The five chapters of Part 3 deal with a wide range of issues in implementation including a chapter on phonological development by Christine Hardman, a speech pathologist, and an unexpected section on the potential use of signing with language-delayed children – always a controversial issue! Chapter 14 describes the authors' experience with the Laurel House Early Language Programme, upon which much of the book's content is based, and provides some illustrative data on the programme's effectiveness. It perhaps underestimates the considerable impact programmes such as that at Laurel House have had upon the techniques of early childhood teaching. Chapter 15, on working with children from bilingual backgrounds contains some excellent points. The eight appendices contain most of the materials necessary for implementation of a transactional-type programme, together with details of useful resources.

I believe that *Child Language Development: Learning to Talk* is an accurate reflection of much current work in the area of early language teaching and a very useful compendium of appropriate methodology and materials. Its most striking feature, however, is the obvious wealth of experience, experimentation and analysis that emerges on every page. It is clearly written, and it is pleasing to note that the authors have managed to avoid the use of excessive technical language without trivialising the account. This will certainly commend it to many! They are to be congratulated for producing a well-informed, useful and, hopefully, influential book that should attract a wide readership.

James Ward,
formerly Foundation Professor of Special Education and Director,
Centre for Research into Special Education and Rehabilitation,
Macquarie University, Sydney, Australia
April, 1997

Introduction

This book is about language acquisition. Its specific focus is on young children who experience difficulties in early communication. Among the many skills that children must acquire during the first few years of life, language is one of the most important and the most difficult. Problems can be encountered as a result of a variety of factors, including those that the child brings to the learning task such as a limited attention span, a hearing problem or difficulties in fine movement of lips and tongue, and those associated with the context in which the child is acquiring language, such as lack of opportunity to hear good language models or to take part in conversation-like exchanges with familiar adults.

Most children learn to talk in the years prior to school entry. However, a small number experience difficulties and this can sometimes result in extreme frustration both for the child and his or her family. Children need to learn to communicate, to express their feelings, to convey ideas and information, to interact socially with adults and other children. Once they enter school, their language skills become the building blocks for learning to read and write. The early acquisition of appropriate language skills does not guarantee later success in learning at school. However, initial poor development is often difficult to overcome, so it is important to ensure that assistance is given as early as possible to children who are encountering difficulties in the early stages of language development, or to those who are known to be at risk for problems in the area of language.

Since the early 1970s there has been a dramatic increase in knowledge about the processes involved in children's acquisition of language. Much of this expansion resulted from the work of psycholinguists such as Brown (1973), Bruner (1976), Halliday (1975) and Nelson (1973), who extended the work of linguists to explore cognitive, social and emotional aspects of the language acquisition process. These developments occurred at a time when McVicker Hunt had already challenged the notion that intelligence was fixed from birth (Hunt, 1961) and Bloom (1964) had documented the rapid rate of cognitive development during the early childhood years and the effect of experience on this process. Piaget's studies had also emphasised the importance of the environment and of the active role of the child in early cognitive development.

Recognition of the significance of early experience for children's subsequent development led to the concept of early compensatory education as a means of offsetting the negative impact of social and environmental disadvantage on children's progress at school (Chazan, Laing and Jackson, 1971). In England, local education authority (LEA) nursery schools and classes provided programmes for some children from socially disadvantaged backgrounds. In the USA, Headstart programmes, introduced in 1964, provided compensatory educational experiences to socially disadvantaged, primarily inner-urban, black children in the period immediately prior to school entry. From 1972, following recognition that children with disabilities would also benefit from these programmes, legislation was enacted that required that at least 10% of the children who enrolled in these compensatory educational programmes should be handicapped. At about this time, early education programmes were also being established in the USA for groups of children with specific handicaps, including children with Down syndrome (Hayden and Dimitriev, 1975) and children with severe visual impairments (Fraiberg, Smith and Adelson, 1969). These programmes were characterised by a consistent, structured approach to teaching with clearly defined objectives and parental involvement in planning and decision-making (Pieterse, 1988). They provided a model for exemplary early intervention services for children with disabilities, which were imitated in the United Kingdom, Canada, Australia and other developed and developing countries. It was within this context, in Australia, that the language programme described in this book was developed.

About the language programme

The programme described here is derived from a theoretical model that assumes that early language skills are acquired through children's meaningful and active involvement with people, objects and events in their environment. According to this view, cognitive, social and linguistic aspects of children's experiences contribute to early language development. It is argued that 'first words' emerge out of children's earliest experiences with adults, particularly in situations that provide opportunities for infants to observe their carers' faces and listen to their voices. During routine activities and simple games, adults' facial expressions and the intonation of their voices encourage infant attention and engagement. Over time, infants learn both the actions and sounds associated with daily routines and familiar games and, eventually, begin to take an active as well as a passive role in the social exchanges that are embedded in these events. These experiences provide children with opportunities to begin to produce sounds intentionally, to communicate specific, if primitive, meanings with familiar interactive partners. These are the contexts in which most children acquire language and they provide a model for the intervention ideas proposed here.

The language programme outlined in this book comprises a set of procedures that can be used to assess children's current language skills and, using this information, to design a series of activities and experiences that will increase their level of communicative competence. Teaching ideas are organised around a developmental sequence that moves from the prerequisite skills of taking part in a joint activity within a shared context to the more complex skills of asking and answering questions. Suggestions are made to help children progress through these levels. Other issues, such as the place of signing and the needs of children whose language backgrounds are other than English, are also explored.

How can the book be used?

The book was written for use by early childhood teachers, nursery nurses, special education teachers, speech and language therapists, speech pathologists and other professionals working with young children with language difficulties. It may also be useful for parents who have a child who is slow in acquiring language. It is suitable for use in initial training and professional development programmes in the areas of special education, early childhood education and care, and speech and language therapy or pathology. Procedures are described that can be used to facilitate the acquisition of early language and communication skills in young children with developmental delays and learning difficulties, either through direct intervention or by working with parents who will implement language development procedures at home.

Language activities can be carried out in one-to-one situations, with professionals working directly with a child in a clinical context, or supporting a parent who is implementing ideas from the programme at home. Alternatively, programmes can be implemented for individual children within group settings such as an early childhood programme, a child-care centre or a special education classroom. In these contexts, language goals can be practised with the child individually or within group activities that provide opportunities for specific language objectives to be implemented with a specific child or group of children.

Which children will benefit from the language programme?

The procedures described in the following chapters were designed for use with any child who is not talking at a level appropriate for his or her age. The programme can be implemented with children who are having problems because of learning disabilities, developmental delay or intellectual impairment. Teaching ideas can be implemented using a language other than English. They should facilitate the acquisition of early communication and speech in children who have little or no expressive language, or who are just beginning to put two words together. The programme is *not* designed for children who have adequate language skills but are experiencing difficulties in specific aspects of language development such as pronunciation and morphology.

The approach to language development that underlies the procedures described in this book has been described as *interactional* or *transactional*. According to this view, children acquire language through interaction with familiar adults, usually their mothers or other consistent carers, who engage the children in shared activities within familiar contexts. During such exchanges, adults provide clear models of appropriate language that children, in time, learn to imitate and then use meaningfully. If the transactional view of language acquisition is accepted, then failure to acquire early language skills can be explained, in part, as a failure to acquire the skills needed to interact successfully with others. This can result from factors associated with the interactional context, or those inherent in the child. Factors associated with the context may include:

- Limited opportunity to participate in interactive exchanges with adults. The child's usual adult carer may be too busy or too preoccupied with other problems or responsibilities to provide the child with sufficient opportunities for interaction. Such opportunities occur most naturally during daily routines such as feeding, bathing and dressing.
- Lack of consistent adult partners. If the caring figure changes too often, the child may not have time to build up the set of interactive routines, shared with a familiar adult, that provide the basis for language acquisition.
- Lack of recurring experiences with adults. The child's daily routines may change too often, as when a child is frequently moved from one setting to another, so that there is little continuity in his or her daily experiences.
- Provision of poor language models. These can include adult speech that is too complex or too fast or where there is more than one language spoken. Many children do learn to speak in spite of such difficulties. However, the presence of other inhibiting factors may compound the child's difficulties and contribute to problems in acquiring appropriate language skills.

Factors associated with the child may include:

- Lack of skills that are necessary to enable the child to participate in relevant activities. This can involve a very short attention span or an inability to attend to salient aspects of a situation, as when a child looks at a trivial part of a picture in a book, such as a leaf on a tree, rather than attending to the main topic which is a boy fishing.
- Inability to initiate. The child may not be aware that he or she can cause events to occur or that he or she can act independently. A concept of the self as 'me' may not yet have been acquired. Once the child demonstrates the capacity to take both roles in a game like 'Peek-a-boo', acting as either the surpriser or the more passive surprised, then you can assume that the concept of 'me' has been learned.
- The presence of a disability that interferes with the child's effective participation in social interaction. This can include mild to severe, or fluctuating, sensory impairments (primarily visual and auditory), restriction of movement arising from a physical handicap, or any intellectually disabling condition.

About this book

The book comprises 15 chapters and, for convenience, is divided into three parts. Part 1 comprises the first four chapters and provides a background to the language teaching ideas presented in later chapters of the book. The theoretical context in which the language programme was developed is described in Chapter 1. Chapter 2 gives an overview of the developmental sequence followed by most children as they acquire language skills. Chapter 3 explores the language contexts in which children are engaged during the day, exploring both daily routines and play as important elements in the process of acquiring language. The way adults talk to children has a significant role in children's language acquisition and some of the strategies that they can use to help children learn to talk are reviewed in Chapter 4.

The language programme is outlined in the six chapters that comprise Part 2 of the book. The first chapter in this section, Chapter 5, gives an overview of the steps to be followed in starting a language programme. The five levels of the language programme are described in the remaining chapters in Part 2 (Chapters 6–10). Each chapter sets out details of procedures for assessing a child's current level of communication and for extending these skills using appropriate teaching strategies. Chapter 6 focuses on the preliminary skills that are the first steps in learning to talk (Programme Level 1). Chapter 7 looks at children's skills at the point when they begin to communicate, using sounds, gestures and idiosyncratic words (Programme Level 2). The single-word stage is explored in Chapter 8 (Programme Level 3). Early sentences are discussed in Chapter 9 (Programme Levels 4 and 5) and ways of helping children to use their language skills effectively (pragmatics or communicative intentions) are considered in Chapter 10.

Part 3 includes the final five chapters. Children's phonological development, the production of speech sounds, is described in Chapter 11. Suggestions are made here for helping to improve the intelligibility of speech. For some children, consistent hand gestures or signing can be used in the early stages of acquisition to supplement speech that is not readily intelligible. This issue is considered in Chapter 12.

Those who are working with groups of children will find Chapter 13 particularly useful. It is concerned with the implementation of language objectives for individual children in situations such as a preschool or crèche, where many children are present and one-to-one interaction is difficult to arrange. Chapter 14 focuses on procedures developed within an intervention programme that assisted parents to implement language-development activities at home.

The ideas presented in this book are based on experiences gained through this community-based programme. Resource materials developed for use with parents attending the language programme, including information sheets, assessment protocols and record forms, are appended. Those working with children whose home language is other than English will be interested in the issues examined in Chapter 15.

Child Language Development: Learning to Talk is intended to be a practical guide for those interested in helping children who are experiencing difficulties in language acquisition. It is not necessary to read all the chapters sequentially, although this will provide the clearest understanding of the language programme. Information about the theories that provide a background to the language teaching ideas suggested here can be found in Part 1 of the book (Chapters 1–3). The final chapter in this section, Chapter 4, is concerned with how adults talk to children and is particularly important for anyone working directly with a child. We urge all our readers to study this chapter.

Readers who are primarily interested in finding ways to help a particular child might focus on the six chapters that comprise Part 2. Chapter 5 provides an overview of the main features of a language programme. Such readers should then look at each of the chapters that describe the five levels of the language programme (Chapters 6–10) and decide the level that the child has reached. Some suggestions to help with this decision are included in Chapter 5. Readers who are uncertain should begin with Chapter 6, which is concerned with the early skills that underlie language acquisition. The skills described here are crucial for later development, so it is a good idea to check that the child can do the types of activities discussed in this chapter.

Special education teachers, speech and language therapists or pathologists, and early childhood teachers or carers will be interested in all the sections of the book. However, the chapters in Part 3 (Chapters 11–15) were written specifically for professionals involved in language intervention activities.

The language programme presented here is based on ideas included in an earlier publication on language intervention (Bochner, Price and Salamon, 1988). These ideas were strongly influenced by the theoretical work of McLean and Snyder-McLean who developed the transactional model of language acquisition (McLean and Snyder-McLean, 1978) and by MacDonald and his associates at the Nisonger Center, Ohio State University, who were instrumental in translating theory into practice through their programme 'Ready, Set, Go; Talk to Me' (Horstmeier and MacDonald, 1978). The contribution of these sources to the ideas set out in this book is acknowledged. We are grateful for permission to reproduce selected signs from the book *Sign It and Say It: A Manual of New South Wales (Australian) Signs for Use with the Revised Makaton Vocabulary Adapted for Use in Australia at Stockton Hospital, NSW, for Communication with Intellectually Handicapped Residents* (Cooney and Knox, 1980).

Part 1
Background to the Language Programme

The purpose of this part of the book is to provide a general introduction to the theories and research data that have influenced the ideas about language development presented in later chapters. In selecting goals and strategies for helping children to acquire early language skills it is important to have some understanding of the explanations of language development that have influenced work in this field. It is also important to have some knowledge of the results of relevant research.

Since the 1960s there has been considerable expansion of interest, particularly among linguists, psychologists and educators, in the processes that underlie the emergence of speech in very young children. Much of the research that has been reported has focused on developing language in children whose communication skills are delayed or disordered in some way. Most children acquire language very rapidly. Data derived from studies of emerging communication skills in children whose development is less rapid are particularly useful because they provide researchers with opportunities to explore and begin to understand the factors, both within the child and within the child's environment, that facilitate language acquisition. Knowledge derived from these studies has been particularly useful for those wishing to help children experiencing difficulties in acquiring effective language skills. It was within this context that the language programme outlined in later parts of this book evolved.

Chapter 1
Explanations for Language Development in Children

What is language? How do children learn to talk? Why do some children have difficulty in learning to use words? These are some of the issues that are discussed in this chapter.

Before you begin to help a young child to communicate more effectively, you need to know something about the term 'language' and the theories that have been proposed to explain its development.

What is language?

What is meant by the term 'language'? How does it relate to words like 'communication' and 'speech'? It is generally accepted that the term 'communication' refers to the process whereby information, ideas and messages are transmitted between people. In a very general sense, roads, cars and aeroplanes, as well as telephones, radio, television, books and newspapers are part of our system of communication. Roadside signs and symbols such as a red cross, a church spire or a McDonald's big M communicate a message to those who understand the meaning of the symbol. A scream or cry of pain is usually understood by anyone who hears the sound. A touch or smile can also convey a message of sympathy or understanding. Communication in a very simple and direct form can occur without a formal language, without words. It involves the transfer of some message, or meaning, from one person or group of people to others.

Language is one form of communication. It involves an organised system of signs or symbols that are used by a group of people to share meaning between themselves. The signs or symbols can take the form of voiced sounds, written symbols or, for people with very poor hearing or vision, hand movements or raised dots as in sign language and Braille. Language in an oral form involves the use of speech.

All formal language systems, such as English, German, Mandarin or Hindi, have four main components:

- *Use* (pragmatics), function or purpose: what we want to do when we communicate. Some examples include uses to: attract attention ('look!'), obtain information ('how far?'), protest ('No. I don't want to!') or show ownership ('my ball!').
- *Meaning* (semantics) or the intended topic of communication. This may be represented in words (spoken or written) or through gestures, hand movements or symbols that represent the objects, events or experiences that we want to communicate about.
- *Rules* (syntax and morphology) or the grammatical system that defines ways of combining words to convey meaning. For example, the expression 'Mummy washed the red cup' is meaningful because the words are combined according to accepted rules, whereas 'cup red washed Mummy' is less clear because the words are not combined in an order that is grammatically correct. Meaning is also conveyed through the way a word is formed. For example, final consonants are added: to indicate plurality ('one hat, two hats'), to indicate possession ('the girl's ball'), to indicate tense ('the boy jumped').
- *Sounds* (phonology) or the mechanisms by which intended meaning is conveyed to others. This may involve use of the voice to produce speech sounds, or a pen or pencil to write strings of letters to form words on paper. Alternatively, hand movements may be used to convey meaning through sign language. For example, if a precise meaning is to be conveyed by both speech and writing, then a specific set of sounds (phonemes) and letters (graphemes) must be selected to go with that meaning, as in:

'd' + 'o' + 'g'

or   =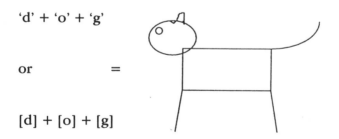

[d] + [o] + [g]

In planning a language programme for children, we need to take account of these four aspects of language. Initially, children must learn that they can communicate meaning to another person using their own sounds, gestures and body language. For example, they need to understand that they can attract attention or obtain assistance to reach a toy by using sounds like 'oo-oo' or gestures such as pointing. Later, they will replace these primitive forms of communication with words. Once they have begun to use words intelligibly they will learn to combine these words according to the rules of their language group. When they reach this stage and can produce simple two- or three-word sentences it can be claimed that they have acquired the beginnings of a language system.

When thinking about the problems that a child is having in learning to talk, it is necessary to consider each of these aspects of language as a possible source of the difficulty. For example:

- *Use* (pragmatics). Has the child learned to use sounds, words, gestures or body language to communicate specific meanings to others, such as to protest, obtain help or attract attention? (See Chapter 10.)
- *Meaning* (semantics). Does the child understand that messages, including requests, comments and complaints, can be conveyed to others through voiced sounds, gestures, words and other means? (See Chapter 8.)
- *Rules* (syntax and morphology). Are the child's words combined correctly to make meaningful sentences? Can the child modify words appropriately to indicate meanings such as tense, as in 'I fell down', or possession, as in 'Daddy's car'? (See Chapter 9.)
- *Sounds* (phonology). Are the words intelligible? Are they produced in a form that can be understood by others? (See Chapter 11.)

Background to the language programme

In order to help children acquire appropriate language skills, some understanding of the processes involved in learning to talk is needed. Ideas for intervention are likely to be most effective if they are based on a theory, or explanation, of how language develops and on information from relevant research. The theoretical background and some of the research findings that influenced the language programme described in this book are reviewed below.

Various accounts of how children learn to talk have been proposed. These different explanations can be compared in terms of the relative weight that they give to two key aspects of the language acquisition process: first, the child's innate ability or the role of brain function in language behaviour and, second, the child's environment, particularly those aspects of the social environment that enable language to be acquired. These various explanations can be classified in terms of broad descriptive categories, for example:

- *nativist*, or concerned with innate linguistic knowledge;
- *behaviourist*, or concerned with observable stimulus–response associations;
- *cognitive*, or concerned with the role of cognition or thinking processes; and

- *interactional* or *transactional*, or focused on the contribution of social interaction to the language acquisition process.

Each of these explanations is based on a different set of assumptions about how children learn to talk and why some children have difficulties. Moreover, each explanation leads to a different solution to the question of how to help a child who is having difficulties in some aspect of early communication. In the following discussion, the four explanations for language acquisition – nativist, behaviourist, cognitive and interactional – are described in terms of their underlying assumptions. Implications for facilitating children's development in terms of the four approaches are also considered. The first and third are mainly concerned with cognitive aspects of language acquisition, while the second and fourth concentrate on the role of contextual or social aspects of children's experiences in learning to talk.

Nativist or innate linguistic knowledge explanations

Some theorists (Chomsky, 1986; McNeill, 1970) have argued that learning to talk is a natural process involving an innate *language acquisition device* (LAD). According to this view, children are born with 'a number of formal and substantive linguistic mechanisms' (Cromer, 1991, p. 10), including, for example, knowledge of basic grammatical relationships or the ways in which words can be classified and combined to create meaning. The concept of a language acquisition device helps to explain the remarkable achievements of children as they acquire language. Nativists argue that the primary task faced by children is to use their innate knowledge to learn the particular language that they hear being used around them: English, Danish or whatever is spoken at home.

At the time when this argument was proposed, research into mother-infant interaction appeared to demonstrate that the speech directed to young children at home was degraded (disjointed and grammatically incomplete) and provided an inadequate language-learning model. It was suggested, therefore, that children's very rapid acquisition of complex language skills during the first three or four years of life could not be explained simply on the basis of their exposure to speech. A more satisfactory explanation involved acknowledgment of the existence of innate linguistic structures that were applied to the specific language system to which children were exposed. Evidence from cross-cultural studies of universal aspects of children's speech, such as the noun form, appeared to confirm the existence of an inborn predisposition for language. The fact that children are able to produce unique sentences that they cannot previously have heard was used as further evidence to support the argument that children have an innate capacity for language.

The remarkable linguistic achievements of children during the first years of life can be contrasted with accounts of attempts to teach language to apes. Studies such as those reported by Gardner and Gardner (1989), Patterson (1978), Premack (1976) and Savage-Rumbaugh (1986) demonstrated that while apes can be taught to communicate using plastic symbols, gestures and computer keyboards, they only produce very limited numbers of word or sign combinations and even these may have been memorised or prompted (Terrace, 1981). Overall, the amount of language that apes have learned is insignificant when compared with the language-learning achievements of even very young children. According to nativists, such language competence is best explained in terms of a genetic predisposition for language, or the language acquisition device.

However, recent studies of early language development in children (see Howe, 1993; Snow, 1995) have raised questions about the adequacy of 'innate knowledge' explanations for language development. Although it may be acknowledged that children are born with an inherent predisposition for language learning, it is argued that the process of language acquisition cannot be explained adequately by assumptions about innate capacities. Other factors, including the increasing sophistication of children's perceptual skills and their expanding cognitive and social abilities, appear to contribute to the emergence of early language behaviour. More detailed studies of adults or older children interacting with infants have also demonstrated that while the language used in these exchanges differs from that used with peers, it is not degraded, as had previously been thought, but is finely tuned to the child's level in terms of simpler syntax and vocabulary, with higher pitch and exaggerated intonation in response to the infant's vocalisations and smiles. Cross-cultural studies have also highlighted the significance of speech addressed to children in the language-acquisition process while challenging nativist claims about the universality of specific language mechanisms (Snow, 1995, p. 162).

Other criticisms of nativist explanations for language acquisition have focused on its negative view of the language potential of children with learning and other developmental difficulties on the basis that the problems experienced by such children are associated with limitations in innate abilities arising from the child's learning problems or disability. However, it must be acknowledged that biological factors contribute to language development. For example, it is argued that there is strong evidence to support the claim that 'the human face has special, species-specific visual significance for the infant from birth onwards' (Slater, 1989, p. 66). At the same time, Locke (1995) argues that the helplessness of new-born infants, coupled with the length of time that they remain helpless, ensures that they are placed in situations which involve close contact and interaction with a consistent carer, in most cases, the mother. Early discrimination of the mother or primary carer's face, voice and smell may reflect the learning competence of the new born, but may also result from *endogenous maturational processes* (Slater, 1989, p. 69). Undoubtedly, maturation contributes to the child's increasing ability to learn from exposure to language-learning experiences and endogenous or inborn factors may also influence the relative success of this process.

Behaviourist explanations

Behavioural explanations for language acquisition (Skinner, 1957; Mowrer, 1960) focus exclusively on the contribution of environmental aspects of the learner's experience. Language acquisition is explained in terms of observable phenomena. According to this view, children's behaviour is shaped by stimulus–response associations or the rewarding of appropriate behaviour. Children are encouraged to imitate the sounds they hear and to use them again by praise and other rewards. Appropriate communicative behaviour is reinforced by parents, with the child's responses shaped to achieve closer approximations to intelligible speech. Children are rewarded when they make speech-like sounds. According to Winitz (1969, cited in Ingram, 1989), acquisition begins when mothers vocalise during feeding. Following a classical conditioning model, the infant learns to associate these voiced sounds with feeding, a pleasurable event. The mother, in turn, is reinforced by the sounds made by her infant which seem, to her, to be an imitation of her own vocalising. In this way, the sounds produced by both mother and infant become mutually reinforcing. This association is strengthened when the mother rewards the baby's vocalisations, particularly those that sound adult-like, such as 'mum-mum' and 'da-da'. These experiences encourage the child further to imitate adult speech models.

Behavioural explanations for language acquisition have a positive view of the potential of intervention programmes designed to assist children with learning difficulties and delays. As a result, behavioural techniques such as shaping, modelling, imitation and reinforcement have been used to teach early language skills to children with learning difficulties and disabilities (Gray and Ryan, 1973; Kent, 1974; Stremel and Waryas, 1974). In general, these studies have shown that a behavioural approach can be used successfully to teach children to use new words. However, follow-up studies (see Garcia and De Haven, 1974; Snyder, Lovitt and Smith, 1975) have shown problems in generalisation of the children's new language. For example, the children tend to use their new skills only when they are with the language teacher, rather than spontaneously when they are away from the training situation, either at home or playing with other children.

Overall, it has been concluded that behavioural techniques can be used to teach both expressive (uttering or using language) and receptive (understanding or comprehending language) skills to children with delayed language. However, their use is limited. For example, behavioural techniques may not be effective in the very early stages of communication development when the child needs to learn that he or she can initiate contact with others. This is a particular problem with children whose difficulties are severe or profound in nature. Problems have also been encountered in ensuring the generalisation of newly trained skills to settings outside the teaching situation. These difficulties are associated with the fact that a purely behavioural approach takes no account of mental or cognitive aspects of learning. It also neglects the significance of the social relationships that are an essential component of language learning.

Behavioural techniques do, however, provide some very useful tools for those working with children who need assistance in acquiring early language. In particular, techniques such as modelling, imitation and reinforcement of desired behaviours can be used effectively in conjunction with other approaches to facilitate acquisition of specific skills during regular language-practice sessions.

Cognitive explanations

The main issue addressed by those interested in cognitive explanations for language acquisition (Bernstein, 1961; Bever, 1970; Cromer, 1991; Piaget, 1962: Vygotsky, 1986; Werner and Kaplan, 1963) concerns the relationship between developments in the areas of cognition and language. For example, does the child acquire the concept of an object before learning an appropriate label for that object? Or does the acquisition of specific words (such as 'gone') contribute, for example, to the development of the concept of object permanence? Is the attainment of a specific level of cognitive development such as Piaget's stage six (object permanence) a prerequisite for the acquisition of words? Are some cognitive abilities, such as the transfer of information from one sensory modality to another, dependent on language? To what extent is intellectual development dependent on language?

Piaget's cognitive view of language development is similar, in many respects, to that of the nativists such as Chomsky (Cattell, 1980, p. 8; Cromer, 1991, p. 14; Ingram, 1989, p. 27). For example, both Piaget and Chomsky believed that linguistic knowledge gradually becomes available to the child through heredity and maturation. However, where Chomsky emphasised the significance of an inborn 'biological clock' in this development, Piaget placed much more emphasis on the contribution of experience to the language acquisition process. Thus, whereas nativists believed that the processes underlying the development of linguistic knowledge were innate, cognitive theorists believed that the child had an active role to play in the development of cognitive structures. Both cognitive development and language acquisition were the outcome of the child's activity in exploring objects, events and people in the immediate environment. This approach suggests a very positive view of programmes designed to assist children experiencing difficulties in learning to talk, with clear implications for intervention involving manipulation of children's experiences within their social and physical worlds.

One of the issues that has concerned both practitioners and researchers in the field of language acquisition has involved identification of the developmental level or sensorimotor stage that a child has to reach in order to acquire his or her first words (Bates and Snyder, 1987; Bloom, 1970; Brown, 1973; Ingram, 1978). (The term 'sensorimotor' refers to the level of development reached by the child within the first of Piaget's stages of cognitive development, namely the sensorimotor stage. This, in turn, is divided into six substages.) Early studies suggested that the attainment of means-ends (Piaget's sensorimotor stage 5) was critical. Scales such as those developed by Uzgiris and Hunt (1975) provided a tool to assess children's cognitive level as a basis for determining eligibility for a language programme. However, subsequent research has focused more closely on other cognitive-language issues such as the specific links between cognitive and linguistic skills, as demonstrated in studies of event knowledge and language (Nelson, 1986).

Cognitively-based research on early language acquisition has focused particularly on issues such as the relationship between the acquisition of a concept and related vocabulary. For example, does concept acquisition precede lexical development? Are new words mapped onto existing concepts? Does the acquisition of a word facilitate concept learning, or is the word (a set of sounds that co-occur with instances of the concept) acquired as part of the concept? Can learning to read (recognise sound-symbol correspondences) be used to facilitate language development? Questions such as these have provided a trigger for a considerable body of research on the relationship between language and cognitive development (see Barrett, 1995; Cromer, 1991). In his review of the development of language and thought, Cromer (1991) concludes that general cognitive development is not an essential prerequisite for the acquisition of language, and that the two systems, cognitive and linguistic, develop in parallel, but independently. Shatz (1987) identifies 'bootstrapping operations' whereby children's development in one area, as in the use of a language phrase that has been heard but is not fully understood, contributes to development in another area, such as concept acquisition, by drawing children's attention to aspects of their experience that had previously been unnoticed. In this way, development in one area may facilitate or trigger progress in another. This view has influenced the development of intervention procedures to facilitate language development in children experiencing problems, with the use of strategies for mapping new language onto existing cognitive schemes, while at the same time using emerging vocabulary as a pointer for the selection and introduction of new concepts.

Interactional explanations

It is now generally accepted that children learn to talk through interaction with familiar adults. According to this explanation, language skills are acquired as children take part in routine exchanges with the adults who care for them. This process begins from the time of birth, or perhaps even earlier.

Certainly there is evidence that new-born infants have an innate predisposition towards other humans which helps to ensure that they survive an extended period of extreme helplessness. For example, from the time of birth, infants appear to be attuned to visual stimuli that are face-like – those that are moving, three-dimensional, with high contrast and involving patterns that are curved rather than straight (Slater, 1989). Studies of infants show that a neonate can recognise his/her mother's face, voice and smell (Bushnell, Sai and Mullin, 1989; DeCasper and Fifer, 1980; Lipsitt, 1977; Porter, Makin, Davis and Christensen, 1992). Early behaviours that engage adult attention through eye contact, smiling, cooing, crying and, in particular, rooting (the feeding reflex in new-born babies that causes them to turn, mouth open wide, to whatever touches the cheek) and sucking, ensure the survival of the infant and provide a trigger for contingent interaction with care-givers. Studies reported by Kaye (1982) have explored the feeding cycle of babies in terms of 'jiggle and suck' sequences; babies suck then pause, and during these breaks mothers tend to jiggle, stroke and talk to them. Debate about who controls the timing of this pattern of interaction has concluded that it is the baby, rather than the mother, as was initially thought. Clearly, babies appear to be 'pretuned' for social interaction, in terms of visual acuity and sensitivity to sounds, smells and touch.

Care-giving adults respond to infant signals of dependency and interpret these signals as communicative long before it can be claimed that the infant's actions are intentional and fully communicative. From the start, adults try to 'read' infant behaviour as if it conveyed meaning (hunger, discomfort and pain, pleasure, recognition). They respond to infants as if they were communicative partners from the age of two months (Schaffer, 1989), if not earlier. This behaviour provides a scaffold (Bruner, 1983) for the later emergence of intentional communicative behaviours and, subsequently, first words.

As children's awareness of objects increases, they acquire skills in integrating interactions with both objects and people, using objects to attract attention and adults to obtain desired objects. As these skills increase, they will combine familiar action patterns into more complex routines involving interactive partners. Bruner's descriptions of 'boo' and the 'disappearing clown' games (Bruner and Sherwood, 1976; Ratner and Bruner, 1978) are examples of this stage. Such routines, shared with a familiar care-giver, provide a very important first step in the development of language. According to Piaget (1962) it is through such recurring experiences that children develop schemas (concepts, collections of ideas) about objects, events and people.

Learning to play with a ball provides a good example of the way that children's 'schemas' for objects and events develop. Children need to touch, smell, roll, drop and throw a ball in order to develop a concept of 'ball'. Part of this concept includes the sound of words that are used by familiar adults when playing with balls; for example, 'roll', 'push', 'kick', 'up', 'gone' and, of course, 'ball'. Most of this learning occurs when children play with balls regularly with a parent, sibling or other consistent partner. Then there are opportunities to imitate what the other person says and does, to take turns in familiar routines and to practise new skills. Note that this explanation of language learning integrates physical, social and cognitive aspects of the child's experiences in acquiring language concepts. It also allows for some contribution from naturally occurring opportunities for imitation and reinforcement of appropriate behaviour by interactive partners. In a sense it combines aspects of all the views of language development described in this chapter. This approach assumes that all children can acquire the skills needed to enable them to communicate effectively with others.

According to the interactional view of language development, parents or other adults and older siblings can help children learn to talk by spending time with them, providing the children with opportunities to listen, watch, imitate and practise appropriate language skills. This model of language acquisition provides a particularly useful framework for developing an intervention programme that is based on parents, teachers or other familiar adults acting as agents of change for children with language difficulties. Using an interactional framework, adults can be taught to recognise both children's current level of communicative competence, and the contexts in which appropriate opportunities may arise to introduce and practise new language skills.

The ideas set out in the remaining chapters of this book for teaching language to children whose language acquisition is delayed are strongly influenced by interactional explanations for language learning and, in particular, by the transactional model of language acquisition described by McLean and Snyder-McLean (1978) in their comprehensive review of language teaching strategies for children with disabilities and delays.

Other sources of influence include the research reported by psycholinguists and psychologists such as Bates (1976), Bruner (1976), Dore (1978), Greenfield and Smith (1976) and Halliday (1975), theoretical accounts of early symbolic behaviour by Piaget (1962), Werner and Kaplan (1963) and speech act theory outlined by Austin (1962) and Searle (1969). These various sources emphasised the significance of cognitive development, socially interactive experiences and the emergence of communicative behaviour in the acquisition of early language skills. Useful reviews can be found in Fletcher and MacWhinney (1995), Ingram (1989), Gallaway and Richards (1994) and Locke (1993).

Summary

In this chapter, the meaning of words like 'communication', 'language' and 'speech' were defined. Some of the theoretical explanations for the processes involved in language acquisition were considered. These included ideas involving innate knowledge (nativist explanations), imitation, modelling and reinforcement (behavioural explanations), concept development (cognitive explanations) and social interaction (interactional or transactional explanations). The implications of each of these theoretical approaches to the difficulties faced by some children in learning to talk were considered. It was concluded that the interactional explanation, focusing on the role of parents, teachers and other interactive partners, provided the most useful model for helping children learn to communicate more effectively.

The next chapter will describe the stages that children pass through as they learn to communicate as a basis for understanding how children begin to talk and how they can be helped in this crucial area of development.

Chapter 2
Acquiring Language: the Developmental Sequence

In this chapter, the processes underlying language development are described in terms of the sequences that children pass through as they learn to talk. These sequences provide a framework for the language programme that is set out in the second part of this book.

How does language develop?

The process of language acquisition is often described in terms of a continuum or process of gradual change, starting soon after birth at a point that precedes intentional communication and leading to the stage where children are able to use language in more complex ways, such as asking questions and indicating plurality. However, this process does not always proceed evenly. There are often growth spurts, when change is very rapid, as well as plateaus, when progress seems to slow and little change in skills is evident.

Language development is also frequently described in terms of a sequential set of milestones, steps, or stages of achievement, such as 'the pre-verbal stage' or the 'single-word stage'. These labels refer to a cluster of related behaviours that tend to occur together as children begin to communicate. For example, children often use both consistent sounds and gestures in the pre-linguistic stage. Later, in the single-word stage, they begin to use labels for objects, actions and people. Ages are often attached to these stages which can then be described as a 'developmental calendar' (Kent and Miolo, 1995).

Various models of the stages in language development have been proposed. For example, Ingram (1989, p. 53) identifies five major periods in the language acquisition process based on detailed descriptions of emerging child language by three linguists: Brown (1973), Nice (1925) and Stern (1924). An alternative model, based on Piaget's six stages in the sensorimotor period, is presented by Goldbart (1988, p. 23). In each case, it is assumed that individual children will progress through the stages in the predicted sequence, although the transition from one stage to the next will, at first, be only partial as current skills are gradually replaced by more complex behaviours. Patterns of development may also be uneven, with some aspects of behaviour progressing more rapidly than others; for example, receptive skills often appear before equivalent expressive skills. Moreover, once a child has reached a specific stage, such as the use of single words, development may appear to slow down. Occasionally, some form of intervention or change in the child's social environment may be needed to stimulate further progress. Overall, the concept of stages provides a convenient way to talk about children's language development, as in 'Josh is at the single-word stage'. Ingram (1989) has a detailed discussion of this topic.

Other sources of information about the sequence of skills that emerge as language develops include studies of early language in small samples of children, such as those reported by Bates (1976), Bloom (1970), Brown (1973) and Halliday (1975). Useful data can also be found in large-scale surveys of emerging language skills in children who are developing normally. Information of this latter type is often reported in standardised tests of child development that cover an aspect of language (Knobloch, Stevens and Malone, 1980; Uzgiris and Hunt, 1975) and in standardised child language tests (Hedrick, Prather and Tobin, 1984; Kiernan and Reid, 1987). The model proposed below is based on data derived from all these different sources.

What are the stages of language development?

The language programme set out in this book covers the stages that occur in the period described at the beginning of this chapter. It starts before the emergence of first words and continues to the point where the child can demonstrate acquisition of the more complex language skills achieved by most children in the years prior to school entry. The first stage is concerned with skills that emerge when the infant begins to attend to objects and events, as well as people, and to use objects appropriately – not just mouthing or holding them. This is sometimes described as Piaget's sensorimotor stage three (see Golbart, 1988, p. 23).

From birth, care-givers attribute meaning to infants by 'interpreting' their behaviour. However, as infants gain increasing control over their actions and interactions with others, it becomes obvious that they can now use consistent sounds, gestures or movements intentionally to convey meaning. This is the point where the language programme begins.

The first stage of the programme is concerned with developing skills that are considered to be prerequisites for language. There are three categories of related skills here:

- *looking together:* joint attention or the ability to look at something of interest with a partner, to follow a care-giver's gaze and look at what he or she is observing;

- *turn-taking and imitation:* the ability to interact with a partner and copy his or her actions;
- *appropriate play:* the ability to play in a commonly accepted way with a variety of familiar objects; for example, by shaking, putting in, dropping, waving, pulling and pushing, rather than just holding or mouthing.

The programme continues to the stage where single words are combined into more complex utterances, to ask questions, or indicate location or possession (see Table 2.1).

A more detailed discussion of these stages of development is set out below.

Pre-linguistic stage: early vocalising; adults attach meaning to sounds that are not yet intentional

As noted in the previous chapter, the origins of language development can be traced to the infant's earliest experiences. Studies of babies during the very earliest stages of development (Halliday, 1975; Green-field and Smith, 1976; Kaye, 1982; Trevarthen, 1979) have shown that the foundations of language are laid when infants start to show an interest in people and in the objects that surround them. They learn to

Table 2.1: Developmental stages in learning to talk

Pre-linguistic stage	Early vocalising: parents attach meaning to infant sounds that are not yet intentional		
Stage 1	Preliminary skills		
	Looking together	Turn-taking and imitation	Appropriate play
Stage 2	Pre-verbal skills		
	Performatives ('brmm', 'quack-quack')		
	Protowords (word-like vocalisations)		
Stage 3	First words ('dog', 'Mum', 'car')		
Stage 4	Early sentences ('Daddy car', 'dog gone', 'boy fall down'; 'cat go there')		
Stage 5	Extending meaning (adding English morphemes, such as the plural 's' as in dogs)		

follow a carer's eyes to see what he or she is looking at. They also learn that when something interesting attracts their attention the carer will notice their interest and comment on it, or move them closer so that they can touch the object or see it more clearly. Infants are very interested in anything that is unusual or different. They like complicated patterns and will look longer at things that are colourful, move or make interesting noises.

Babies' first apparently 'communicative' acts often take the form of cries and calls, often triggered by physical events such as hunger, cold or colic. They make different sounds when they are tired or in pain and parents often interpret these sounds to mean that the baby is hungry or wants to be comforted. It is some months before the infant can actually produce sounds intentionally to indicate pleasure, hunger or pain.

Very young babies also learn to gurgle and coo, and make other interesting sounds for their own entertainment; these noises can often be heard when they are alone, either before or after a nap. From soon after birth, care-givers begin to attribute meaning to these early sounds: 'the baby's hungry/tired/upset about something'. These judgements are often based on the context, such as 'baby is crying and it is four hours since the last feed so she must be hungry' or past experience as in 'yesterday he cried like this after a feed and finally went to sleep for a long time'. Of course, care-givers cannot know what causes infant behaviour and their interpretations may not be accurate. But over time, as they respond consistently to infant actions and sounds, the first steps towards social interaction and communication begin.

Stage 1: Preliminary skills: looking together, turn-taking and imitation; appropriate play

From about six months of age, most infants begin to learn that sounds can be used to make things happen around them. At about this time they are also acquiring more complex strategies for exploring and interacting with their environment and learning about the objects and people in it. Initially, they learn about objects by putting everything into their mouths but, gradually, they learn to drop them, give them, bang them together, wave them, put one thing inside another and so on. Eventually, these strategies become more complex: the spoon is put into the cup, the blanket is piled up on top of the Teddy and pillow. Objects can now be picked up, as well as dropped, and small items can be held one in each hand at the same time. Some of these actions are learned by accident while others are learned by watching and participating with others in daily routines like eating, bathing or dressing. At these times, the child and an adult or other children often look together at interesting objects or events such as a new bath toy that pops, or a book with flaps that can be lifted up. They also take part in games like 'Boo' or 'Incy, Wincy

Spider' that involve the infant and partner in taking turns or imitating each other's actions.

In all of these experiences, babies are learning about the people, objects and events in their world. They are learning appropriate play skills: that balls can be dropped or put into a bucket and are sometimes blue and sometimes red; that balls can be rolled back and forth to a partner. These experiences help infants to develop receptive understanding of words like 'ball', 'gone', 'roll', 'more' and 'blue'. At the same time, they take the first steps in expressive language by learning that they can use actions and sounds to make things happen; if they cry long and loudly enough, someone will come; if they stretch out and point to something interesting, someone will bring it closer or lift them up to see it better; if they call 'more', someone will play the ball game again.

Early games are also very important for language development because they give adults topics that they can talk about when they are with babies; experiences that both have shared. Of course, these games also give the babies something that they can share with the adults who interact with them: 'boo' will remind an older sibling to play the game again and 'open' might remind Daddy to read the book with the pages that unfold wide. Learning to talk involves more than learning about objects: it also involves learning to interact with other people, sharing ideas, remembering past experiences as well as asking for help or information. Communication involves interaction with others, so infants need to learn to take turns in activities with others: 'my turn to roll the ball; now it's your turn'. They also need to learn to watch others and imitate what they are doing, since imitation is a powerful tool for acquiring new behaviours. Joining in activities with others is the best way to learn these things.

Stage 2: Pre-verbal skills – performatives: 'oops', and protowords: idiosyncratic or 'made up' words

Performatives are consistent sounds, often linked to actions or entities that are associated with a specific sound, such as 'whee' when sliding down a slippery slide, 'br'mm' while pushing a toy car or 'woof woof' when looking at a picture of a dog. Performative sounds usually involve a repeated pattern that is easy to remember, and sounds that are easy to produce such as simple vowel-consonant or consonant-vowel combinations like 'bye-bye', 'er-er' when rocking and 'oh-oh' when something falls down.

The earliest signs of language appear when infants begin to combine their contact with objects and their interactions with adults into one event. For example, the infant has watched entranced as a wind-up car turned circles and has also watched his father wind it up and activate it. Later, the child will attract his father's attention to activate the toy by using a consistent gesture such as pointing, or sound such as 'er-er'. The production of performatives is a sign that the child is gaining some control over the sounds that he or she is able to make.

Information about performative sounds is gained by infants when they begin to attend to what is happening around them, not only what can be seen, but also what can be heard. The kettle makes an interesting whistle when it boils, the telephone rings, a clock goes 'tick tick'. The dog's bark sounds like 'woof' and the cat makes a 'miaow' noise. As babies learn about the different events in their lives they are also learning about the sounds that are associated with them, as well as the sight, touch, taste and smell of those events. When they remember what they have seen and heard they recall the sounds as well as the other sensory images.

Gradually, infants begin to use the sounds that they have learned to represent the objects and events that they are associated with. For example, if you push the toy car, you can make a 'br'mm' noise. When you make the 'br'mm' noise and point, Mummy will get the toy car out of the cupboard. If Auntie comes to visit, 'boo' will remind her to play the hiding game and when Daddy comes he will show you his watch if you say 'tick tick'. Most children produce these early sounds in the period before their first words. Initially, the sounds have no meaning: for example, 'boo' and 'boomps-a-daisy'. Eventually, the sounds begin to be used to represent the game or activity with which they are associated. Later, these early sounds will be replaced by proper words, but in the earliest stages of language acquisition they provide a very useful transition into first words.

Protowords are word-like vocalisations used intentionally in a consistent context to convey a specific meaning (McCarthy, 1954, cited by Ingram, 1989, pp. 170–1). Halliday (1975) argued that they are created by children from their own vocalising, as a means of expressing their own meaning. Examples could include the sounds used consistently for a favourite toy or food. These words are not like the words they replace but they have recognisable tone and pitch. They are often used when the child has discovered that words can be used to achieve a purpose, such as to attract attention or obtain a desired object, but has not yet learned to utter the appropriate sounds. Twins sometimes develop quite extensive private communication systems using protowords. However, children need to learn the language of their group so that they can communicate with people outside the family. Eventually, more conventional word forms are acquired, as when 'car' replaces 'br'mm br'mm' or 'bottle' is used instead of a sucking noise or an idiosyncratic word created by the child.

According to Halliday (1975), children use their early 'word-like' sounds and, later, first words to fulfil a basic set of purposes or functions:

- instrumental: 'I want';
- regulatory: 'do as I tell you';
- interactional: 'me and you'; and
- personal: 'here I am' (Halliday, 1975).

As expressive language skills increase, the heuristic 'why?' and imaginative 'let's pretend' functions are added. These developments are considered in more detail in Chapter 10.

Stage 3: First words: 'dog', 'Mum', 'car'

The first words produced by children often seem to be used sporadically, over a period of time and are only intelligible to a direct care-giver. These words are usually labels for objects and people, as in 'cup', 'shoe', and 'Daddy', 'Mummy', although a range of other words are also acquired to represent actions, 'up', 'see'; locations, 'there', 'down', 'in'; modifiers, 'hot', 'big', 'there'; and other socially useful meanings such as 'bye', 'no' and 'more'.

There is some evidence (Dore, 1978; Nelson, 1973) that children's initial interests in objects and people are shaped by the major orientations of their primary care-givers. Some children seem to use more general object labels first, while others are more interested in social activities and the regulation of another's behaviour. These differences can frequently also be observed in their carers (Dore, 1978). Observational records show that, while children in the first group produce words like 'dog', 'ball', 'car', those in the other group are more likely to produce words that are useful in social interaction, such as 'hi', 'bye', 'nite-nite', or socially appropriate formulaic expressions such as 'have-a-cup-of-tea?' or 'how do you do?' The latter are often uttered in a continuous stream with appropriate intonation but the individual words are largely unintelligible.

It is important to remember, here, that while care-givers are usually very interested in pinpointing when a child actually begins to talk, as in 'I'll give her a canary when she says her first word!', this interest is focused on only one aspect of language use, namely expressive language skills. Of equal importance is the child's acquisition of receptive language or the skills needed to listen to and comprehend language. Studies of word comprehension in infants and young children (Benedict, 1979; Bates, Bretherton and Snyder, 1988; Bates, Dale and Thal, 1995) suggest that children begin to understand words well before they are able to use them. Interestingly, the first words that children understand appear to be mainly words associated with actions, such as 'give', 'get', 'no', 'kiss' (Benedict, 1979), whereas, as noted above, the first words that they produce are more likely to be general or specific labels for significant people or objects such as 'Daddy', 'Mummy', 'dog', 'cat', 'car', 'ball', 'shoes' (Nelson, 1973).

Stage 4: Early sentences: 'Daddy car', 'dog gone'

Once children have about 50 words in their spoken vocabulary and understand almost 200 words (Bates *et al.*, 1995), they begin to combine them into simple sentences in a sequence that directly reflects their experience or perception of the world. At first, words are produced separately, as single words on the same topic, each with a distinct intonation pattern and uttered sequentially. Later, the words begin to merge together into a coherent string. Soon afterwards, the child combines them into one utterance.

Children usually combine words into two-word phrases in predictable ways. The words used represent the semantic categories: agent, action and object. They can also be described in terms of grammatical categories such as noun and verb. The first single words used are mainly general labels that represent a variety of meanings, for example, 'drink' can mean a glass of milk or the act of drinking. Later, action words are acquired such as 'eat', 'go', 'fall-down'. These are then combined in different ways with labels for people and objects, as in 'eat bickie', 'go car' and 'Winnie fall-down'. The next step is to add words that modify the object labels, such as 'more bickie', 'my ball', 'little car'. Other useful words are learned, including words to greet ('hi', 'bye'), to describe ('wet', 'little', 'yellow'), to show possession ('my', 'mine'), to indicate location ('there', 'on', 'up'). These are then combined with other words to express specific meanings more clearly. In forming such sentences, children are mapping words onto elements of the entities and events that they experience and want to talk about. Their sentences are formed by following familiar word-combination patterns (Howe, 1993).

Children's first two-word combinations can be described as following a pattern that is comparable to an event script or a child's mental image of a familiar occurrence, such as having a bath or going to visit an aunt (Nelson, 1986; see also Chapter 3). The child first learns the main elements of the event, such as getting undressed, getting into the bath and getting out, for the 'bath' example. Later, other different components are added, such as whether soap or bubbles are put into the bath, which toys are played with in the bath, and so on. These less critical, more varied parts of the bath script are called 'slot-fillers'. For the child who is learning to talk, key action words such as 'go', 'see' and 'eat' are combined with a variety of labels for objects, people's names and other types of words as in 'Daddy go', 'go car', 'see cat', 'Mummy see', 'eat (ba)nana', 'Jamie eat', 'eat more'. Later, as the child's speech becomes more fluent, the listener will begin to hear multi-word utterances that include even longer chains of key words linked with different slot-fillers. These different semantic combinations demonstrate the gradual emergence of rule-bound speech.

After children learn two-word phrases to express a variety of meanings, they begin to combine these to produce sentences of three words or more, as in:

'me want' + 'want drink' = 'me want drink'

'go car' + 'Mummy car' = 'go Mummy car'

By this stage children can also express more detailed information by using modifying words for colour, size, possession and so on, as in 'me go big red car', 'want my blue ball'.

Stage 5: Extending meaning: using English morphemes

At about the same time as children begin to combine words into sentences, they also begin to acquire morphemes or the small words or parts of words that are used to add meaning to other words, such as a plural '-s' or '-es', prepositions such as 'in' and 'on' and articles such as 'a' and 'the'. According to Brown (1973), the first to appear is '-ing', followed by 'in', 'on' and the plural 's'. For the child, the addition of a morpheme to a word, as in the use of '-ing' to make 'eating' or 'sitting', is the equivalent of saying two single words. So examples of 'two-word' combinations produced at this time might include: 'putting', 'washed', 'shoes', 'a cup'.

Once children can combine words into more complex sentences there is often a rapid expansion, both in the size of their vocabulary and in their overall language skills. At this stage they are learning to use language in a variety of ways: to ask and answer questions, to give and obtain information, to protest, and to discover new words. These pragmatic uses of language began much earlier, when the child learned to use sounds, gestures and words to draw the attention of others to objects and events of interest, to obtain desired objects or help and to protest or attract attention. The different communicative functions of language have been described in greatest detail by Dore (1975) and Halliday (1975). Ingram (1989) and McLean and Snyder-McLean (1978) give a clear overview of pragmatic aspects of early language development.

Once children are using language in more complex ways, both in terms of pragmatic functions and the range of morphemes observed in their utterances, it can be assumed that they have mastered the most difficult tasks in learning to talk. Further progress will involve expanding the lexicon and learning to use more complex aspects of the grammatical system.

Summary

In this chapter, the stages that children pass through as they learn to talk are described and some reference is made to the ways in which adults help in this learning process. It is important to have some idea of these stages when beginning to help a child who is having language difficulties. For example, how do children move from just looking at interesting things with adults to being able to use words as part of a game or to describe what they are doing? If we can understand what is happening as such developments take place, then we can use this knowledge to help children who are experiencing difficulties to progress in the same way.

In the next two chapters, we will look more carefully at the way in which adult–child interaction and the context in which it occurs contribute to the development of early language skills.

Chapter 3
Contexts for Learning:
Routine Events and Play

This chapter is concerned with the contexts in which children acquire language. These include situations where they learn new skills, but also those where they practise what they have already learned. Many of these contexts involve daily routines at home. They also include other times when children and adults interact, talk, look at a book or play a finger game like 'Round and Round the Garden' or 'This Little Piggy'. Other important contexts for language involve activities described as 'play'.

Play is particularly important for children who are learning to talk. It provides situations within which real learning can occur, where children have both the time and the opportunity to explore thoroughly new objects and materials, to discover new ideas and test what they have learned in a safe environment that they can control. Play provides opportunities for children to be challenged in their thinking and learn how to solve problems. It is also the best place to learn how to interact successfully with others.

The chapter begins with a review of two research studies that explored the relationship between specific contexts and children's use of language. This is followed by a discussion of the significance of naturally occurring situations, including daily routines, stories, action songs, nursery rhymes and play as contexts for encouraging and practising early language skills. The characteristics of children's play at different stages of language development are then described and the role of parents and other carers in children's play is also considered.

Contexts for learning to talk

As noted in earlier chapters, children learn to talk by taking part in activities within the natural environment that involve interacting with others who can provide good models of appropriate language. Many of these situations occur daily: while eating breakfast, having a bath, or waiting for the bus. Others occur during games and social activities when children interact with adults and other children. Within these contexts partners follow the child's lead, modelling appropriate actions, sounds and words, taking turns with the child to throw a ball, push a car or put another block on the tower. They also respond appropriately to the child's attempts to communicate.

Studies of children's language development have demonstrated an association between specific natural contexts and language use. For example, Wells (1985), in a longitudinal study of Bristol families, tape-recorded samples of children's language in their homes over a three-year period, beginning when the children were aged around 15 months (younger group) and 39 months (older group). In exploring the relationship between language use and context, Wells showed that the most speech occurred in domestic 'non-play' situations where the child was simply an observer and not directly involved in any activity. Over 20% of all the speech recorded in this study occurred in such contexts. Relatively high percentages of speech also occurred when the child was playing alone (self talk) or with other children, or while simply 'talking' with an adult (being engaged in a conversation).

Among the daily routines that children experienced, speech occurred most often during eating, dressing and toileting. From around 42 months, children began to talk more when they were 'helping' an adult. Interestingly, the percentage of speech associated with looking at books and reading decreased over the time period observed. Wells comments that this activity was, at first, used by parents to teach children vocabulary. It gradually declined as the children's language skills began to develop more rapidly.

A second study that identified specific contexts associated with high and low language use was reported by Sylva, Roy and Painter (1980). As in Wells' study, observations were made of children (aged three to five years), but in this case, the children were attending nursery schools, nursery classes and playgroups in the Oxford area. These data showed that child–adult exchanges occurred most often when the children were engaged in tasks associated with early attempts at reading, writing and counting and, to a lesser extent, with materials such as puzzles, pegboards and posting boxes. The highest rate of child–child language occurred during informal games where children held hands and giggled, hid in corners and took part in activities described as 'rough and tumble'. The children were most likely to be silent when engaged in adult-directed activities where the aim was to improve skills like cutting, tracing, pasting and colouring in, and during activities that involved manipulation of materials such as sewing, sorting, or playing with dough or water.

The results of the studies by Wells and by Sylva *et al.* confirm that language interaction tends to occur more often in some contexts than in others. At home, most language occurs at times when the child is interested, but not always directly involved, in some ongoing domestic activity, or when the child and an adult converse about topics of interest. Mealtimes also provide opportunities for conversation. In an early childhood setting, most child–adult exchanges occur when children are not physically involved in an activity, or when they are involved in tasks that require relatively high levels of concentration, including pre-reading and mathematics, or structured materials involving fine motor skills and hand–eye coordination.

Not unexpectedly, they talk less with adults when involved in gross motor activities like running, climbing, chasing and jostling. They are also less talkative during tasks that require very high concentration such as those involving fine motor skills, such as playing with plastic building bricks (Lego). Activities that involve co-ordination of fine movement and senses such as play with sand, dough and water, or sorting and arranging objects, are also less conducive to language use. Children are most likely to talk with other children during informal games.

Daily routines and familiar situations

In earlier chapters we talked about the ways in which children learn about objects and people. For example, they learn about balls by playing with balls and they learn to recognise the characteristics that distinguish Mummy, Daddy or a regular carer from other people by their look, sound, smell, touch and so on. Children also learn about their daily life by recognising the pattern of recurring events. They learn what happens first and what happens next, what they have to do, and what others do. They are often more interested in sorting out these sequences ('now I have breakfast, then I go to playgroup') than in the more unusual and exciting things that engage the interest of adults, like the birth of a sibling or a forthcoming holiday (see Nelson, 1989, for a fascinating account of the topics covered by a two-year-old child during pre-sleep monologues). Children acquire what has been called 'event knowledge' as they learn about the different activities that they take part in each day, such as having a bath, going to bed, visiting the doctor or going to the shops (e.g., Nelson and Gruendel, 1979). All of these events involve a fairly predictable sequence of actions, as well as having a predictable set of words to accompany the actions. These words can be used as goals in a language programme for a child who needs help in early communication.

The sequence of actions and words that recur within daily routines and familiar events are sometimes referred to as forming a 'script' of the routine or event. For example, here is a possible script for having a bath:

A script for having a bath

Actions	Language
Put in plug and turn water on/off	'plug in', 'water on/off', 'sh-sh-sh'
Take clothes off	'shirt off', 'pants off'
Get in bath	'in'
Wash, play with bath toys	"wash face/arms/legs', 'boat', 'woosh', 'duck', 'quack quack'
Get out	'finished', 'out'
Dry face/arms/legs	'pat pat', 'rub rub'
Empty bath	'plug out', 'gurgle gurgle', 'water gone'

Obviously, not every bath will follow the set of actions and words outlined here. Each family will have its own procedure and that sequence will be repeated every time the child is bathed. The main events of taking off clothes, filling the tub, washing, getting out, drying, dressing and emptying the bath will be shared by many children. The language that accompanies the actions will also be fairly similar for a particular child and care-giver and can be targeted during activities designed to encourage the acquisition of new language skills. For example, the child at the performative stage can be encouraged to say 'sh-sh-sh' as the tap is turned on; the child at the single-word stage can practise saying 'in', 'finished', 'out' and so on. Other recurring events that could provide useful opportunities to encourage and practise new language skills include:

waking up and getting dressed
mealtimes
visits to aunts, uncles, grandparents
arriving and leaving crèche, play-group, preschool
going shopping
going for a walk
going to church
having a picnic
birthdays
eating at McDonald's
getting ready for bed
saying good-night

You can think of other similar activities that children and their carers take part in together, and of the sequence of actions and words that the child is learning to associate with these events. These 'scripts' will be useful when you begin to select language goals, and plan activities to learn and practise new language skills.

Stories, action songs and nursery rhymes

Familiar stories, read or told, songs and nursery rhymes, particularly those that accompany physical movements like bouncing on the knees or finger play, provide another context for language acquisition. When such experiences are repeated many times, children become familiar with the structure and content of the stories and songs that they hear.

As adults, we usually do not read a newspaper article or a book more than once, but children enjoy repeated retelling of a favourite story or nursery rhyme, as well as singing familiar songs. They learn the words, rhymes and rhythms, and can predict the relevant script or schema for the story (Mandler and Johnson, 1977), who the actors are and what will happen first, next and last. As in the example of script-learning arising from participation in recurring daily routines and events, so, too, repetition of favourite stories, songs and rhymes gives children opportunities to remember predictable sequences of actions and associated words and sound patterns. These experiences are highly motivational. They also provide children with valuable opportunities to practise their language in a safe and predictable environment.

If the story includes the repetition of specific words, as in 'The Three Bears' ('Who's been eating my porridge?'), the children do not even have to find appropriate language, but can just say the words used in the story. If they sing a familiar song such as 'Twinkle, Twinkle Little Star' or 'Happy Birthday to You', a listener will quickly recognise the tune, if not the words, and respond appropriately. These experiences can be a useful place to begin to encourage talking. Ideas for using stories, songs and nursery rhymes for encouraging and practising early language-related skills are included in Chapter 6.

Children's play

To many adults, 'play' is thought of as something that we do when we are free to decide how to spend our time. Play is something that is fun, where we can follow our own interests. There are no fixed goals and, as a result, little possibility of frustration or failure (Sylva, Bruner and Genova, 1976, p. 244). In contrast, 'work' is usually associated with tasks that have a specific goal and, with this, the potential for frustration and failure if the goal is not achieved. There is usually little flexibility about the way the task is carried out and participation is often not voluntary. This distinction is worth keeping in mind when considering suggestions for engaging children in 'play' activities as a means of encouraging and practising new skills and behaviours. Children may be more willing to join in the game if they know it will be fun.

When children are left to amuse themselves, to do what they like with their time, we usually describe their activity as 'play', but can all of the

things that children do at these times be called 'play'? Is it also possible
to distinguish between different types of play in children's activity? Can
you tell when children are 'playing' and when they are not? Which are
the more effective play contexts for language learning?

Some people argue that it is possible to make such distinctions when
you watch children playing. For example, studies of three-to-four-year-
olds in preschools (Hutt, Tyler, Hutt and Christopherson, 1989) have
shown that some differences can be identified in the various activities
that the children engage in during periods of what we might call 'play'.
Some activities are chosen by the children because they are fun. Their
main purpose is self amusement (Hutt *et al.,* 1989, p. 12). Children
involved in such activities are relaxed and happy; their behaviour is
unpredictable and sometimes highly creative or unusual. When these
activities cease to be fun, the children simply stop doing them. Examples
of such games include playing with trains and model cars, tea parties,
doll's corner, dressing-up and imaginative games where children
interact and assume different roles.

Other types of play activity that children become involved in are
mainly concerned with acquiring information. Such games require very
high levels of concentration, as, for example, during exploration of unfamiliar materials, acquisition of new skills and problem solving. During
this type of play, children's attention is highly focused and their actions
are very predictable. Examples of such activities include exploring interesting objects, such as finding out how to start a new mechanical toy,
making something like a rocket out of boxes, learning new skills like
riding a tricycle or skipping, and solving problems, as in doing a puzzle
or threading beads to match a pattern.

Sometimes children who have been left to play do not seem to be
doing anything. They wander about indecisively or flit from one activity
to another, not really being involved in anything. These children may not
yet have decided what to do with their playtime, but they may also not
know how to play. Most children learn how to play by watching other
children or adults and imitating what the others are doing.

Interestingly, all the studies cited earlier reported relatively high
percentages of time spent by children in 'looking' and 'watching'. For
example, Hutt *et al.* (1989, p. 72) reported that over 20% of the time
spent by children they observed in nursery schools, nursery classes,
playgroups and day nurseries were involved in this type of activity. Some
of these children may not previously have had opportunities to watch
other children playing. They will become more active when they feel
confident enough to join in. However, some children lack the skills
needed to learn spontaneously from simple observation. Such children
need access to stimulating environments, and in some cases, assistance
or 'scaffolding' to ensure that they benefit from periods of 'watching and
looking'. The term 'scaffolding' is used to describe the behaviour of a

responsive adult when interacting with a young child. The adult's aim is to involve the child in dialogue and to provide a context or meaning for the child's gestures and early utterances. One of the adult's tasks is to adjust the interchange to ensure the participation of an immature partner. Scaffolding assists the child to move from an immature level to that of a mature language user.

Of course, it is not always possible to tell why children are doing something or whether they are really enjoying what they are doing. Sometimes the children themselves are not sure; the different kinds of games are mixed up together. Nevertheless, it is often possible to distinguish between the play and other types of activity in children's games. In general, 'play' activities can be distinguished by the following four characteristics:

- play is fun; children stop playing when the game is no longer enjoyable;
- play is voluntary; children play because they want to, not because they have to;
- play is flexible; goals can change: what children do is the most important part of the game;
- play has no failure; achieving a goal is not important; you can 'lose', as in Cowboys and Indians, but you cannot 'fail' during play (Sylva *et al.*, 1976, pp. 244–5).

When children's activities do not conform to these four qualities (when they are not enjoyable, voluntary, flexible and without failure) then they are probably more like 'work' than 'play' to the children. So if you sit down to play with a child and find that you are directing the game, setting the rules and insisting that the child 'finishes' what he or she is doing, there is a risk that the activity will not seem like play to the child. When introducing a new activity, you need to ensure that it is fun for the child. You can encourage the child to participate but do not insist if he or she is not interested.

Why is play so useful for helping children to learn to talk? In the early stages of learning to talk, children need to have some control over the situations that they are in. They need to learn that they can use their own actions or sounds to make things happen. They have to understand that we use particular sounds and gestures to represent specific objects, people and events. They also have to learn to produce the sounds and gestures themselves, in order to have the means to interact with others; for example, to say 'boo' and pull the cloth off your face, instead of always waiting for you to pull the cloth and say the word. This learning can occur in naturally occurring situations such as those discussed earlier. It can also occur when you and the child share an entertaining or interesting activity. In other words, when early communication skills are being encouraged, activities need to provide a context that encourages children to communicate because they want to and are involved in a shared activity with a partner.

Later, when you begin to help children who can already talk to improve specific aspects of their language, the activities you choose for practising new skills can be more formal, with an expectation that the child will stay and finish the task, in spite of the fact that it may be difficult and not much fun.

Stages in learning to play

In Chapter 2, we described some of the changes that take place as children learn to talk: progressing from the pre-verbal skills of taking turns, imitation and so on to more complex verbal skills such as asking and answering questions. In the same way, children's development in learning to play can be seen in terms of their progression through a series of stages.

Currently, much of our understanding about the development of children's play skills is based on the work of Jean Piaget (1962) who observed his own children very carefully and, from the knowledge gained, developed a theory about how children learn. Piaget's ideas are useful in drawing attention to the ways in which young children explore and learn about the objects that they encounter around them. Most children progress through this stage of learning relatively quickly, but those whose development is slow in some areas, including language, are also sometimes slow in developing these exploratory play skills. When this happens, we may need to help the children to move on to more advanced play and language levels.

In the following discussion, the characteristics of children's play at different developmental levels are described. The relationship between these levels of play and the stages of language development outlined in Chapter 2 is set out in Table 3.1.

Levels of play

Exploring objects or simple actions with one object

Initially, babies seem to learn about things in their immediate environment by looking very intently and by putting things into their mouths. As their skills in grasping and holding improve they will wave objects in front of their eyes, drop them or, as they learn to release things at will, give them to you. At this stage, infants' ability to learn about objects is limited by their physical skills in grasping, holding and releasing.

Table 3.1: Levels of children's play and stages of early language development

Levels of play	Stages of language development
Exploring objects	Pre-verbal stage: uncontrolled vocalising; parents attach meaning to infant sounds that are not yet intentional
Combining objects	
Using objects in play: functional use of objects	Stage 1: Preliminary skills: looking together, taking turns and imitation, appropriate play
Simple pretending using real objects	Stage 2: Pre-verbal skills: performatives (for example 'brmm', 'quack quack'), protowords (non-conventional or 'made-up' words)
Simple pretending using substitute or imaginary objects	Stage 3: First words (for example 'dog', 'Mum', 'car')
Imaginary play	Stage 4: Combining words into sentences: putting two words together (for example 'Daddy car', 'dog gone'), making simple sentences (for example 'boy fall down', 'cat go there') Stage 5: Extending meaning (for example adding plural 's', asking 'wh' questions)

Combining objects

Gradually, manipulative skills improve and babies begin to use more complex strategies to explore the things that they encounter. They learn to hold two objects at the same time and combine them in some way, such as putting the spoon into the cup, banging two objects together, or putting one object on top of another, as when a blanket is piled on top of a pillow or one block is carefully placed on top of another. Now, you can help them learn to put in, pull out, put on and so on. Gradually, the children begin to explore the things around them, seeking out new objects and new ways of using materials already encountered. The traditional activity of exploring the kitchen cupboard is a good example of appropriate play at this stage. Playing with water and sand is also exciting as the children learn, amongst other things, what can and cannot go into the mouth.

Functional use of objects

By this stage infants have acquired some knowledge of the ways in which familiar objects are used. If you give them a cup they will attempt to drink from it and will use a hairbrush to brush their own or your hair. They have usually learned that a book is to be opened and the pages turned, and know that the sight of their bottle and blanket means that it is time to go to bed. If you want to know something about the language skills of children at this stage of development, give them a toy telephone. Most children will immediately lift the receiver and begin to babble. They have watched adults use a telephone and can imitate what they have seen. Once children have reached this stage they need a variety of materials such as tea sets, toy cars and farm animals that can be used in simple lifelike games that can lead into creative or pretend play.

Simple pretending: real objects

Once children have begun to associate specific uses or routines with particular objects, they are ready to begin to take part in games that involve simple pretending, for example, 'drinking' from an empty cup, 'eating' the cakes in the picture book and even 'feeding' Teddy and 'putting him to sleep', wrapped up in a blanket. At this stage, the children should be using performative sounds in their games, such as pretend drinking and eating noises to accompany their actions.

Simple pretending: imaginary objects

Early games involving appropriate use of real objects are gradually replaced by games using substitute or imaginary objects. Children are now able to use small pebbles to represent the cakes needed for tea and will happily put Teddy to sleep in a box. Single words begin to be used during these games.

Imaginary play

Children move into the creative-symbolic stage by extending their games with Teddy, the tea set, the farm animals, the garage, the train set and other culturally-appropriate objects and activities. Functional play becomes imaginative as children pretend to have a tea party with a fairy, set up the train so that people can board it and go for a trip to the moon, make a box into a space rocket or build a pirate ship and set sail to find treasure. At this stage children should be combining words into sentences and taking part in conversations.

Parents and carers as 'managers'

Many parents and other carers spend much of their time directing children; telling them what to do, or how and when to do it. This tendency to 'manage' is a particular problem when children are developing slowly or are having problems in some area of learning. In this situation, it can be very difficult for carers to stop managing and leave the children to choose what they want to do for themselves. To compound this problem, children who are developing slowly often have not developed the skills needed to play independently, to explore and learn about objects and then begin to enjoy using the objects in different 'fun' ways.

One of the main things that parents and other carers need to do if they are to help children begin to talk is to recognise that they will need to spend time interacting with their children. This will include the opportunities that arise naturally, during daily routines such as washing up, washing the car, gardening and going for a walk. It may also involve special times in the day. The best conditions for children to begin to explore and learn about new objects and materials, and then use their new knowledge in creative or fun ways, is when they are in situations that they can control, where they feel safe and are in the company of children and adults whom they know well. In other words, the best place to learn to talk, for most children, is in a familiar context, either home or another familiar setting, and during activities with parents or carers who are closely involved in their daily care.

Summary

Experience working with children who are having problems in the early stages of learning to talk has demonstrated the importance of natural environments as contexts for language acquisition. In particular, language is acquired through the child's participation in daily routines and recurring events, such as going to bed, eating a meal and washing up. Other important contexts include the stories, finger plays, nursery rhymes and songs that carers share with children. Finally, children's play provides opportunities for children to interact with others, taking turns to roll a ball, knock down a block tower or pour a cup of tea. Parents, teachers and others can learn to use these naturally occurring situations and play situations to help children begin to communicate more effectively. In the next chapter, the way that adults talk to children during these encounters will be explored in terms of its place in children's acquisition of language.

Chapter 4
Talking to Children

Communication is, by definition, interactive. Children cannot learn language alone. They are completely dependent upon concerned parents or care-givers to help them accomplish this most complicated but necessary task. In their transactional model of early language acquisition, McLean and Snyder-McLean (1978) emphasised the importance of interacting cognitive, linguistic and social factors in the acquisition of communication skills. They stressed that above all, children will not learn to talk unless they have a reason to communicate and someone meaningful with whom to interact. Evidence from studies of children placed in residential institutions at an early age supports this view (Bochner, 1986). This chapter is concerned with the role of parents and other care-givers in the process of language acquisition. Information is given about the way adults interact with young children who are acquiring early language skills, the contexts in which this interaction occurs, and strategies that can be used by communicative partners with young children.

Interaction and language learning

Research into the earliest interactions between care-givers and children (see Conti-Ramsden, 1994) suggests that the origin of communicative behaviour lies in the early social exchanges that occur between infants and their carers. In these situations, the adult is usually intent on responding to the baby's needs, while also concerned about the infant's capacity to take part in communicative exchanges. Within this context, meaning is shared between adult and child, although the role of the child is initially passive, not active. Ultimately, this interaction contributes to the child's achievement of independent communicative functioning.

As their communicative competency increases, infants begin to engage in language-learning partnerships with mature users. The roles of both members of the partnership are important. Typically, mature language users facilitate the learning process by reacting to meaningful elements of an event and providing appropriately modified language models. At the same time, infants must bring to the partnership the skills needed to attend to the object or event of interest, listen to their partner's language and respond appropriately.

It has long been noticed that adults modify the language they use when interacting with young children (see Snow, 1994). The term 'motherese' has been used to describe such speech. Even children as young as four years of age modify their speech when interacting with younger, more immature siblings. Their speech is slower, clearer, more fluent, with shorter, simpler utterances, more exaggerated pitch, stress and a greater-than-usual use of rising tones. Words, phrases and whole utterances are frequently repeated and topics tend to be restricted to current activities, objects and events (Snow, 1994).

Questions that arise from the findings reviewed here concern the purpose served by the modifications and adjustments made by adults when they communicate with young children who are acquiring language. Are such modifications essential features of language-learning environments or is it possible for young children to acquire language without them? Is adult input the same for children who learn language easily as for those who experience difficulty? Much research has been undertaken to try to clarify these issues. Some studies have explored the strategies used by mothers in interaction with children who are developing normally and those used by mothers of children who are delayed in the area of language. Other studies have involved attempts to change parent interaction styles, to see if this has any effect on the achievement of language skills in their children. To date, the outcomes of this research have not provided clear guidelines for parents and others to follow in their interactions with children who are experiencing problems in learning to talk, although much has been learned about the processes involved in language acquisition. In particular, there is now a body of knowledge about the ways in which children acquire language, the types of social interaction that they experience, the settings where these experiences occur and the changes that are observed as language competence progresses. So although we cannot offer a 'recipe' for language learning, there are many suggestions that can be made to help those caring for children to facilitate the process of language acquisition through their interactions with the children.

Some relevant information about the way adults interact with children is set out below. See also Price (in press) for further discussion of these issues.

Interacting with the pre-linguistic child

Communication begins in infancy, long before the child is able to produce his or her first words. This stage is crucial for later language development because it is the period when all the prerequisite skills are established. Care-givers are often unaware of the importance of this period. This is the time where mothers respond to the child as if the signals were meaningful, for example, while feeding, changing or soothing a crying child. Through this reciprocity the child learns that he or she can cause things to happen. This is the beginning of joint attention. During this period responsive parents and other carers 'teach' the child that attempts to communicate will be rewarded, thus consolidating the child's motivation to communicate.

As the child's repertoire of actions and sounds increases, the responsive adult will begin to join in the child's 'game'. Early sounds are imitated back to the child, introducing the earliest form of turn-taking. Mother will put out her tongue, shake her head and imitate the gestures of the child. Again, this involves an interactive sequence and encourages communication. When the child looks at something or points to it, the adult will follow the child's gaze and hand-pointing and will pass the toy or move the toy car as if in response to a request to do so. Soon the child makes the gesture or sound with intent, and the interaction is truly communicative. The child raises his or her arms to be lifted from the cot and the carer says 'up'. It will not be long before the child learns to signal that he or she wants to be lifted out and, as sounds develop, the child will make approximations of the sound 'up' as arms are lifted to say 'take me out of here!'

These early 'games', in the context of the baby and carer's shared interactions in everyday routines, become the basis for all later language learning. The carer is responsive to the child's needs, and to early communicative attempts. As the child's competence grows, gestures turn into sounds and babbling sounds become more specific. Gradually, the carer extends what is expected of the child, waiting for the sound to go with the gesture before lifting the child from the cot. As noted in Chapter 2, this process is sometimes described as 'scaffolding' and helps the child move to a higher level of language use (Vygotsky, 1978).

There are four major factors which affect the acquisition of language, and these are summarized below. Full details and examples are given in Appendix H.

•   Responding to the child

The most important factor in facilitating language acquisition is the responsiveness of the mother or care-giver to the child. This has been discussed for the child in infancy but it continues to be of paramount importance at all stages of the child's development.

-     Acquiring effective conversational skills

The task of acquiring adequate conversational skills begins in earliest infancy, when the carer infers intent to early infant sounds and actions and although initially the adult takes both roles in the interaction, the infant will eventually begin to take part (see Appendix H).

-     Helping slow, non-initiating children

The importance of 'responsiveness' has been a recurring theme in the discussion on how adults interact with young language-learning children. Children who are passive and seldom initiate sound or activity will need special treatment (see Appendix H).

-     Strategies to use when interacting with children

There are many strategies that can be used in interacting with young children who are learning to talk. There are no clear guidelines about when any particular strategy is appropriate but each one can be useful in stimulating more effective language skills in young learners. See Appendix H for details.

Summary

What children need most when they are learning language is responsive parents or carers, quick to identify opportunities for interaction, and sensitive to the stage that the child has reached in learning to communicate. What adults need most is to understand how children learn language, what stages they pass through, and how they can facilitate the language-learning process. Adults cannot 'teach' children language but they can provide an optimal learning environment by observing and responding to all the communicative attempts that children make.

Part 2
Designing and Implementing a Language Programme

In the following six chapters (Chapters 5–10), guidelines are set out for designing and organising a language programme for a child who needs help in the early stages of language development. Chapter 5 provides a general overview of the procedures to be followed in establishing a language intervention programme. The remaining chapters (Chapters 6–10) focus on each of the five programme levels described in Chapter 2 (see Table 2.1), ranging from the preliminary skills of shared attention and shared activity to the more complex skills of combining words into sentences, expressing ideas about possession and tense, and asking and answering questions. Three of the main components of language identified in Chapter 1 are also explored: meaning or the intended topic of communication (semantics), rules or the grammatical system that defines ways of combining words meaningfully (syntax and morphology) and use, function, purpose or the intentional use of language to communicate meaning (pragmatics). The fourth component, speech sounds or the mechanism by which meaning is conveyed to others (phonology), is considered in the first chapter of Part 3 of the book, Chapter 11.

The aim of the chapters that follow in Part 2 and Part 3 of the book is to provide a very practical description of procedures that can be used to help children with problems in the early stages of communication. Information in these chapters is presented in a direct and highly personal style, with the expectation that this will make the ideas more readily accessible to the reader. Remember that these suggestions are intended for use by early childhood and special education teachers or carers, speech and language pathologists and therapists and parents who have the support of a professional.

Chapter 5
Organising a Language Programme

In this chapter, we consider the steps that need to be taken if you want to help a child begin to communicate more effectively. First, you need to watch and listen to the child to find out exactly how he or she is currently communicating. You also need to identify culturally appropriate activities and toys or other materials that the child enjoys. With this information, you can begin to select some appropriate language goals and plan activities for teaching. By the end of this chapter, you should have ideas on ways to find out exactly how the child is communicating now, examples of specific language teaching goals and activities that might be suitable for teaching new communication skills, and where and when your teaching games could be carried out.

Before beginning to talk about actually planning and implementing a language programme, it is a good idea to review the basic principles or assumptions upon which the ideas used in the programme are based. These principles are derived from the interactional view of language learning described in Chapter 1.

Basic principles underlying the language programme

It is sometimes difficult to recognise and write down all of the assumptions and basic principles that underlie programmes such as that described here. Some can be stated readily but others may not be obvious to those closely involved in the programme. In thinking about the procedures that comprise the programme, six major principles can be identified:

- First words emerge as a result of children's daily experiences with people, objects and events.
- Children acquire language through interaction with consistent caregivers, at first, parents and then teachers and others.
- When children have difficulty in learning to talk, experiences can be provided that will encourage their language development.
- Language activities are best carried out in children's natural setting by familiar adults.

- Teaching activities need to be frequent, with opportunities to practise the new skills occurring throughout the day. Clear speech models provided by interactive partners should accompany these games. These will ensure that children learn to associate specific speech sounds with their actions.
- Necessary preliminary skills need to be acquired. These include attending, turn-taking and imitation. Appropriate play skills also need to be developed, as first words will emerge out of children's play activities. Children need to learn to produce sounds intelligibly. Initial attempts to say a word may have little resemblance to the adult form of the word. These efforts should be accepted and a clear model of the word that the child is trying to say should be provided so:
      child: 'Ba'
      adult: 'Yes, it's a ball'

The basic principles set out here demonstrate that the programme described in this book is based on the assumption that children learn to talk by interacting with others. The active role of the child is central to this process. He or she has to learn to initiate, not just to respond. The child also has to make sense of all that is being experienced. Cognitive processes are involved here. Learning to talk involves learning about the environment. The content of the language programme will be derived from aspects of the environment that interest the child. A linguistic system is also involved in that the child must learn the language of his or her community. The programme is, therefore, based on three main components:

- the child's active participation in social exchanges;
- the child's knowledge of the physical world and the relationship of objects and actions within it;
- the child's gradual acquisition of a shared system of symbols that can be used to communicate meaning to others.

The remaining sections of this chapter give an outline of the general procedures that you should follow to help a specific child who is having difficulties in the development of early language skills. Specific details of assessment methods and intervention strategies are described in Chapters 6 to 10.

How to set up a language programme

It is a good idea to begin by collecting information about the child's current communicative behaviour. This process is sometimes called *screening*. Here your aim is to collect simple information, using quick methods, as a first step in identifying the skills that the child has already acquired. Once you have collected this information, you can begin to assess the child more carefully and plan an intervention programme.

Initial screening of current communication skills

The best way to find out how a child is communicating is by observation. You will also need to write down examples of what is said or done. You can do this by watching the child carefully in everyday situations. You may also need to give the child a set of tasks that provide an opportunity to demonstrate current skills. Ask significant others who spend time with the child, including parents, teachers and other carers, to help you collect this information.

Here are some examples of the kind of information that you could collect. Remember to note what the child does and says, and the context in which this occurs:

- How does the child attract your attention?
- How does the child tell you something important, such as 'Daddy is coming'?
- How does the child tell you what he or she has found, or what he or she is doing or looking at?
- How does the child tell you that he or she is hungry, or cold?
- How does the child tell you other interesting things?

Try to collect up to 10 examples of the way that the child communicates this type of information. Write down what the child does or says as exactly as you can. If some words are not clear, write the sounds that the child makes. Then write the word that you think the child is trying to say in brackets beside the sounds, just to remind yourself of what you think the child wants to say.

Taking a language sample

Another way to find out how a child is communicating is to collect a sample of language or other communication skills. To do this, you need to make a tape or video-recording of you or another person playing with the child. Try to record at least 10 minutes' play. Use some toys or picture books that the child likes. The adult should try not to talk too much during the session. The aim is to encourage the child to talk. You can replay the tape or video and write down exactly what the child said or did later. Try to collect at least 20 utterances, whether they are sounds, gestures or words. Guidelines for taking a language sample are set out in Appendix A.

Once you have collected some information about how the child is communicating, you will be able to work out what stage of language development he or she has reached. The material you have collected will also be useful when you begin to plan a programme, as a source of ideas about the actions, sounds or words that you can begin to teach.

Identifying what the child likes to do

When you begin to plan ways to help a child learn to talk, you need to identify some of the activities, games and toys that the child is very interested in or enjoys. Children need to feel relaxed and confident in any activity that they share with you. They need to feel that the activity is fun and that they are taking part because they want to, not because you expect them to. It will be easier for you to engage their attention if you select something that you know will attract and hold their attention.

Here are some examples of activities that most children enjoy:

- games with a ball;
- playing with blocks and model cars and trains;
- drawing;
- games with dolls and soft toys;
- looking at books;
- going for a walk or driving in the car;
- doing jigsaw puzzles;
- running, hiding;
- tea parties;
- preparing food and eating;
- talking.

Watch the child and make a list of the activities, toys or events that he or she particularly enjoys. Try to find activities that are associated with different times of the day and with different locations, such as during quiet times after waking up from a sleep, after tea, during the bath if it is not too hectic, outside in the garden, at the park and so on. Also think about the types of toys that interest the child, such as balls, model cars, soft toys and dolls, books about trains, and wind-up toys. Make a list of about five activities and objects that might be appropriate for using in language games. This will give you ideas about the contexts in which you can practise language skills. You will also know which materials will engage the child's attention. Now you will need to assemble any equipment that you have planned to use. A list of the materials that parents and others have found to be very useful in engaging children's interest in language games is set out in Table 5.1.

Identifying the appropriate language level

Once you have observed the child and collected information about how he or she is communicating now, and any preferred activities and toys,

Table 5.1: The essential collection (toys and other useful teaching resources for children at all levels of development)

Balls, blocks of all sizes and shapes, cars, planes.
Simple train set or something similar.
Model farm or zoo animals and people.
Cups, bowls, spoon, tea pot, cooking utensils.
Playdough, rollers and cutters.
Containers: all sizes and shapes for bath, washing up bowl and so forth.
Cloths, face washers.
Teddy, soft dolls with removable clothes.
Bed and bed clothes; cardboard box or cushion for a doll's bed.
Old cloths, nappies/diapers, hats.
Glove or finger puppets.
Purses, bags, boxes of all sizes for small objects to be put in and taken out.
A 'posting box' or 'gone' box; this is made from a cardboard box with a flap cut in the lid to put small objects in.
Large cardboard boxes in which a child can sit.
Noise-makers; xylophone, bells, shakers, drum and so forth.
Simple puzzles.
Picture books; make your own from photo albums, plastic folders clipped together, magazines, cards and so on (involve other members of family in making these).
Paper and crayons for drawing.
Junk; for example, plastic bottles, cotton reels (use your imagination).
Mirror.
Surprise bag (small cloth bag with drawstring or elastic around the top; opening big enough to allow child to feel what is inside and pull objects out).
Jack-in-the-box.
Tapes of music; bought or make your own of music and songs that the child enjoys.

For children with more advanced skills
Lottos, dominoes, colour matching games, and so forth.
Early reading books.

---

you can decide the programme level that you think the child has reached. Ideas for more detailed assessment of children's current communication skills are included in the remaining five chapters in this part of the book (Part 2). Each of these chapters is concerned with a particular programme level and you need to decide which chapter is likely to be most relevant for you and your child. For example, if the child is not yet using consistent sounds, gestures or words you should turn to programme level 1 (Chapter 6) which is concerned with the preliminary skills of looking together, turn-taking and imitation, and appropriate play. If the child has these early skills but does not use intelligible words, you should begin with programme level 2 (Chapter 7). If the child is just beginning to produce single words, turn to programme level 3 (Chapter 8). If the child is beginning to put two words together, look at programme level 4 or, perhaps, programme level 5 (Chapter 9). Issues associated with appropriate use of language (communicative intentions) are considered in Chapter 10 and you should refer to this information as the child's skills increase since development in pragmatic skills increases at the same time as other aspects of language development. Each chapter begins with suggestions for more detailed assessment of the child's language skills in the particular aspect of language that is the focus of that chapter.

When selecting an appropriate level at which to begin you need to remember that it is advisable to start at a point where the child will experience success. This will help to ensure that he or she enjoys interacting with you and co-operates in your planned activities. Look at the language level that the child is at now, as a starting point for your programme, rather than moving too quickly to a level where the child is likely to experience difficulties and lose interest in your games.

Selecting language objectives

You can select some initial teaching objectives on the basis of information obtained from assessment of the child. These will comprise the specific actions, gestures, sounds, words or simple sentences that you have decided the child could learn. How will you decide what to teach the child? A number of factors are important in choosing teaching objectives. Who are the most important people in the child's life? Are there favourite objects, games or events? What does the child like to eat or drink? Does he or she have a security blanket or similar favourite object? There are unlimited possibilities for topics from which you can select items to teach but it is important that the ones you choose are appropriate for this particular child. They will help the child move to a higher level of language functioning.

It is usually appropriate initially to choose four or five actions, gestures, sounds, words or phrases as your first teaching objectives. Later, when you and the child are familiar with the new routine, this list can be extended to include 10 items. At the start of a programme it is a good idea to include a few items that you suspect the child already knows. We call these 'success' items. They help to make the child feel good about taking part in the programme and be willing to participate in your planned activities. Once you begin you will need to monitor progress in the items you have chosen. Those that are learned can be dropped from the list and new items selected. Those that are not learned will also need to be replaced with other items that may be more successful. Details about the implementation of this process are described in the next five chapters.

Planning where, when and how to implement language activities

Now that you have decided what to teach and which activities to use in your teaching you need to plan where the teaching will take place and at what time or times of the day. You will also have to think about how you will introduce the activities. What role will you take? Answers to these questions will be determined by the specific goals and activities that you have chosen. For example, words associated with water, taps and washing will be taught at bath-time and, if you are patient enough, while you are washing up or hanging out the clothes. Words to do with eating are best taught at meal or snack times. Some of your teaching should be carried out during special times that you set aside to spend with the child. You will need to choose a time when you and the child will be fairly free from other distractions and a place where you will both be comfortable. If necessary, you might have to organise activities to occupy other children while you are busy, although they can often be included in the activity. You might be able to find a time when others are not at home, or already well occupied.

In developing a plan for teaching the child, you will need to decide when, where and how you will implement this plan:

When?   In the morning, after tea, before bed.
Where?   In the kitchen, the garden.
How?   While sitting on the floor playing with a car, having a tea party or getting ready for bed.

Language teaching is best carried out in three types of situations:

- within daily routines;
- at appropriate times that occur spontaneously during the day;
- as part of planned activities that have a high level of interest for the child.

Much learning occurs during routine events. These types of situations recur often and have a predictable format or script (see Chapter 3). Examples include:

- eating lunch;
- washing up;
- reading a book;
- playing in the park;
- visiting grandmother;
- going to bed.

Within the relatively fixed set of activities associated with these types of events, opportunities should be planned for children to practise appropriate language skills. For example, level 1 turn-taking can be practised while throwing a ball at the park, saying 'my turn, your turn'. Level 2 performative sounds such as 'whee' and 'oo-oo' can be practised on a swing. There are many opportunities for using the single words and simple sentences of levels 3 and 4 during mealtimes, as when adult says 'do you want egg or tomato?' and the child replies 'egg'. On family visits, the child can practise saying 'hello Nana', 'hello Auntie' or count the stairs, 'one, two, three, four'. The more advanced skills of level 5 can be practised while shopping, with the child asking questions about what is needed and describing what has been bought. It is important to take advantage of these recurring situations because they provide a rich source of opportunities for children to practise simple language skills. Similarly, nursery rhymes and familiar stories with repeated dialogue such as 'The Three Bears' and the 'Three Billy Goats Gruff' also allow children to practise talking.

Many opportunities for teaching language occur spontaneously during the day. For example, the child at level 1 can be encouraged to imitate Mummy clapping her hands or drinking tea. Skills such as waving 'goodbye' can be learned when someone leaves or arrives. Similarly, performative sounds can be practised: 'br'mm' and 'toot toot' when talking about going for a ride in a bus or a car, or 'woof' and 'prrr' or 'miaow' when the child sees a dog or a cat. There are many occasions when the single words, simple sentences and more advanced skills can be practised, such as while unpacking a shopping bag or going for a walk. These kinds of situations are particularly appropriate if language-teaching experiences can only be provided within normal daily activities, either at home or in an early childhood group setting.

Planned activities that are highly interesting to the child can be used to practise language. For example, for the child at level 1 in the language programme, activities involving blocks, pop-up toys, puppets, finger plays and 'boo' games are a good way to teach the preliminary skills of looking and attending, taking turns, imitation and appropriate play. At level 2, activities with dolls or soft toys, small cars, model animals and musical instruments provide opportunities to encourage performative sounds like 'br'mm', 'moo' and 'bang'. Matching objects to pictures is a good way to encourage a child at level 3 to label these objects, while games such as Lotto or Snap are useful for teaching the level 4 and 5 skills of early sentences and asking questions.

To be successful, the same games are usually repeated over a number of days or weeks. This gives the child time to learn the skills that have been selected for teaching. Often, three or four different games are included in each practice session, with new games introduced and old ones discarded according to the interest and progress of the child. Children need time to learn and enjoy doing familiar activities and playing with favourite objects over and over again.

Playing with children

If you are not used to sitting and playing with the child, or if you are a little unsure about how to begin, here are some suggestions about ways of sharing in games, encouraging play and introducing new toys. You should remember that the world is very big and threatening for many children; they like to be close to a carer for security and support. The child will be happy that you are near, showing an interest in what he or she is doing. Sharing the game will give you both a sense of togetherness.

If you find it difficult to begin a game with the child, try starting off by just sitting nearby. Get down on the floor if you possibly can. If this feels strange, try sitting down with something to occupy you such as a book or some work. Give the child some toys to play with and when the child is happily involved with the toys, you can look at what he or she is doing. The child will just be happy to have you near and watching. In time, the child will come close to you, perhaps showing you a toy. Then you can comment on the toy or on what the child is doing. Before you know it, you will have begun to follow the child's lead and you will have joined in the game. You still need to remember to stop, sometimes, to watch and listen to the child as he or she plays. Once this joint attention is established, you will be in a position to guide and extend the child in the game. At this stage, your smiles and laughter will tell the child that you approve. In this way you build up the child's confidence.

If a child seems to lose interest in an activity, you might decide that this is a good time to introduce some simple songs and rhymes. You can change the words of the songs to suit what you are doing, incorporating key words or sounds that you want to teach into your song ('This is the Way we Roll the Ball', for example).

When you and the child are comfortable, sitting together and playing, you can start introducing new toys and actions as well as new ways of using familiar toys that you have planned; feeding and bathing Teddy, building a bridge for the cars and pushing them through it, rolling the ball back and forth. These simple routines will encourage the child to take turns with you in a game, and help to develop new play skills. Do not expect the child to follow all your ideas. Encourage the child when he or she discovers new ways of doing things without your help. Remember, as you play, to comment on what both you and the child are doing and to use appropriate noises and gestures or words during the game, such as 'br'mm', 'boo', 'gone' and so on.

At this stage, it is also important to have a variety of things to play with so that the child can choose what is most interesting. These items need not be expensive: blocks, balls, old containers into which things can be put to roll and shake, cardboard boxes and kitchen utensils are all interesting to children. It is a good idea to have a box or cupboard where the child can have ready access to the toys and be free to explore. New items can be added from time to time and broken items, or those that are no longer interesting to the child, can be removed. Simple toys are best. By sticking to simple toys that the child can easily manipulate, you will avoid or lessen the inevitable frustration that comes with a toy that breaks too easily or is too difficult or complicated.

If possible, you should try to select language objectives to practise in all three of the types of situations described here. If it is too difficult to include a special playtime in your daily routine, make sure you look for appropriate opportunities during the day and try to identify some regular event where a relevant language task can be practised.

If you cannot provide individual sessions and must incorporate your language teaching into an early childhood context that involves groups of children, then the routine situations described here are particularly important as a means to teaching appropriate language skills to a child. Moreover, once you know the objectives that are appropriate, you can include specific language goals for each of the children involved in a group activity. For example, at eating and drinking times, or when asking for equipment or permission to go outside, children can be taught to use appropriate actions, gestures, sounds or words to get what they want or need. Group situations have the advantage that each child can see and hear peers model appropriate actions and speech. This issue is discussed in more detail in Chapter 13.

Involving all the family

Finally, you should try to involve the whole family in your language programme. At home, ensure that everyone knows what you are doing and has an opportunity to join in. Older brothers and sisters are often interested and have time to help when parents are unable or too busy. All those involved with the child need to be told about your current language objectives. This will help to ensure that the child is encouraged to use any new skills at every opportunity, not just when you are there to give encouragement.

Once the child begins to use the new skills that you have been teaching, tell others such as grandparents, aunts and uncles and the babysitter what the child has learned to do. At home, write it on a card and tape it on the refrigerator. Write a note to the preschool teacher or other helpers so that they can encourage the child to use the new skills at appropriate times. Some parents, teachers and care-givers find it useful to keep a record of what they are working on and how the child is progressing in a communication or language book. Such a book provides a good source of information for everyone who is helping the child or is interested in his or her progress. Involving everyone in your programme ensures that the child has plenty of practice with different people. This will help him or her to progress more quickly to the next level in the language programme.

Checking progress

Once you have begun to implement some specific teaching objectives you will need to carry out some form of evaluation to check whether or not your objectives have been achieved. Here, you will be interested in:

- progress on specific objectives;
- progress on programme levels.

Progress on specific objectives

Sometimes it is helpful to monitor a child's progress on a current language objective by noting at regular intervals whether a particular action or sound is produced successfully by the child. If you wish to record this information formally, some examples of data collection sheets are included in Appendix B. These sheets are most appropriate if you are using planned games in your language programme. Videoing an activity can also be helpful; it will enable you to check how the child is progressing, particularly when you do not have time to record what is happening during a game and find it difficult to remember what happened later. This type of information is useful in two ways. It is helpful as a means of deciding when to move on to a new activity or higher level in the language programme. It can also help you realise that the child is learning the skill you want to teach and this can be important if progress is slow. Very slow progress may result from the child's lack of interest in the activity you have chosen, or because the task is too difficult. In either case, you may need to abandon that activity and choose another one.

Progress on programme levels

When a child appears to be learning the tasks you have planned quickly, without much practice, you should find out if it is time to move on to the next level in the language programme. To check the child's progress, you can re-use the tasks you gave the child initially or find a similar set to check on current skills.

Once you have assessed the child and know the level of his or her current skills, you can begin to plan your teaching programme. Details of planning at each language level are set out in Chapters 6 to 10 that follow. The general procedures involved in setting up activities to practise new language skills have been described in this chapter. Some hints for setting up a successful language programme are set out below.

Hints for setting up a successful language programme for a child

Assessment

Take time to assess the child's current language competence before you start. This will ensure that you have identified the appropriate level to begin teaching. Several periods of both formal and informal observation are better than one long period.

Seek information about the child's communication abilities, styles and strategies from relevant adults, including parents, other family members, teachers and other carers. Ask about how the child communicates with them.

Selecting teaching objectives

Identify at least one activity that interests the child. This will be the context in which you will implement your objectives.

Think of four or five actions, sounds or words to introduce within this activity. These will be the specific items that you will plan to teach. Include at least one or two that the child can already do as 'success' items. Note that in some cases, such as where the aim is to encourage the child to look at something of interest with you (see the early part of Chapter 6), the specific objective will be 'looking together'. Here, your goal will not involve identifying specific sounds or words to teach.

Choose achievable targets at first. Do not worry if some appear too easy. They will give you the opportunity to provide lots of praise and allow the child to experience success. You can always move on quickly, once you and the child have become accustomed to the procedure. This is much better than letting the child become 'stuck' on difficult targets.

Do not be worried about dropping an unsuccessful item. It may not have been appropriate or of interest to the child at the time you introduced it. If it is one you would like him or her to achieve, try it again later after the child has experienced success with other items.

Organising a practice session

Decide how to set up the activity to ensure that there are opportunities for the planned words or actions to occur.

Collect the materials you will need. Try to keep them ready to use when a suitable opportunity arises. Make sure you are organised before you invite the child to play with you.

Introduce only a few new target items at a time. Initially, both you and the child will need to learn the rules of the new game. Once you have developed your relationship within the activity, the child's communication behaviour will tell you when it is time to introduce some new items.

Choose targets that are easy for you to implement. In particular, they should interest the child and be relevant to his or her needs.

Remember to provide ample opportunity for the child to practise with as many people as possible in a variety of situations. Several short sessions, lasting five to ten minutes, or opportunities to practise during the day are better than one long session. Periods of play and routine activities usually provide the best times to practise. Make as much use as possible of opportunities that arise spontaneously during the day.

Give lots of praise. Young children really respond to intrinsic reinforcement such as a quick hug or pat and the sound of pleasure in your voice.

Slip in occasional opportunities to practise recently learned target items in your play to ensure that they are remembered. Practice is the key to retaining newly acquired skills.

Involving family and friends

Make sure that everyone who has contact with the child, including parents, siblings, other family members, teachers, the babysitter and other carers know about your current goals. Encourage them to practise these goals with the child if there is an appropriate opportunity. Use a communication or language book to let others know what you are doing and encourage them to keep you informed about anything relevant. Put notes on the fridge and family or staff notice-boards to remind relevant adults about your current goals.

If the child has interested siblings or friends, encourage them to become involved. It is amazing what a child can learn from another more competent child. This also helps overcome the difficulties that are sometimes encountered when one child appears to get more adult attention than others. The 'helper' will be rewarded by the attention given to his or her 'helpfulness'.

Selecting new goals and moving on to the next programme level

Once the child shows that an item has been learned, as when he or she can tap the table and say 'bang' on three separate occasions, drop this item from your list. Choose a new task. Refer to the following chapters for criteria to use when deciding the time to move from one language level to the next.

If the child does not appear to be learning a particular item that you have been practising for at least two weeks, you may need to reconsider its interest or difficulty level. It might be appropriate to replace that item with a new one.

At all times, avoid confronting a child with demands to 'look', 'do' or 'say'. The child will usually try to join in your tasks if they are embedded in an interesting activity or game. If the child does not want to join in, you may need to change your plans. Perhaps the activity is not interesting, or the child may not like sitting with you. You may need to look for naturally occurring situations in which to embed the practice. The tasks you have selected may be too difficult and you may need to move back to an earlier level in the programme to establish the new routine. Above all, make it fun and you and the child will be soon enjoying better communication.

The most important points to remember when you begin to practise language tasks are to follow the child's lead, ask only three times and avoid confrontation.

Summary

This chapter made suggestions about the steps that you will need to take before you can begin to help a child learn new language skills. Strategies are outlined to find out how a child is currently communicating, what his or her main interests are, which teaching goals you might select and how to set about achieving these goals.

In the next chapter, specific ideas are given for helping children who lack the preliminary skills of looking together, turn-taking and imitation, and appropriate play. Subsequent chapters in this part of the book focus on the pre-verbal skills of performatives and protowords, and then first words and beyond. Each of these chapters describes ways to assess a child. Help is then given in selecting and practising appropriate language and communication goals. Practical ideas for a variety of suitable activities and games are included here. Finally, each chapter ends with suggestions about how to decide when it is time to move on to the next level in the language programme.

Chapter 6
Preliminary Skills
(Programme Level 1)

While the sounds that an infant makes are important precursors of language and, in particular, later phonological development, babbling does not lead directly to speech. First words are derived from the child's earliest experiences with objects and, more particularly, people. So if children are delayed in learning to talk, attention needs to be paid to their daily activities and their interaction with familiar people and objects. In this chapter, suggestions are made about ways to find out whether a child has acquired three of the key skills needed to interact with people and objects: looking at something of interest with an adult (this is sometimes called 'joint attention' or 'shared gaze'), taking turns in an activity and knowing how to play appropriately with a variety of objects and materials. The chapter is divided into three sections, each of which is concerned with one of these three key skills. Each section includes details of procedures to assess a child's performance in the focus skill. Practical suggestions are then made about activities and materials that can be used with the child to improve performance in the target skill. Assistance is then given for checking the child's progress and deciding when to move on to the next task.

Research evidence suggests that language development depends on three major types of experiences involving both people and objects:

- *looking together or joint attention* – learning to look with an adult at something interesting, such as a butterfly, the moon or a picture of a puppy;
- *turn-taking* – learning to take turns with an adult in a shared activity. This involves imitation, which is a powerful means of helping a child to acquire and practise the skills needed to take part in a conversation. It might involve learning to take turns with a special toy, or imitating actions to wave 'goodbye';
- *appropriate play* – the acquisition of strategies needed to explore and manipulate the variety of objects and materials that children encounter each day, such as learning to push a toy car or build a tower from blocks.

Children can learn these skills in any order but the child usually needs to learn to look at something interesting with another person first and some children begin to play appropriately before they learn to imitate or take turns. However, each of these three skills is important if a child is to learn to talk appropriately. So, whatever the language level of your child, you will need to check each of these areas and be prepared to give the child more practice if the skills appear to be lacking.

Looking together

In Chapter 2 we reviewed research on the sequence of stages that children pass through as they learn to talk (Bates, 1976; Bloom, 1970; Brown, 1973; Halliday, 1975). These studies suggested that the origins of communication lie in activities that involve the child and an adult in jointly attending to objects and events that interest them both. Check whether your child will follow your lead and look at things with you.

Suggested assessment activities

The main goal here is to find out whether your child can follow your lead to look at something. You may check these skills by observing the child at different times during the day. Alternatively, you can set up a special time and check the child's responses to selected activities. Here are some ideas to check these skills. Notice that the four activities described here range from relatively simple tasks like looking at a moving, colourful toy to the more difficult task of looking at a book with an adult. You should substitute other similar activities if you feel those suggested here are not appropriate for your child. Your aim is to find out whether the child has the skills identified below.

Whatever activities you decide to use, you must remember to allow enough time for the child to respond to each task. Some children react very slowly and you need to allow them enough time. You might be able to record the assessment with a video-recorder. You can then check the child's responses more carefully later. In recording the results of your assessment you may wish to use the summary assessment sheets set out in Appendix C.

Assessment of looking-together skills

Will the child look at an interesting toy that is put in front of him or her?

- Find a toy that moves, makes a sound or is colourful, such as a Jack-in-the-box or pull-along toy with moving parts that makes a noise. Encourage the child to watch it. Does the child look for at least five seconds?

- Will the child look at a paper bag in which you have hidden a surprise? Hide a small toy, such as a ball, in a paper bag. Attract the child's attention and make sure that he or she knows something is hidden in the bag. Open the bag slowly and let the child find the toy. Does the child look for at least five seconds?
- Will the child look at your hands while you play a finger game or a hiding game with a favourite soft toy? Sing a nursery rhyme that has hand movements, such as 'Twinkle Twinkle Little Star' or 'Open, Shut Them'. Play a game with a favourite toy, first hiding it and then letting it appear gradually or suddenly. Does the child look for at least five seconds?
- Will the child look at pictures or a book with you? Take a favourite book or one with clear simple pictures. You could use pictures cut out of magazines in a scrapbook or a photo album with pictures of the family. Sit beside the child and look at the pictures in the book, talking about them and pointing to aspects that should interest the child. Does the child look at most of the pictures you talk about for at least five seconds?

If the child attends to three of the four activities, you can assume that he or she has the target skill and can move on to the next task. If the child is only able to do one of the four tasks, he or she probably needs to practise very simple 'looking together' activities such as following a colourful and noisy toy that moves into his or her line of vision. If the child is able to do two or three of the tasks then more practice is needed in this skill.

Suggestions for practising looking-together skills

Think of a number of activities that are likely to interest your child and provide opportunities for developing looking-together skills. These could include playing with interesting toys, finger rhymes, games with puppets or looking at simple, colourful picture books. Remember that you can repeat a game that interests the child several times during one practice session and over several days. You can repeat a game until you think the child is beginning to lose interest. Stop well before the child is bored.

Play these practice games with the child sitting close beside you or on your lap. If appropriate, try to keep the activity close to your face and exaggerate your facial gestures so that the child learns to look at your face as well as the toy. Keep the toy under your control and close to you. Look at the child and, as appropriate, talk about the toy's colour, movement and sound. Give the child plenty of time to react to what is happening and respond positively when the child looks at the toy. Your aim is to teach the child to pay attention with you when something interesting is happening.

Interesting toys

Most children enjoy and will watch toys that move, make a sound and are colourful. Here are some suggestions for such toys:

- balls;
- favourite soft toys;
- Jack-in-the-box or pop-up toy;
- wind-up toys, pull-along toys;
- toys with moveable parts such as a bus with people inside, a fire engine with a crane, a garage with opening doors;
- blocks (build a tower and knock it over, build a tunnel);
- model cars, cars that make a noise, trains;
- model animals;
- water and sand play: pouring, splashing, patting;
- play dough: rolling, squashing, cutting;
- musical instruments: banging, shaking.

Finger games and nursery rhymes

Try to choose songs and rhymes that are brief and interesting for a child who are not yet able to attend for long. Make the actions near your face to encourage the child to look at your lips and eyes as well as your face. Or play a finger game that involves touching some part of the child's body. Sit on the floor with the child beside you in front of a mirror. Do the actions with your hands beside the child. You can use any favourite family songs. Your aim is to do the songs and rhymes together, with the child watching and listening. It does not matter which songs and rhymes are used. Here are some examples of suitable songs and rhymes:

- Twinkle, Twinkle Little Star;
- Incy Wincy Spider;
- This Little Piggy;
- Round and Round the Garden;
- Open, Shut Them;
- Roly Poly.

Puppets

Simple but attractive puppets can be made out of old socks. Put your fingers in the toes of the sock and bend your fingers to touch the heel, to open and shut the puppet's mouth. Or draw a face on the inside of your fingers. Bend and dance your fingers to accompany a song. Most children are fascinated by the movements and sounds made by puppets which can be a powerful means of drawing their attention to you.

Pictures and books

Looking with a child at pictures and books is a very effective way for a child to practise attending closely to an activity with an adult. This is also a time when the language that the adult uses with the child is important. Remember that Chapter 4 and Appendix H set out clear guidelines on how to talk to children so that they hear good models of appropriate language.

When selecting books for language development experiences, begin with very simple picture books that have clear illustrations of familiar objects like an apple, cup, keys, chair, plate, spoon and shoe. Books can be made to suit children's particular interests by cutting pictures from magazines and pasting them into a scrap book or mounting them in picture albums. Family photos can also be used. Albums have the advantage that the pictures can be changed as the child's interests change. Use albums with pages that are strong enough to be handled often by a child.

While looking at books, point to anything that is likely to interest the child, commenting with clear simple words. Allow time for the child to look and respond. Remember that children with poor skills need many more opportunities than other children to practise a new task, so look at the same book or set of pictures for as long as the child remains interested.

Taking the next step

When should you decide to move on to the next skill? You need to check to see whether the child is progressing in the tasks you have been practising. Select at least two toys and two finger plays that are not familiar to the child. Show them to the child and see if he or she will attend to them for at least five seconds. If the child does not watch at least three items you need to give more practice. If the child watches three of the four items, it is probably time to move on to the next section.

Taking turns and imitation

Two important skills that underlie learning to talk are taking turns and imitation. Both these skills reflect the social bases of language. Learning to speak involves not only understanding the meaning of words and how to produce them, but also when to talk and how to take turns in a conversation. Imitation is important because it is a means for the child to learn how to produce words. So if a child is to acquire effective language skills, he or she will need to learn how to take turns with a partner and how to imitate what the partner is doing and saying. Some children who can talk still need practice in turn-taking skills so that they can begin to use the words they know to communicate effectively.

Initially, turn-taking and imitation skills are learned through games that involve the child in cooperative activities with an adult. Including a sound in the game (for example, when playing 'Boo') gives the child an opportunity to imitate both actions and sounds. Eventually, the sound rather than the action part of the activity becomes significant for the child. This is discussed in more detail in the next chapter (Chapter 7).

Does your child know how to take turns and imitate what is done by the partner in a game? Here are some suggestions for checking these skills. Note that if the child is unable to do one of the suggested tasks, it is suggested that you give the child some practice and then repeat the task. This strategy (check-practise-check) is followed because it is important to know if the child is, at this stage, able to learn from even a very brief practice session. If the child is ready to acquire these skills, he or she will probably respond to more practice. If there is no change in skill levels after some practice, it is likely that the child is not yet ready to learn these skills.

Suggested assessment activities

You can assess a child's skills in turn-taking and imitation by observing the child carefully during appropriate daily activities, or by setting up a series of tasks. Here are some suggestions for assessing these skills. Substitute alternative activities if you feel these suggestions are not appropriate for your child.

Assessment of turn-taking skills

- Will the child join in a game with you that involves taking turns with a toy? Sit opposite the child on the floor or at a table. Push a toy car towards the child, roll a ball, or throw a bean bag. Encourage the child to return the object to you. Does the child return the object? If you answered 'no', give the child some practice. Model the task again and encourage the child to take a turn in the game. Now re-administer the task. Does the child take a turn after practice?
- Will the child take turns with you in an activity involving objects? Sit opposite the child with an activity that includes small parts that can easily be put in/on or taken out/off, such as a peg board, small blocks or other items that can be put into a container or a ring game. Demonstrate an action. For example, take a peg off the board and put it into the container or take a block and begin to build a tower. Say 'look, my turn'. Model the action. Encourage the child to take a turn in the activity. Say 'your turn' or '[child's name]'s turn'. Does the child take a turn in the game? If you answered 'no', give some practice and re-administer the task. Does the child take a turn after practice?

Assessment of imitation skills

- Will the child join in a game with you and imitate what you do? Hide your face with your hands or a scarf and, as you uncover your face, say 'boo'. Does the child copy you and hide, or accept your help to hide and then reappear? If you answered 'no', help the child to imitate this action. Model the task again and encourage the child to imitate you. Shape the child's hands to imitate the actions. Now re-administer the task. Does the child do the action after practice?
- Will the child imitate simple actions that you model? Sit opposite the child. Select four simple actions, such as: clap hands; hit table; rub tummy; drop a toy. Model the action and encourage the child to do it too. Does the child imitate the action? If you answered 'no', provide some practice. Model each action again and encourage the child to imitate you. Shape the hands. Now re-administer the task. Does the child imitate the action after practice?

If the child is able to do three or four items on the first attempt, you can move on to the next section. If the child is not able to do at least two actions after practice, then he or she is probably not yet ready to begin these activities. If the child can only do two items after practice, you should continue to practise these games.

Suggestions for practising turn-taking and imitation skills

Think of a number of activities that involve you and the child in taking turns and imitation. It is important to select activities that interest the child and that he or she will enjoy repeating over several days. Remember that you have two goals:

- to teach the child to take turns; and
- to teach the child to imitate your actions.

Both these skills are very useful for helping the child to acquire good play skills, as well as for learning to talk. Remember to say 'my turn' and '[child's name]'s turn', so that the child learns the rules of the game. A physical prompt such as patting the child's hand or chest may help. When you are teaching a new activity, always demonstrate it first before asking the child to imitate you. For example, if you want the child to build a three-block tower, say 'watch me' or 'look'. Then build the tower. Give the blocks to the child and say 'now you do it'. If necessary, help the child to pick up a block and put it on top of another. When the child can do the activity with a model, then just say 'you build' or '[child's name] build'. Say 'my turn', 'your turn' if you want the game to include turn-taking. When selecting activities or actions for the child to learn to imitate, select a sound or word that you can pair with each action. For example, you could label each action, or make an appropriate sound during a game with a soft toy or doll ('smack lips', 'yum yum', 'eat', 'drink', 'sleep', 'walk'), or accompany an action such as rolling a ball or pushing a model car with a sound like 'oh!' or 'br'mm br'mm'. This will allow the child to begin to associate particular sound patterns with specific actions or games, and will provide a basis for you to begin to teach early sounds (see Chapter 7) and words (see Chapter 8).

When introducing a new activity, you will first need to model appropriate actions and then encourage turn-taking and imitation. This can take place in situations that allow for relatively informal play, such as with water, or in a sand pit. Play these activities with the child close to you so that he or she can watch you easily. Model appropriate actions. Show the child what you are doing and encourage imitation. Say, 'look, you do this' or 'Jason's turn'. Informal games for turn-taking:

- soft toys and dolls   wash face, brush hair, set table, eat
- kitchen corner   cook dinner, pour tea, drink, wash up
- water play   pour, empty, fill, splash
- sand play   dig, fill bucket, build castle, make cakes
- dough   roll, pat, cut, pile up
- blocks   build tower and push over
- cars and trains   push cars down ramp, under bridge
- balls, small bean bags   put into bucket and empty out
- outside equipment   take turns on slippery dip, climb through tunnel
- mechanical toys   take turns to operate a wind-up toy
- commercial games   take turns with a picture lotto

Actions to imitate (sit opposite child or in front of a mirror):
- Roly Poly with hands;
- touch parts of the body: head, nose, lips, knees, toes;
- shake hands: clap hands;
- hammer fists together;
- stamp feet;
- touch finger to lips;
- make a kissing noise;
- bang two blocks together;
- bang a drum or other musical instrument.

Action songs and games

Children usually enjoy action songs and will often produce appropriate sounds in such songs. Here are some suggestions for songs that are

Mary Immaculate College
Issue Receipt

Customer name: Sejal Toca Yarza

Title: Born to talk : an introduction to speech and language development
ID: 0103344124
Due: 11/11/2014 21:45

Title: Language development
ID: 0103445880
Due: 11/11/2014 21:45

Title: Child language development : learning to talk
ID: 0101194674
Due: 11/11/2014 21:45

Total items: 3
10/28/2014 10:55 AM

Thank you for using the Self Service System
Please retain this receipt for Due Date

particularly appropriate to use in turn-taking and imitation activities. They are also useful if you are working with a child in a group situation (see also Chapter 13). Where the song can include a variety of actions, let each child suggest what to do. Some examples of appropriate action songs include:

- Ring-a-Ring-o'-Roses;
- Row, Row, Row your Boat (for children facing in pairs);
- Here we go Round the Mulberry Bush;
- Everybody do this;
- The Wheels of the Bus;
- Simon Says.

Taking the next step

If you think the child has learned to take turns with you and imitate your actions, check by introducing four new activities that you have not already practised. If the child is able to do at least three, you can probably move on to the next section. Remember to provide plenty of opportunities to take turns during each day because you will base your teaching of first words on the skills the child acquires during turn-taking and imitation activities. If the child does not succeed in at least three items you need to give more practice.

Appropriate play

Language emerges out of a child's experiences, particularly from those experiences involving actions with toys and objects, as well as people. For example, before using a word to represent an object, the child must acquire strategies for exploring and learning about the object. Initially, a baby will mouth an object, wave it, drop it and bang it, but over time these strategies are combined to become more complicated, as in waving and then dropping, or putting the object into a container. New ways of exploring objects are also learned, such as squeezing, biting, pushing, hiding or throwing. Sometimes a sound is added to an action sequence, for example, dropping it and saying 'oh-oh' or pushing it and saying 'br'mm'. Often these sounds have been heard by the child while playing the dropping game with a parent or while playing a game of pushing cars with a sibling.

Over time, the child will begin to use a part of the game or familiar routine to indicate that he or she remembers it and wants to do it again. The remembered part could be a gesture (hand movements to represent pushing the car) or a sound ('br'mm'). Such actions and sounds may be used to represent other daily routines in the child's life such as a grasping action to indicate that the child wants a toy that is out of reach, or smacking the lips to indicate thirst. The significant point is that the child develops a repertoire of actions and sounds for using and playing with the objects encountered each day. This is important as these experiences are the substance out of which words emerge.

Suggested assessment activities

Does your child know how to play appropriately with a variety of toys and objects? Here are some ideas that you can use to assess play skills. You should substitute other activities if you feel these suggestions are not appropriate for your child.

Assessment of appropriate play skills

- Will the child play appropriately with familiar toys? Put a toy car, soft toy or doll in front of the child and encourage the child to play with it. Does the child push the car, or pat, cuddle or walk the stuffed animal or doll? If not, model an appropriate action. Put the child's hand on the car and push it, or put the soft toy or doll in the child's arms and rock it. Now re-administer the task. Does the child play appropriately after practice?
- Will the child use familiar household objects correctly? Put a cup, hat or hairbrush in front of the child and encourage play. Does the child use these items appropriately? If not, model appropriate actions, encourage imitation and recheck. Does the child use the objects appropriately after practice?
- Will the child look at books, or draw on paper with a pencil or crayon? Put a book in front of the child, or a pencil or crayon and piece of paper. Does the child look at the book or use the drawing material appropriately? If not, give some practice and recheck. Does the child look at the book or use the drawing material correctly after practice?

If the child did three or four of the tasks on the first attempt you can move on to the next chapter. If the child is not able to do at least two of the tasks after practice, then he or she is probably not yet ready to begin these activities. You should spend more time practising looking together, turn-taking and playing imitation games. If the child can do two or more of the tasks after practice, you should continue to practise appropriate play activities.

Suggestions for practising appropriate play skills

To help a child acquire appropriate play skills, you should follow the same procedures as were suggested earlier for turn-taking and imitation.

Model appropriate behaviour and encourage the child to do as you do. Involve the child in the game. Keep accompanying the child in the game until you are sure that he or she can continue without you. Then you can withdraw and leave the child to play independently.

Many of the activities that are appropriate for practising play skills can be introduced when the child is in a group with other children. This issue is discussed in more detail in Chapter 13. In this case you can involve a few more competent children in the activity so that the child has good models of appropriate play skills, as well as partners for turn taking. It is often a good idea to begin practising new play skills in one play area, such as with blocks and cars, or with soft toy animals and dolls in a tea party. Once these skills are established you can extend the practice activities to other areas of play.

When you begin to help a child develop play skills, it is a good idea to select activities to practise in play contexts that allow for relatively free or unstructured activity, such as in a doll corner, with blocks and model cars or in the sand pit. Children engaged in these types of activities can choose what they want to do. There are few rules about how to play these games. In contrast, activities described as structured include mechanical toys (for example a pop-up toy, a wind-up dog), board games (such as animal lotto and puzzles) and construction toys (for example Duplo). Even bikes, slippery-slides and swings can be described as 'structured' because children are limited in the way they use such materials. Play equipment that can be described as 'structured' is very useful when you are teaching a child more advanced language skills and you need some control over what the child does and says (see Chapters 9 and 10). In the very early stages of learning to communicate, however, unstructured materials are more useful because they can be used flexibly, in accord with the child's current interests. Examples of unstructured activities suitable for learning appropriate play activities include:

Indoors:

- games with soft toys and dolls;
- tea parties, cooking;
- blocks and cars;
- dressing up and pretend games.

Outdoors:

- sand pit;
- water play;
- outdoor blocks;
- informal games without rules.

In the types of activities listed above, children are often left to play relatively independently. However, children who have not yet acquired a variety of play skills may need help to begin to use more sophisticated strategies. To help the child progress, you will need to organise the child's experiences in these areas to ensure that the child is both learning appropriate ways of playing with different materials and also hearing appropriate sounds and words. Remember that children who have had difficulty acquiring adequate play skills and speech may not attend to the language they hear, so it is a good idea to encourage the child both to watch and to listen to you as you model new actions and appropriate words during a game (some suggestions are included in the next chapter). This will help the child begin to associate particular words and sounds with the activity.

Remember that to help a child begin to play appropriately the child needs to learn how to explore and manipulate different toys and materials, and needs to hear clear models of appropriate sounds and words during this activity.

Games should have a high level of interest for the child. You should play them briefly (for about five minutes), but often (daily if possible) and in the early stages when the child is still learning what to do, preferably with the same partner.

The adult should model appropriate actions and encourage the child to imitate. Once the child can imitate an action, encourage it without a model.

Comment on the child's actions, using clear, simple words (see Chapter 4). Try to limit your language to key words. Follow the child's lead as far as possible. Remember that the aim of these games is for the child to learn how to play appropriately with a range of objects and materials.

Taking the next step

Once the child demonstrates appropriate play with a variety of materials, shift your focus during the games from acquisition of appropriate play skills to activities that are accompanied by sounds and early words. This transition is discussed in the next chapter.

Summary

Suggestions were made in this chapter for setting up language acquisition activities with a child who does not yet have the preliminary skills of 'looking together', turn-taking, imitation and appropriate play. Suggestions were made about ways to assess the child's current skills in each of these areas, and for setting up games and other opportunities for acquiring and practising these skills if necessary.

It is important to remember that children who appear to be more advanced in their development than this level but who are having problems in acquiring speech, may, in fact, lack some of the early skills described in this chapter. It may seem inappropriate to consider working on these skills with a child who appears to be relatively competent and perhaps has a few recognisable words and phrases, but these skills are the foundations upon which language is based: the child needs to be able to do these tasks if you are to help with the development of his or her language. So before you begin to focus on more advanced aspects of language, check that the child has these skills and is willing to use them.

Finally, it should be noted, again, that while the skills of 'looking together' should precede the other skills discussed in this chapter, there is no fixed order in which the others should be learned. The sequence of 'looking together', followed by 'turn-taking and imitation', and then 'appropriate play' was chosen because it seemed to be a logical progression. In fact, play skills can be taught through turn-taking and imitation. Later, all these skills will be needed when the child learns to talk. They function as tools that are used to acquire other skills, including language, so there is a good reason for helping children to acquire these basic 'tool' skills first. However, the order in which they are introduced should be decided on the basis of the interests and needs of both adult and child.

Chapter 7
Pre-verbal Skills
(Programme Level 2)

Before children begin to produce recognisable words they usually acquire a range of sounds that they use consistently with particular events or during specific activities. Sometimes the event associated with these sounds is easily recognised, such as a sucking noise for a drink, or 'tick tick' for the clock or watch. Others sound like words but have no recognisable meaning although the child appears to understand them and uses them intentionally to convey a message. For example, Alice uses 'ot' when she wants a special toy and 'bah' when she has wet her nappy. These consistent sounds or 'words' are sometimes called *performatives* or *protowords*. They are important because they represent a definite stage that generally occurs after the child has acquired early turn-taking, imitation and play skills and before a variety of clear words are produced.

Performatives refer to sounds produced by children as part of an activity, often involving a game with an adult. 'Boo' is a good example of a performative learned as a key part of the 'Peek-a-boo' game. Other examples include 'br'mm' which many children learn to vocalise while playing with toy cars, or a sound like 'ee-ee', used while playing with a model aeroplane. These performative sounds are initially not used by the child to represent or indicate but are simply part of the routine associated with a particular activity or toy.

Children probably learn performative sounds earlier than words because they are usually easier to say. They are also often produced in an extended or repetitive form, such as 'oo-oo-oo', 'quack quack', 'woof woof' or 'bang bang'. Such repeated sounds must stand out in the confusion of speech sounds that the child hears. Moreover, they are often associated with physical movements that are related to events that have high interest for the child. 'Bye bye' is a good example here. It is usually paired with a waving movement and is probably produced by children, initially, as a noise paired with an action that is modelled and shaped by an adult at appropriate times. You should encourage children who are not yet talking to use some performatives that imitate you, since, in learning such sounds, the child will also be learning to attend to and imitate the speech model you provide.

Some examples of common performatives include:

drop/fall down	'oh oh'
food	lip-smacking noise
swing	'whee'
fire engine	'ee-or-ee-or'
bus	'toot toot'
dog	'bow wow'
aeroplane	'whoo-oo-oo'
kiss	popping lips sound
favourite blanket	'er-er'
general excitement	'yabba-dabba-do'
waving/going out	'ta-ta'

Protowords are consistent, often word-like sounds, produced by some children. Such children almost seem to develop a 'private language' with a range of protowords but the meaning of these 'words' is only recognisable through their obvious association with specific objects or events. Thus, a sucking noise can begin to be used to indicate 'drink' in a picture of a cup, or that the child is thirsty. Some protowords have no recognisable origin in the child's experience but their meaning can be recognised if you observe when they are used by the child. Sometimes, the child uses such words in so many different contexts that it is impossible to discern any precise meaning. It is almost as if the child knows that a 'word' is needed, but does not know which word to use.

While protowords are an early or immature form of language and can be used by a child to communicate successfully with another person, such words represent a primitive language system. They will not enable the child to communicate with people outside the immediate circle of familiar family and friends. Therefore, it is important to encourage the child to begin to substitute conventional word forms for private protowords. Many children make this transition without special help, provided they hear clear models of the conventional word forms and do not find that their idiosyncratic words are sufficient to convey their meaning to others. If your child has developed a number of protowords, you should try to provide clear models of conventional words.

No suggestion is made here for assessment of the child's use of protowords, since it is not appropriate to 'teach' them. It is, however, a good idea to note whether the child is using protowords because this is further evidence of progress in acquiring language skills. Make a list of any protowords that you hear and their meaning. This will be useful information for teaching first words (see Chapter 8).

Suggested assessment activities

Check to see if the child is using any performatives. Make a list of any sounds you hear and the situations in which they occur. Here are some suggestions for assessing performatives:

- Will the child produce an appropriate sound as part of a familiar game? If yes, is the sound produced spontaneously or only in imitation? Play Peek-a-boo. Does the child say 'boo' when it is his or her turn? Play Ring-a-Ring-o'-Roses. Does the child say 'a-tish-oo' or 'down'? If the child does not make the sound spontaneously, will he or she do it if you prompt? Repeat each task and model an appropriate sound. Does the child produce the modelled sound?
- Set up a game with model cars, trains, a fire engine or an aeroplane. Does the child make any performative sounds during this game, such as a screeching noise, 'toot', 'ee-or-ee-or' or 'whoo-oo-oo'? Set up a game with a tea-set and doll or soft toy. Does the child make any performative sounds during this activity, such as eating or drinking noises? If the child does not make any sounds spontaneously, will he or she do it if you prompt? Repeat the task and model an appropriate sound. Does the child produce the modelled sound?
- Set up a game with model animals. Does the child produce appropriate sounds while playing with the toys, such as 'quack quack', 'baa', 'woof woof' or 'moo'? If the child does not make any sounds spontaneously, will he or she do it if you prompt? Repeat the task and model an appropriate sound. Does the child produce the modelled sound?

If the child is able to make most of these sounds spontaneously, you will not have to give more practice. If a model is needed, you will need to provide more opportunities to use these sounds. Remember that children who are already using a few clear words may not like to produce performatives. Some of these children may be ready to move on to the single-word stage. You should look for ideas in the next chapter (Chapter 8) to help these children.

Sometimes children begin to produce single words as if they are performatives; for example, 'gone' and 'bye' are often used in this way. These children probably need more practice in producing performative sounds before they move on to single words. If the child does not make many sounds, you need to provide opportunities to practise such sounds in a game or other activity. Children who are having difficulty using consistent and intelligible words to communicate can often be helped to make a start by learning to produce these sounds in association with a familiar activity. Ideas for activities you can use to introduce the child to performative sounds are set out below. You will need to model the sounds yourself while taking part in each activity. Once the child is familiar with a sound, encourage imitation. Then watch to find out if the sounds are being used spontaneously during play. Once the child is using some sounds, either alone or with others, you can anticipate the next stage by substituting an appropriate word for each sound; for example, 'car' for 'br'mm', 'duck' for 'quack' and so on (see Chapter 8 for more on this).

Suggestions for practising performative sounds

All the activities listed in Chapter 6 for practising turn-taking, imitation and appropriate play can be used here. Choose activities that can include a sound, such as 'oops' or 'br'mm'. Here are some more ideas.

Activities associated with soft toys and dolls, tea-sets or blocks and cars and other familiar household objects provide good opportunities for using performative sounds. Some appropriate activities and sounds include:

doll eat	smack lips, 'yum yum', 'mmm'
pour tea	continuous 'sh-sh-sh' noise, 'pour-pour'
teddy drink	click tongue, 'drink-drink-drink'
teddy sleep	humming and rocking movement
push car	'toot', 'br'mm', 'bee-beep', crashing noise
plane dive	'whoo-oo-oo'
blocks fall down	'oh-oh', 'oops'
push fire engine	'ee-or-ee-or-ee-or'
train go	'chuff chuff', 'choo choo'

Model animals have been shown to be particularly effective for stimulating performative sounds. Use models of familiar animals that make a sound that the child can imitate. Some appropriate animals and sounds are:

dog	'woof woof'
sheep	'baa'
duck	'quack quack'
donkey	'ee-or'
cat	'meow'
pig	'oink oink'
turkey	'gobble gobble'
cow	'moo'
bird	'tweet tweet'
rooster	'cock-a-doodle-doo'
horse	'neigh' or tongue click
bee or fly	'bzzz'

Once the child knows a range of sounds, you should encourage their use during play with other related materials such as animal puzzles and picture books. Appropriate songs can also be taught. These are particularly effective if they can be sung in a group, for example, 'Old MacDonald had a Farm'. Many children are more likely to produce such sounds if they can hear other children first (see also Chapter 13).

Some children are interested in the sounds produced by musical instruments. You can introduce a child to these sounds during a game with such instruments. Talk about the sounds that each instrument makes as you play with them, or look at pictures of the instruments. For example:

drum	'bang bang'
bells	'ding ding'
horn	'beep beep'
trumpet	'toot toot'
triangle	'ting ting'
tambourine	'ring ring'

Once the child is familiar with these sounds, they can be included in action songs like 'We can play on the Big Bass Drum and this is the way we do it'. As with the animal sounds, this type of activity is very effective if played with a group of children who can model appropriate noises and actions for the child.

Use your imagination to find sounds that go with other familiar objects and events. For example:

water	'drip drip', 'whoosh'
flower	'mm-mm', 'sniff sniff'
broom	'swish swish'
tree and wind	'oo-oo'
smoke	'sh-sh'
something sticky or messy	'ugh', 'yuk'
going up stairs	'up, up, up' or 'one, two, three'
taking off clothes	'off'
something good	'yum yum'
starting off	'one, two, three, go', 'ready, set, go'

Sometimes, at this stage, you can link actions with words by using the words as if they were performatives. For example, saying 'up, up, up' as you climb stairs, saying 'up' as you put your arms up in a game or as you pick a child up from the floor or out of bed. Similarly, you can label actions like 'walk, walk, walk' as you walk together or make teddy or dolly walk. Other ideas include:

- 'run, run, run';
- 'jump, jump, jump';
- 'down' as the child goes down the slippery slide; or
- 'in' as you put the blocks away into a box or cupboard.

Even though children are not yet ready to use the full word, they will often be able to produce an approximation, for example:

Adult	Child
'up'	'u'
'walk'	'wa, wa, wa'

When a child has learned some performative sounds, you should provide a variety of situations where the sounds can be practised. Some useful games include using a 'gone' box, a 'surprise bag' or a matching game.

To play the 'gone' box game, cut an opening in the top of a shoe box, large vegetable box or ice-cream container. Collect six to eight objects you know the child associates with particular sounds, such as a clock ('tick tick'), a car ('br'mm'), a cow ('moo') and a toy horn ('toot, toot'). Demonstrate to the child that the object can be posted in the opening after the appropriate sound is made. You will need to keep your hand over the opening and only allow the child to post the object when the sound has been produced. As you post the object, say 'gone' or 'bye'. Make the game fun. If the child does not make the appropriate sound after a few opportunities, model the task: make the sound and post the object. When all the objects are 'gone', empty the box, reassemble the collection of objects and begin the game again. You can also play this game using pictures instead of objects.

A similar game can be played with a 'surprise bag'. Hide six to eight familiar objects in a cloth bag or pillowslip. Let the child feel in the bag for an object and bring it out to show you while making its sound. Once the object has been taken out of the bag, play with it or do an appropriate action, again making a sound; for example:

car + push + 'br'mm'

teddy + hug + 'ah'.

Alternatively, you can collect a set of pictures to match the objects. The child can match each object pulled out of the bag to a picture and make the appropriate sound.

Other games can be devised to practise performatives. For example, make a tunnel out of cardboard or a cardboard cylinder. Slide a variety of small objects, such as a car, keys, comb or animals down the tunnel.

Make an appropriate sound as the object disappears and reappears again, such as:

'whee'	'whoo'
'br'mm'	'boom'
'oo-oo'	'bang'
'moo'	'crash'

All these games can be played individually or in a small group. They can also be practised, without the 'gone box' or 'surprise bag', during daily routines like bath-time and snack-time. 'Hide' a floating object under the bath water and make a noise as you release it. A ping-pong ball works well in this game. Or put a biscuit or piece of fruit in a paper bag and let the child reach in and find it. Pair a sound with the food as it appears, such as 'mm-mm' and 'yum yum'. The 'surprise bag' game with its objects is a useful activity to take with you on car outings, or to appointments with the doctor. It will help to keep the child occupied.

It is a good idea to set yourself the aim of trying to use a sound or word to accompany your own and the child's actions as you play together or carry out daily activities. Some examples include:

'out' as you go out of the door
'whee' as you spin the child around
'oh oh' when you drop an object or stumble
'on' as you put on socks and shoes
'rub rub rub' as you wash arms and legs at bath-time

This way you will be constantly providing models for the child to imitate while reinforcing the idea that sounds go with actions.

Taking the next step

When the child has acquired some performatives, you can begin to pair a single word with these objects or events to encourage the child to replace the sounds with appropriate words. Once children begin to use performatives spontaneously you will find that they gradually substitute words for the sounds without any extra help from you. Now it is time for you to move to the next level in the language programme. The next chapter provides an outline of procedures to use for helping a child begin to use single words.

Summary

The idea of performative sounds and protowords was introduced in this chapter. This level is regarded as an important intermediate stage for the child who has the preliminary skills described in Chapter 6 but is not ready to produce recognisable words. Over time, most children begin to substitute words for performative sounds and protowords. However, experience with children who are having difficulty in acquiring speech skills has shown that learning to produce performatives can provide a very useful bridge between meaningless babble and first words. An understanding of performatives and protowords enables you to recognise the progress that a child is making on the road to fluent expressive language and spontaneous talking.

Chapter 8
First Words
(Programme Level 3)

Children's first communicative acts are usually related to real events that have a high level of interest for them, such as Daddy's car, a passing aeroplane, or the family pet. Later, the child learns to use gestures, sounds and words to make things happen or to obtain desired objectives, such as food, drink or comfort. This chapter is concerned with children's language development at the point where they begin to utter their first words. It begins with suggestions for assessing the current communication skills of children who are starting to produce intelligible single words. Specific words that are likely to be acquired by children at this stage of development are identified, together with ideas for games and other activities that may provide opportunities for practising these words.

As discussed in Chapter 2, detailed studies of children who are just beginning to talk have shown that, initially, they use words to:

- indicate the existence of something that interests them (for example, 'look');
- obtain objects and services that they want (for example, a toy, food or help to climb onto a swing);
- regulate other people's actions. This may include *protest* (for example, 'don't do that'; 'no') or *a request for attention or service* (for example, 'watch me'; 'come and play'; 'wash hands').

Once children begin to communicate these types of meanings intentionally with others using a few consistent gestures and sounds, opportunities can be provided to help them learn some useful words to use during such communication. This learning process can take place in a variety of different situations during the day. However, before introducing games to stimulate early speech, you will need to find out what gestures, sounds and words a child is already using to communicate with people. The best way to do this is through unstructured observation. For example, you may decide to observe the child carefully during daily routines, ask a parent or carer what meanings the child is expressing and how these are expressed, or take a language sample. You can also assess the child's production and imitation of single words by using a structured activity. These different methods of assessment are described below. Suggestions are then made for selecting new words to practise. Issues associated with the emergence of the communicative intentions identified above are explored more fully in Chapter 10.

Choice of language for children whose home language is not English

Many children belong to families where the language used in the home is not English, although English is the main language used outside the home: at the shops, the school, the church and so on. As these children begin to talk, their parents are sometimes uncertain about which language the children should be learning, the 'home' language, or that of the dominant group in the community. If you are worried about this issue and wonder which language you should encourage the child to learn, it is probably a good idea to choose the language that you are most comfortable using. Children are very adaptable, and once they have begun to use one language they are usually able to recognise contexts where 'other' words should be used: for example, when they are thirsty, they learn to say 'num' at home and 'drink' at preschool, or 'shi-shi' at home and 'wee' at school. If you are the child's main carer, you should probably decide to begin by helping the child to learn the language you like to use at home. If you are working with the child outside the home then you may not know the child's home language and so may have no choice about which language to use in your practice games. It may, however, be a good idea to talk to the child's parents or carers to identify some words from home that you can include in your programme. This issue is discussed in some detail in Chapter 15.

Suggested assessment activities

Children's communication skills can be assessed in a variety of ways that can be described as 'unstructured' or 'structured'. An 'unstructured' assessment technique means that the methods you use are quite informal and flexible, mainly involving careful observation of communication in everyday contexts. A 'structured' assessment is more formal, meaning that the procedures are implemented by following fairly specific rules or guidelines. Both these approaches will give you useful information. You may decide to begin with an unstructured assessment technique, such as a language sample, and supplement the information by using a structured assessment procedure. Examples of both unstructured and structured procedures for assessing children's communicative behaviour are described below.

Unstructured assessment of first words

Make a list of the meanings the child is able to express through gestures, consistent sounds or recognisable words. This information can be collected in three ways:

- *Observation.* Over a period of several days, make a list of all the gestures, sounds and words that you observe the child using. Also note the meaning of each item. If this is not obvious, follow the clues you use to recognise whether the child is expressing some communicative intent, such as any actions that occur, or the activity in which the gestures, sounds or words are used. It is sometimes helpful to record whether the item is used spontaneously or in imitation, what is going on at the time, who the child is talking to, and what you think he or she is trying to say. You may wish to use the observation record form for single words in Appendix D.
- *Parent report.* Ask a parent or carer to make a list of the gestures, sounds and words they know the child uses. They should also describe how and in what contexts these meanings are expressed. You might wish to suggest that they use the communication record form for sounds, gestures, words or phrases in Appendix D.
- *A language sample.* Set up an activity the child likes, such as a game with Teddy or looking at a book. Play the game with the child for five to ten minutes. Keep a note pad and pencil beside you and list all the child's communicative acts (gestures, sounds and words). A tape or video-recorder is useful here because it allows you to concentrate on interacting with the child during the activity. You can check later for any instances of communicative behaviour. Again, you should note any contextual clues that will help you understand the child's meaning. It may be helpful to read the guidelines for taking a language sample that are included in Appendix A.

Having collected a list of the ways in which the child is currently communicating, you can sort them into one of the five broad types of meaning listed below:

People:	Mummy, Daddy, sibling names, family pets;
Object:	labels: real things ('ball', 'car');
Actions:	related to movement ('look', 'fall down');
Modifiers:	related to conditions and states ('more', 'hot', 'blue', 'in');

Other: socially useful words ('bye', 'no'). Include
                            here any items that you are unsure how to
                            classify.

You should also note how each meaning is expressed. Is it by:

Gestures (G):   pointing
Sounds (S):   'br'mm'
Words (W):   'ba' (ball)

Here are some examples of two children's communication lists:

Johan's word list (4 years, 3 months):

People	Objects	Actions	Modifiers	Other
Bubba (W)	car (S)	go (W)	wet (W)	gone (G)
Dada (W)	hat (W)	hide (G)	hot (W)	no (W)
Mummy (W)		fall down (W)	more (G)	ta (W)
Spot (W)		come (G)	out (G)	there (G)
Ya Ya (teddy: W)		look (G)		

Laaya's word list (3 years, 9 months):

People	Objects	Actions	Modifiers	Other
Ibu (Mum: W)	book (G)	shi-shi (W)	hot (S)	kai-kai (W)
Ayah (Dad: W)	(ba)nana (W)	eat (G)	smelly (S)	ta (W)
	plane (S)	go up (G)	in (G)	oops (W)
	car (S)	open (G)		

If you are not sure how to classify a particular item, put it where it seems most appropriate to you. This is your list and you should sort the words in a way that makes sense to you. This information will give you a good record of the way the child is communicating, whether words are only used to obtain objects and never to protest or attract attention, and who the child talks to most often, such as Granny or a helper at the crèche. This information will be very useful when you are deciding which objectives to select for helping the child to learn some single words.

Structured assessment of first words

As an alternative to the informal methods described above, another useful way to assess a child's current communication skills is to set up an activity that the child enjoys, such as a tea party or a car game. While playing the game, you will need to ensure that the child has opportunities to use appropriate words, spontaneously or in imitation, while involved in the game. This information will supplement the list of words and meanings you have collected from parental reports and your own observations. Moreover, since an important aspect of the strategies that you will use to practise new language skills include imitation of an adult speech model, this assessment procedure will help you find out whether the child can imitate a word that has just been heard. Note that some children are more interested in activities than objects, and for these children, action words (for example 'go', 'jump', 'fall down') are often learned first rather than object labels.

When working through the assessment activities described below it is important to allow the child time to respond to each task. Young children often need more time to reply to requests to do or say than might be expected for older children, so try to wait for the child to attempt to do what you have asked.

Spontaneous speech

Will the child label a familiar object or action as part of a 'surprise' bag game? Use the 'surprise' bag that was described in the previous chapter. Find a cloth bag, a pillowslip or a large paper bag. Collect four objects that are familiar to the child. Label the items and let the child watch as you put each item into the bag. Now let the child feel in the bag for one of the objects. As the child takes it out, say 'What is it?' or 'What have you found?' If the child begins to play with the item, say 'What is . . . doing?' Can the child tell you? If he or she cannot label the object or use a word to describe what the object is doing (for example '[car] go'), look at the item carefully and ask again, 'What is it?' Repeat this procedure with the other objects. Keep a list of any words the child says. Your aim, here, is to find out whether the child can label four familiar objects or actions.

Some appropriate objects to use in a 'surprise' bag and words to use with them include:

ball	'gone'
car	'go'
key	'in'
cup	'drink'
spoon	'more' 'eat'
fruit	'banana', 'apple'
shoe	'on'
doll	'baby'
book	'open', 'read'
hat	'off'

brush	'brush'
duck	'quack'

- Use any other objects that you know interest the child. Does the child label three or four of the objects?
- Will the child label a familiar object or action in a picture book? Find a set of pictures or a picture book that includes objects or people that are familiar to the child. Sit beside the child and look at the pictures. Ask 'What's that?' 'Who is that?' or 'What is . . . doing?' Keep a list of any words the child says. Does the child say an appropriate word for three or four of the pictures?
- Imitated speech: will the child imitate a model of an appropriate word during an activity with an adult? Repeat the 'surprise' bag game described above but this time use four objects or pictures of objects that you think the child might recognise but which the child cannot already label. As the child takes each item out of the bag, ask 'What is it?' or 'What is happening?' If the child cannot reply, model an appropriate word. Say 'It's a . . .' or 'She's . . . ing.' Then encourage the child to repeat the word. Say 'You say . . .' Remember that your aim, here, is to find out whether the child can imitate your words. Keep a list of any words the child imitates. For this activity, you should select object labels and action words that are relatively easy for the child to say. For English-speaking children, some suitable words could include:

bell	pom pom	pig	kiss
bird	comb	mop	pull
bath	cow	mat	eat

You could include any other objects that may interest the child. Try to select items that have only one syllable and begin with a consonant such as 'b', 'm', 'p', 'c' or vowel sounds such as 'e' or 'a' that you know the child can say. Keep a record of what the child says. Does the child imitate at least four words appropriately?

- Will the child imitate a model of an appropriate word while looking at a book with an adult? Find a set of four pictures or a picture book that includes objects and activities that the child cannot already label. Repeat the procedure that was described in the previous activity. Try to elicit an appropriate word and, if the child cannot say the word, model it and encourage imitation. Does the child imitate at least four words appropriately?

If the child is able to label at least two of the items spontaneously or in imitation, he or she has appropriate skills to take part in the language activities described in this chapter. If the child is unwilling or unable to say the words or imitate your model you may need to go back to the imitation and turn-taking section in Chapter 6 (programme level 1) and encourage further use of performatives (Chapter 7: programme level 2).

Suggestions for practising first words

Once you have pinpointed precisely the meanings that the child is communicating and how this is done, you can begin to develop ideas for new words to practise. Look at the list of words, gestures and sounds that you compiled during the assessment activities you have just carried out. If most of the list comprises gestures you should look at the previous chapter which outlines ways of helping the child to produce performative sounds. Such sounds are often a useful bridge for the child who has acquired a range of gestures to express meaning but who does not use many clear words. If the child has a rich collection of gestures and is communicating quite complex meaning through them, but lacks intelligible words, you should consider including some signs among the ideas you are developing for practice activities. Indeed, when working with any child who is experiencing difficulties in learning to talk it can be helpful to pair either a natural gesture or sign with a new word that is being practised. Such signs and gestures provide a visual prop for the child and facilitate, rather than interfere with, the process of learning to use intelligible words. The use of signs and gestures to supplement speech is discussed in Chapter 12.

The strategy suggested to help your child begin to produce new words is derived from skills acquired during turn-taking and imitation games. In these games, the child learned to watch and copy actions and sounds. It is also based on the strategy, described in Chapter 4, which is used by carers with infants when they ask a question and then answer it themselves, knowing that the infant does not yet have the skills to reply. Examples might include the sequences: 'What will we do now? Have a bath!' and 'Where's your bottle? There!' Children who have problems learning to talk need:

* to hear clear models of new words; and
* to have opportunities to practise these words.

The child needs to be reminded of an appropriate word to use in a particular situation, to hear a model of the word that can be copied, and then to have an opportunity to use the word without a model, soon after it has been practised and before it is forgotten. This has been called the *conversation-imitation-conversation* or *C-I-C* strategy (Horstmeier and MacDonald, 1978).

The C-I-C strategy has three parts:

- conversation (C1);
- imitation (I);
- conversation (C2).

Here are some examples of the C-I-C strategy in use.

Jara is washing Teddy in home corner:

| C1 | Adult: | 'Jara, what's happening?' |
| | Jara: | no reply |

| I | Adult: | "Jara, say 'wash'." |
| | Jara: | 'Wash' |

| C2 | Adult: | 'Jara, what's happening?' |
| | Jara: | 'Wash'. |

Ben wants something to eat:

| C1 | Adult: | 'Ben, what do you want?' |
| | Ben: | no reply |

| I | Adult: | "Ben, say 'bickie'." |
| | Ben: | 'Bickie' |

| C2 | Adult: | 'What do you want?' |
| | Ben: | 'Bickie' |

Shauna is trying to show her mother something interesting:

| C1 | Mother: | 'What can you see?' |
| | Shauna: | no reply |

| I | Mother: | "Shauna, say 'balloon'." |
| | Shauna: | 'Balloon' |

| C2 | Mother: | 'What can you see?' |
| | Shauna: | 'Balloon' |

In these sequences the adult first gives the child an opportunity to produce an appropriate word correctly. If the child cannot do this, the adult models an appropriate word and encourages imitation. When the child imitates the word, the adult repeats the original question, giving the child an opportunity to use the word without a model.

It is very important to remember that you should never ask a child to say or imitate a word more than three times. Always avoid confrontation. If the child does not respond to the imitation request after three tries, leave this word and try again the following day. If the child refuses to attempt the word over a number of days, then drop it and find another word to practise or go back to an earlier level in the language programme, such as imitation of performative sounds (Chapter 7).

Selecting new words for practice

To help a child learn new words, first identify which words will be useful for the child. You can begin with four or five words and expand your list to as many as 10 words once the child has learned the rules of the new language game.

Next, you need to select an enjoyable activity or routine which provides opportunities for you and the child to use the selected words, such as during games with Teddy or a doll, during a ride in the car, at snack-time or bath-time. Finally, you can begin to use the C-I-C strategy to help the child learn to use the words appropriately. You may find it a little difficult to use this technique at first but you will be surprised how quickly it will become a natural part of your language with the child. Examples of words that might be suitable to include in a list for a child at the single-word level are included in the first words list in Appendix E.

Children need to acquire a variety of words from the five categories listed earlier, including names of people, object labels, actions, modifiers and other words. At first, they will mainly need words to label objects and familiar people, a few action words and some modifiers. Socially useful words, such as 'bye' and 'ta' also need to be acquired but these are usually learned during the child's daily activities and, as a result, do not need to be taught. However, some children do not acquire these words naturally and need some help.

Finally, it is worth noting that politeness words like 'please' and 'ta' should not be introduced until the child has begun to use a number of different words to communicate. These words often seem important to adults but they can cause difficulties for the child with poor communication skills. Both the child and his or her carer can become very frustrated when the child replies to a question like 'tell me what you want' by saying 'please' or 'ta'. In this situation, the child thinks that the desired answer has been given whereas the adult still does not have a satisfactory answer to the original question that was asked. For example:

Child: 'Ta.' (pointing at the cupboard)
Adult: 'What do you want?'
Child: 'Ta.' (still pointing at cupboard)
Adult: 'Tell me what you want.'
Child: 'Ta.'
Adult: 'I don't know what you want.'
Child: 'Ta.'

It is a good idea to wait until the child has acquired the words needed to express basic needs and interests before you begin to encourage these socially useful words.

Which words should you choose to teach first?

Most children begin to talk using labels for things that interest them very much. For example, apart from 'Mum' and 'Dad', many children say 'ball', 'bus' or 'car' first. Look at the list you have made of your child's gestures, sounds and words. It is a good idea to start with these. If the child is using a gesture or sound to communicate a specific meaning, choose an appropriate word for this meaning and put it on your list of words to teach. This list may include words for objects that are important for the child, for familiar people, actions, or modifier words. Make a list of up to 10 target words, including a few that the child already knows; these are called 'success' items and help ensure that the child feels happy about the activity you are both involved in. Now decide how to practise the words. Some can be taught during daily routines. For example, 'out' can be practised when it is time to go outside, 'come' or 'look' can be practised when the child tugs at an adult's clothing and indicates need for help or attention. Other words like 'car', 'ball', 'baby', 'sit', 'go', 'pat', 'up', 'in' and 'out' can be taught in a game or during daily routines.

Suggestions for practising new words

Having decided which words you will try to teach the child, choose a game or daily activity where the words can be used. Some ideas for appropriate games or activities are listed below. If you decide to carry out your practice as part of a game, then you will need to make a list of the target words and collect any materials needed. You may decide to monitor what happens during the game by keeping running records of target words used by the child using a small note book, 'post-it' notes or a data-collection sheet like the observation record form for single words included in Appendix D.

One of the most effective contexts for practising new words occurs within the events and activities that occur spontaneously during the day. When teaching in these settings it is helpful to have a list of your target words displayed in a place where everyone who has contact with the child can see it, such as on the refrigerator or family notice board at home, or on daily programme sheets or the notice board at preschool or at the day-care centre. A regular babysitter or nanny can be given a copy of the list.

To practise the language goals you have selected, look for an appropriate situation that occurs during the day, or set up an appropriate activity with the materials you have decided to use. Play with the materials while you follow the child's gaze and, at an appropriate time, introduce a C-I-C sequence using one of your target words. You may need to begin practising the word by giving the child an opportunity to hear it used in association with the corresponding object, action or event. For example, before attempting to teach 'Mum', find a photograph of her and ask 'where's Mum?' or 'show me Mum'. If the child demonstrates comprehension of the word 'Mum' then you can begin to introduce the C-I-C strategy.

| C1 | Adult: | 'Who's that?' (pointing to picture of Mum) |
| | Child: | no reply |

| I | Adult: | Say 'Mum'. |
| | Child: | 'Mu–' |

| C2 | Adult: | 'Yes, it's Mum.' |

Keep a check on what the child says for each item on your list. Once a correct word (or approximation for the word) is produced in the C1 condition over a few days, you can probably drop that item from your list and select another word to teach. Now tell everyone who has contact with the child that he or she can say 'Mum' and encourage them to make opportunities for the child to use the word when appropriate. Giving the child plenty of opportunities to use the word throughout the day, with different partners, helps the child both to remember the word and to practise using it. These opportunities ensure that newly acquired language skills are generalised to new contexts, outside the practice situations you are providing. The words you decide to teach should have meanings that are important to the child, and should be useful during daily events and with different partners. This will help to ensure that the child continues to use the words and does not forget them. There will then be less need for you to check, later, that the child has not forgotten the words and is still using them both spontaneously and appropriately.

Finally, try to remember that you should always follow the child's lead. Embed your practice in games and activities that he or she is interested in and enjoys. Encourage the child to respond and always allow enough time. Ask only three times. Avoid confrontation.

Activities to use when teaching a child to use new words

Names of family members, pets or friends

Check your list of the child's gestures, sounds and words. Are there three or four items for family names or the names of pets (if any) or friends? If not, here are some suggestions for ways to encourage the use of these words, using the C-I-C strategy:

- Play a game such as 'Here we go Round the Mulberry Bush' with family members, friends or other children. Let each person call out the name of the next person to model an action for the group to copy.
- Use model people from Lego or a doll's house. Play with the models, label them using the names on your list.
- Use two-dimensional figures such as cut-out pictures of people. Follow the procedure described above.
- Draw faces on your finger tips. Say 'Where's Daddy?' Hide a finger and 'find' it again. Repeat with other names.
- Collect pictures and photographs from home. Put them in an album. Look at the pictures and label them. 'There's Daddy.' 'Look at your new cot.'
- Cut pictures from magazines with the child and label them appropriately; 'Mummy', 'Daddy', 'Rusty', 'boy', 'baby', 'cat'.

Note that the ideas listed above move from the three-dimensional and concrete to increasingly two-dimensional and abstract.

Names of familiar objects (such as 'ball', 'hat', 'car')

Check your list of the child's gestures, sounds and words. Are there up to eight or 10 names of familiar objects? If not, here are some suggestions for practising the use of these words.

When you begin to practise word labels, first check that the child knows the meaning of the words you plan to teach. Before playing a game, ask the child to show you, give you, or touch the items as you label them. If the child is not sure of the meaning of the words you will need to provide him or her with plenty of opportunities to associate the sound of words with the objects they represent. Follow the steps outlined earlier for teaching family names. Here are some suggestions for activities to use:

- Use real objects that interest the child. Put them in a bag. Take turns to take one object at a time and encourage the child to label the object as it is taken out.
- Collect a set of pictures to match the real objects you are teaching. Let the child match each object to a picture and label it at the same time.
- Make a 'gone' box (a box or ice cream container with a hole in the lid big enough to allow the child to 'post' an object or a picture). Only allow the child to 'post' an object when it has been labelled.
- Find a simple game of picture lotto that uses familiar objects. Have the child name the picture before he or she matches it on the board. This is a useful game to play with a small group who will provide good language models for the child.

- Looking at a book provides a good opportunity for talking. Collect the pictures you have used in the activities described above and mount them in a photo album or use clear plastic covers that can be clipped together to make a book. The child should label the pictures before turning a page.

When you are selecting labels to teach the child, remember two points:

- Try to find words for objects and events that are relevant and interesting for the child. Look at the world from the child's point of view and select words that the child will find useful. Remember objects that move, make a noise and are colourful are most likely to interest children. A sample list of words that could be used is included in the first words list in Appendix E.
- Try to select words that the child will not find too difficult to say. Listen to the sounds the child is already making and select words that include these sounds. You should note, however, that children who can make a particular sound during vocal play (such as 'f-f-f') may not be able to make the sound intentionally. So listen carefully before you select a word to teach. A list of the order in which consonants are acquired by most children is provided in the articulation development norms in Appendix G. Suggestions for ways to describe how particular sounds are made are included in Chapter 11.

Words for actions (such as 'go', 'put', 'give')

Check your list of the child's words. Are there at least 10 words for actions? If not, here are some suggestions for practising action words.

Action words are important because the child needs them to make simple sentences. However, these words lack a clear physical referent. For example, you cannot pick up, hide, put or hold 'walk'. As a result such words are often difficult to learn. Many children who have begun to use a number of object labels are very slow to use words for actions. If a child has 30 to 40 object labels it is time to learn some action words as well. One way to begin to teach these words is to pair a word to a gesture already used by the child to communicate an action meaning. For example, many children express 'come', 'want', 'look', 'out(side)', 'all gone' in their gestures and body language long before they use a word. Use the C-I-C strategy to help the child begin to add words to these gestures and actions. Use daily routines such as bath or snack-times, or set up a game that will involve activities appropriate for the words you want to practise. Structure the activity so that the child has to name an action before doing it, or as you do it. Here are some suggestions for suitable activities to use:

- Have a tea party with a Teddy or doll, or play with blocks and cars. Label the actions as you play: 'eat', 'drink', 'pour', 'go', 'stop', 'crash', 'bang'. You can also use this procedure during snack-time. Label what you are doing, as in 'eat', 'drink'. Bath-time can also be used to label what is happening: 'wash', 'pour', 'put on'.
- Look at a book with pictures that involve actions, with adults and children involved in different activities. Label the action component of the pictures as you look at the book: such as 'sleep', 'eat', 'wash', 'run', 'jump', 'push', 'cut'.
- Play 'Follow the Leader'. Let a small group of children play with you, each child taking turns to name an action. Or use the same procedure to play 'Here we go Round the Mulberry Bush'.
- Play charades with a small group. One person can mime an action and the other children guess the action being mimed.

During all the activities described above, remember to ask what the child is doing or what he or she wants you to do. Using the C-I-C strategy, you can teach words like:

tea party, snack-time:	put, pour, drink, eat, cut, all gone
play dough:	cut, roll, poke, squish, put
model cars, animals:	go, stop, walk, run, push, ride, get
soft toys or dolls:	sleep, wash, walk, jump, fall down

Once the child is able to use a few clear action words appropriately, without having just heard a model as in C2 in the C-I-C strategy, use a binary-choice question to provide some help in producing correct words. Ask 'Do you want to cut or paste?' or 'Do you want to build or climb?' This will help the child who is not quite ready to answer such questions spontaneously, without a prompt.

Binary choice is a useful strategy to use in many different situations throughout the day. Use it when you are asking the child what he or she wants at times involving, for example:

food:	'peanut butter or honey?'
service:	'Mummy pick you up or get your blanket?'
play:	'blocks or puzzles?'

Remember to reinforce the child's choice in your response, as in 'You want —?'

Modifiers (for example 'hot', 'wet', 'more', 'big')

Modifier words can be taught in games and activities such as those described earlier. The child will need plenty of opportunities to hear these words in association with the condition they represent before he or she will begin to use them. Most children learn some modifiers early; words like 'wet', 'hot', 'more', 'big'. Others are only learned after the child has a variety of words for entities and actions. Some suitable words to teach include:

prepositions:	in, on, under, up, down
adjectives:	little, my, more
colour names:	red, blue, yellow

Socially useful words (such as 'bye', 'ta')

Words that can be described as 'socially useful' are usually learned during appropriate daily activities. Many children learn 'bye' first. As noted earlier, some children have a problem in communicating their ideas and needs to another person if they have learned to use words like 'ta' or 'thank you'. These 'polite' words convey no information and if the child is only able to use one or two words at a time, words like 'please' and 'thank you' take the place of other words that convey more of the child's meaning. Try to keep such polite phrases for a later stage, when the child is able to use them in addition to the words that carry useful information. However, you should encourage the child to say 'hi' or 'hello' and 'bye' (initially easier to say than 'goodbye') because these words help the child to interact rewardingly with other people. Another useful word is 'goodnight' or 'ni-ni'.

Signs as a supplement to speech

Most children, including those with low muscle tone or a motor disability can be helped to learn words, particularly high-interest words, if a consistent gesture or sign is paired with the word by the child's communication partner. Children often begin to communicate their needs by using a gesture, such as pointing to indicate an object of interest, or a body movement to convey some other meaning. Once they learn to talk, these gestures and actions are replaced by words. In the same way, adults often pair words that have no physical referent with a gesture that helps make explicit a meaning that is being conveyed to children – for example, 'look' while pointing at the object of interest, 'come' plus a beckoning movement, 'stop' plus positioning the hand upright and 'sit' plus pointing downwards. These gestures or physical signs provide a visual or tactile prop that aids comprehension of the speaker's meaning. In addition, the visual cue helps the child in the early stages of language acquisition to associate a particular pattern of speech sounds with a specific referent. If you are helping a child who is at this stage you should consider encouraging him or her to use gestures or signs as a bridge to first words.

Pairing a gesture or sign with a word is one strategy that may help your child to learn labels for objects that cannot always be physically present, such as 'toilet', 'car', 'plane', or actions like 'wash', 'sleep', 'dig', 'gone', and other meanings such as 'more', 'little', 'under'. The child may first learn to use a gesture or sign rather than a word but these are dropped once the child can produce the word intelligibly. The use of gestures and signs as an aid to communication prior to the acquisition of intelligible speech can be particularly useful for children who are not yet physically able to make a variety of speech sounds. (See Chapter 12 for a more detailed discussion of the use of gestures and signs in early communication.)

Learning to use words effectively

Earlier in this chapter it was suggested that children usually begin to use words first to indicate the existence of something that interests them very much, such as an aeroplane overhead or a butterfly in the garden. Later, they use words to obtain objects, such as a new toy, food or a drink and to regulate and control other people's actions by protesting, as in 'stop, don't do that' or requesting attention or services from an adult, with 'look at me' or 'help me climb here'. If the child is not yet using words in these different ways, you may need to help the child learn a variety of words and how and when to use them.

In the early stages of a language programme, the primary goal is to increase the number of different words that the child uses. However, it is also important to check that the child is using these words in different ways, not just to label objects or people. If you are concerned about the way in which a child is using language, read the section in Chapter 10 (programme level 5) on communicative intentions, where procedures are described to help ensure that a child who is only just beginning to talk learns to use language in a variety of ways.

Whatever words you select to practise, here are some important points to remember:

- Follow the child's lead. Try to implement your objectives in activities that have engaged the child's interest.
- Make sure the child understands what is expected of him or her during the activity or game. The child needs to know how the game is played.
- Make sure the child associates a new word with appropriate objects or activities before you expect to hear the word being used, whether in imitation or spontaneously. Provide plenty of opportunities for the child to hear the word used in conjunction with the object or activity.

- In choosing words to practise, always include a few words that the child already knows. This helps to ensure a feeling of success.
- Do not expect the child to learn all the items on your list at one time. It may take several sessions before a child will attempt a new word and only two or three words will be learned at a time.
- Give the child plenty of opportunities to practise the new words.
- Accept any attempt by the child to say a new word. The word should become more intelligible as the child practises it.
- Use naturally-occurring situations as much as possible to introduce and practise new words. This will help ensure that the words are meaningful to the child. Special times are sometimes used to give extra opportunity to practise new words but most language learning will take place in natural contexts.
- Tell everyone who has regular contact with the child about the words that you are practising; parents, siblings, grandparents, the babysitter, preschool teacher and other familiar adults should be aware of your language objectives.
- Keep practice sessions short. Do not expect the child to continue participating in an activity when bored or tired. Several short productive sessions are far more effective than one long one.
- If a child does not attempt to use a word after you have modelled it and after you have encouraged imitation over several days, you may need to drop that item from your list and choose another word to teach.

Ensure that the child has plenty of opportunities to practise new words during routine daily activities. Sometimes, this is the only way teach new words. Some suitable times are:

- At meal and snack-times: ask the child to say 'more', 'eat' or 'juice' before you offer something to eat or drink;
- In the bathroom: ask the child to say 'on' or 'wash' before turning on the tap or washing hands, 'soap' before taking the soap;
- During dressing and undressing: ask the child to label items of clothing as they are put on or taken off. Say 'up', 'off' as pants and socks are pulled on and off.

Taking the next step

Children who have been slow to talk often prefer to communicate using single words only, or, in some instances, phrases associated with daily routines or rituals, such as 'there y'are', 'cuppa tea' and 'ready-set-go'. It is therefore important that, once the child is using a variety of types of words in different situations, you should move on to the next level in the language programme (level 4). This level is concerned with helping the child combine single words into phrases and sentences. Suggestions for helping children begin to combine their words into longer utterances and begin to use the morphemes of English are set out in the next chapter (Chapter 9).

Summary

This chapter has examined issues arising from the acquisition of children's first words. For most children and their families, first words represent a major developmental milestone. The words that children utter first usually reflect the aspects of their experiences that are highly salient, such as objects of great interest or topics that they want to communicate about with others. In this chapter, suggestions were made about ways of assessing the current skills of a child who appears to be at the point of uttering first words. Ideas for words that children often produce at this stage of their development were identified and suggestions were made about games and activities within which these words can be acquired. Once children are producing a variety of single words and beginning to combine them into two-word utterances it is time to move on to the next chapter which examines children's early word combinations and sentences.

Chapter 9
Early Sentences and Extending Meaning (Programme Levels 4 and 5)

Once a child has 10 to 20 words for people and objects, and 5 to 10 action words or other types of words, you may begin to hear these words being combined into simple sentences such as 'ball gone' or 'boy there'. These early sentences reflect the way the child sees the objects and events. They usually involve identification of an interesting object plus a comment about the object ('bird gone', 'dolly eat', 'truck there') or the addition of a word that refers to something or someone associated with that object ('Daddy spoon', 'more bickie', 'go car'). The first part of this chapter is concerned with these early word combinations and sentences. Suggestions will be made about assessing these skills and ways of encouraging further development.

In the second part of the chapter, suggestions will be made about one other useful aspect of language: morphology, or the way that the meaning of words is extended to show, for example, tense, mood and number. It should be noted that this part of the chapter is specific to morphemes of the English language. Anyone who is using a language other than English will need to follow the sequence of acquisition followed by children acquiring that language.

It should be noted that the two topics that are the focus of this chapter (combining words into sentences and using English morphemes further to extend meaning) were identified in Chapter 2 as representing syntax, rules or the grammatical aspect of language – the way that words are combined or modified to convey meaning.

Early sentences

Research has shown that when children begin to combine words, they are expressing their understanding of relationships they perceive to exist between objects and people in their environment. In combining words into simple phrases and sentences, they appear to follow common rules. For example, a child who uses 'Mum' and 'up', might at first combine them into 'Mum up' to ask to be picked up, then say 'Mum pick up' and later 'Mum, pick me up'. The order in which the words are combined reflects the child's perception of the relationship between the events that have been labelled. In the case of the statement 'Mum up', the child first labelled 'Mum' as the person (agent or actor) involved and then labelled 'up' as the action or event that was of interest.

Children usually begin to combine words by using labelling words or nouns that represent people or objects with action words or verbs that represent what happens in an event or what is done to an object. Examples of word labels include 'doll', 'hat', 'key' or 'Mummy', while action words might include 'wash', 'look', 'put' and 'go'. Words to indicate location might then be added, such as 'there' and 'under' and possibly some words to modify the labelling words such as 'big', 'hot' or 'blue', or introducer (socially useful) words such as 'bye'. Other examples of these categories of words are set out in the first words list (Appendix E). The listener often has to consider the situation or context in which the phrase is spoken in order to know what the child means. For example 'Dad car' could mean 'Dad's car', 'Dad drives the car' or 'Dad is in the car'. Knowing the context is crucial for understanding the child's meaning.

Here are 10 rules that children usually follow when they begin to string words together. These rules tend to be acquired in the same order by most children, regardless of the language spoken in the child's environment. The rules are:

Rule	*Example*
Agent + action	Mum get
Action + object	push car
Agent + object	Mummy (gives) bickie
Modifier (possession) + object label	Daddy('s) car, my doll
Modifier (recurrence) + object label	more bickie
Modifier (attribution) + object label	big car
Agent/object + location	car there
Action + location	fall down
Negation + any word	no want, no bickie
Introducer + any word	bye Mum, see train

Once children have begun to use a variety of single words, they usually start to string words together spontaneously. However, experience has shown that children who have had difficulties in acquiring first words are also slow to use simple phrases and sentences. This chapter provides guidelines for helping children move from a single-word stage to the production of two- and three-word phrases and sentences. As in the preceding chapters, suggestions are made for assessing the child's current language skills using both unstructured observation and structured games. Strategies are then described that can be used to help children begin to combine their words and thus move to a higher level in the language development sequence.

Suggested assessment activities

You will need to begin by checking if the child is combining words. You can do this using either unstructured or informal observation or more formal and structured methods of assessment as set out below.

Unstructured observation of two-or-more word combinations

Three procedures, including parent report, systematic observation and language sampling, can be used to assess a child who appears to be ready to combine words into sentences. These techniques were also suggested in the previous chapter for assessing the child at the single-word stage. However this time you will be looking for evidence of the rules that the child is expressing, rather than for a list of the words that are used.

Parent report

Ask a parent or care-giver to make a list of any utterances that the child produces that include two words or more. Request that, if possible, the list should include at least 20 phrases or sentences. You may decide to suggest that the observer use the observation record form for two-, three- or more word utterances that is included in Appendix D. The information recorded on this form will provide information to help you recognise the meaning that the child wanted to convey. You can also classify each utterance listed in terms of the rule that is expressed. For example, here is a list that was collected by Jane's mother. Her teacher classified each two-word utterance in terms of the 10 rules listed earlier in this chapter.

Jane's list of two-word phrases

Utterance	Rule
'Daddy car'	agent + object
'go car'	action + object
'blue car'	modifier + object
'me go'	agent + action
'me there'	agent + location
'go down'	action + location
'me down'	agent + location

Systematic observation

During normal activities with the child, record any two-word or longer utterances that you hear. Use the observation record form for two-, three- or more word utterances in Appendix D. When you have collected about 20 utterances you can classify them in terms of the rules that are being expressed.

Taking a language sample

Your aim, here, is to collect a representative sample of the child's speech by making a tape or video record of a five- to 10-minute play session. You can then replay the tape or video segment and record exactly what the child did and said. Before you begin, you will need to choose two different sets of material for the child to play with during the session. For younger children, suitable materials might include a tea-set and doll or soft toy, some play dough, model cars, box for a garage, and several picture books. Older children could play a card or board game, look at some books or just talk about topics such as favourite games, hobbies or familiar events. You can analyse the taped language sample using the procedures described in Appendix A. Each two-word utterance produced by the child can be classified in terms of the 10 rules listed earlier.

From the information collected by any or all the procedures described above, you will have clear information about the rules that the child is using now. This will enable you to plan which rules you should begin to teach.

Structured assessment of two-or-more word combinations

While you will probably be able to find out which two-word rules the child is expressing from the unstructured observational procedures just described, you may also try to elicit some two-word combinations through structured activities, such as a game with pictures.

Will the child label a picture using two words? Collect a variety of pairs of pictures that have objects, people or animals that the child will recognise and can name. Try to find pairs of pictures that differ on at least one attribute, for example:

> a red car and a blue car;
> a big ball and a little ball;
> a glass full of milk and an empty glass;
> a boy eating and a boy asleep;
> a man in a car and a man in a boat;
> a little puppy and a big dog;
> a woman sitting and a woman standing.

If possible collect pictures that represent each of the 10 rules. Spread some of the pictures out, in pairs, between yourself and the child. Say:

'Let's play a game. We can each have a turn and take a picture. I'm going to start. I want the blue car.' Take the picture with the blue car and begin your pile. Now say to the child 'Your turn. You say which one you want'. Prompt if necessary. Encourage the child to select a picture. If the child does not label it using two words, provide a model. Prompt the child by saying: 'you say, boy eat' or 'boy sleep'. Accept any utterances but encourage the child to use two words. Put your fingers on the picture until the child attempts to say something. If no attempt is made after three prompts, you say the two words and let the child take the picture. Now have your turn. Continue until all the pictures are gone. Record all relevant child utterances. You may find it appropriate to use a tape-recorder for this. The object of this game is to elicit a variety of two-word utterances from the child. As in the unstructured observation tasks described previously, you can classify all the child's utterances in terms of the 10 rules listed earlier. Did the child produce any two-word utterances?

Once you have collected information about the two-word utterances that the child has produced, check these results to show which rules have been learned and which do not yet appear to have been mastered. Here is some information on the rules that Jane used during both unstructured observations and the structured picture games.

Jane's two-word list: number of instances and percentage of use of two-word rules

Rules	Number of instances	Percentage of use
agent + action	15	31
action + object	12	25
agent + object	6	13
modifier (possession) + object	2	4
modifier (recurrence) + object	1	2
modifier (attribution) + object	0	–
agent/object + location	4	8
action + location	8	17
negation + any word	0	–
introducer + any word	0	–

Jane is using mainly the agent + action and action + object rules. More practice could be given in using agent + object and action + location combinations such as 'dolly shoe' and 'go there'.

A few examples of agent + object, modifier (possession and recurrence) + object and agent + location were observed, but no instances of the other three rules occurred in Jane's assessments. She could probably be encouraged, first, to use the agent + action and action + object rules more. However, to do this she will need a variety of agent, action and object words. The following sections of this chapter describe procedures that can be used to help a child like Jane to use more two-word combinations.

Suggestions for encouraging early sentences

Find out if the child is expanding the meaning of the single words that are being used by adding a gesture or other action. For example, the child who pulls a toy car away from another child shouting 'car' and pointing to himself is probably trying to indicate possession. The child could be prompted to use 'my car'. This is the modifier (possession) + object rule. The child who wants you to throw, roll or kick the ball and merely gestures while saying 'ball' could be encouraged to say 'kick ball'. This is the action + object rule. However, try to introduce only one rule at a time, as each one is a new skill for the child to master. If you are not sure which rule to introduce first, follow the order of the rules listed above. Most children use the agent + action and action + object rules first.

Games and activities for encouraging early sentences

A child can be helped to combine words during normal daily activities, or during games with objects or pictures. For example, during regular daily routines and periods of play with a ball or soft toys, encourage the child who is using agent, action or object words to label what is happening with two-word sentences. Instead of saying just one word, prompt the child to say two, as in 'car stop', 'push car', 'Teddy eat', 'wash Teddy', 'ball gone'. Model appropriate two-word phrases during routine activities: 'pants on', 'brush hair', 'wash hands', 'eat bickie'. Prompt by asking the child what is happening or what he or she would like to do. For example:

Adult	*Child*	*Rule*
'What is happening?'	'car gone'	agent + action
	'Mummy car'	agent + object
	'puppy drink'	agent + action
'What are you doing?'	'ride bike'	action + object
'What do you want to do?'	'cut paper'	action + object
	'feed dolly'	action + object
	'brush hair'	action + object
'What will we do now?'	'Mummy bickie'	agent + object

Developing 'scripts' for recurring events

Good opportunities for encouraging early sentences occur during routine events and activities. For example, daily routines that can be used to prompt early sentences include:

- Dressing: ask the child what clothes he or she wants to wear today or what to put on next ('blue shirt', 'new pants');
- Meal or snack-times: encourage the child to tell you what to do next, or what he or she will eat next ('cut bread', 'pour juice', 'eat apple');
- Bathtime: let the child choose what to wash next ('wash tummy', 'wash toes');
- Storytime: ask the child 'what will we do now?' 'turn page?' 'read book?' 'bed time?' 'light off?'

By using similar questions each time you do the same activity, and prompting a response using the binary-choice strategy, such as 'do you want the blue shirt or the red shirt?', or the C-I-C procedure when necessary, the child will soon learn a variety of appropriate responses. These can then be used as a basis for new sentences with different agents, actions and objects. The predictability of these situations helps the child to remember appropriate utterances and he or she becomes less dependent on your prompting and modelling of suitable phrases.

As discussed in Chapter 3, conversational routines or utterances that recur in a predictable way during daily or frequently occurring events, such as those described above, are sometimes referred to as 'scripts'. Greetings such as 'How do you do?' or 'How are you?' and the reply 'I'm fine, thanks' or 'I'm very well, thank you. How are you?' are good examples of conversational scripts that children must eventually learn. Other examples of scripts that govern both behaviour and language in specific situations can be identified for events that most children experience often. For example, birthday parties have some elements that all children learn to expect: the greeting on arrival, 'Happy birthday, Sammy' accompanied by the giving of a present; the birthday cake accompanied by singing of the birthday song 'Happy Birthday to You' and the farewell of 'Bye bye' or 'Good bye. Thank you for inviting me' or 'Thank you for the present'.

One of the ways we can help children acquire language skills is by encouraging them to practise the language scripts used in recurring events such as a birthday party, a visit to the dentist (greeting, sit in the chair, open your mouth), or going shopping (arrive, select items to buy, pay the money, go out). Children who attend an early childhood programme (preschool, nursery school or crèche) can be helped to learn the language associated with the various activities in which they will take part, like snacks and lunch, using the bathroom, story and music times, dolly corner, blocks and outdoor play. In each of these activities, the child will have opportunities to use an appropriate script, including both actions and language. You can help children adjust quickly to new settings by familiarising them with the relevant scripts. These skills can also be taught at home, prior to participation in such programmes.

Structured games for using early sentences

You can help a child begin to combine two words together by setting up games in which the child has to label two objects or ideas consecutively. The two words that must be used should represent one of the early rules described earlier. For example, the child could play with the 'gone' box that was described in Chapter 7. Collect a set of objects that you know the child can label, and a box that is big enough to hold them. Cut a hole in the top of the box, big enough for the objects to fit into it, and let the child post each object in the hole. As the child puts it in, the object should be labelled, and as it disappears, the child should say 'gone'. Phrases like 'cup gone', 'spoon gone', 'Teddy gone' can be learned as each object is posted. As an alternative, the child can learn to say 'bye cup', 'bye spoon', 'bye Teddy' as the objects disappear. Use of an appropriate gesture in conjunction with the word 'gone' or 'bye' may also act as a signal to the child that a word should be said. At first, you will need to prompt and model the correct words. Once the child has learned the rules of the game, you should not let the objects be posted until the two words have been produced.

To encourage the agent + action rule, collect a series of pictures that show one agent, such as a boy or a girl, in a variety of action situations such as eating, running, washing and so on. Your aim will be to encourage the child to describe what is happening in the pictures with phrases like 'boy eat', 'boy run', 'boy wash', 'girl paint', girl brush', 'girl sleep'. Alternatively, select one action with different agents, as in 'Daddy sleep', 'Mummy sleep', 'puppy sleep', 'duck sleep'. Look at the pictures with the child and ask 'what's happening?' Use the C-I-C strategy to elicit a two-word response. Introduce a different agent, such as Mummy or man, using a different set of pictures, or different action words. You can find appropriate sets of pictures in early reading books, or make your own book using pictures cut out of magazines. Try to select general agent words that the child can use in many situations, but you can also encourage the use of names of familiar people, such as Daddy, Mummy, Nanna, and so on. Once the child appears to have learned to use these two-word phrases during the learning games without a model, listen carefully to hear whether the words are also used during other daily activities. If you hear the child use the two-word phrases spontaneously, without having just heard a model, you can assume that the rule has been mastered. Then you can select another rule and begin to teach its use.

Taking the next step

When the child is using most of the rules in two-word sentences, you can begin to encourage him or her to extend these into three- or four-word sentences. For instance, the child using 'push car' and 'boy push' could be moved on to produce 'boy push car', or the child saying 'Mummy go' could be encouraged to say 'Mummy go car' or 'Mummy go home'. The important point to remember is that children can be encouraged to extend their early sentences to include another element, following the sequence listed for the two-word utterances. For example:

Rule	Example
agent-action-object	'girl push car'
agent-action-location	'boy go there'
action-modifier-object	'push big car'
negation-action-object	'no push car'
introducer-agent-object	'bye Mummy car'

Extending language: using English morphemes

At about the same time when the child is learning to use all the rules for combining words in social conversation, he or she should also begin to take the next step in extending meaning by using morphemes to indicate mood and number. For example, the child needs to add some of the morphemes used in the English language to action words to indicate present and past tense, as in 'walk-ing' (present progressive), 'walk-ed' (regular past) and 'walk-s' (regular third person present). Similarly, location needs to be defined by prepositions such as 'in' and 'on'; or plurality and possession by adding a final '-s' to labelling words, as in 'dogs' and 'dog's'.

What is a morpheme? McLean and Snyder-McLean (1978), using Stageberg (1971) as their source, define morphemes as 'a meaningful element which cannot be broken down into smaller units without violation of its meaning or without leaving meaningless parts' (McLean and Snyder-McLean, 1978, p. 80). They go on to distinguish between 'free' and 'bound' morphemes. The former comprise words that can stand alone, such as 'in', 'on', 'the', while the latter include morphemes that are always attached to other words, such as '-ing', '-ed', and '-'s'. This distinction becomes important when the length of a child's utterances is being counted. A decision may need to be made about whether to count the number of words used by the child, or the number of morphemes. For example, 'The bird is singing' has four words, but five morphemes. This issue is relevant for language assessment. Counting morphemes gives a more fine-grained analysis of progress than counting words.

McLean and Snyder-McLean (1978, p. 105–6) review this issue very clearly in terms of its impact on language assessment. See also Appendix A where procedures for taking a language sample are outlined.

Like other children, the child with delayed language usually learns to extend the meaning expressed in early sentences by adding morphemes to words, but often does this at a much slower rate than other children. Therefore, when working with such a child, it may be useful to know the sequential order in which children usually acquire morphemes in English. A list of Brown's 14 grammatical morphemes (Brown, 1973) is set out in Table 9.1 (see also Appendix F). In the remaining section of this chapter suggestions are made for assessing the child's use of morphemes by both unstructured observation and structured assessment activities. Ideas are also included for experiences that should expand the number of morphemes used by children.

Suggested assessment activities

Unstructured assessment of morphemes

In order to discover which morphemes the child is using you need a record of the child's actual words. If a specific morpheme is used in at least 90% of possible instances then the child may be considered to have mastered its usage. Those morphemes that occur less frequently are

Table 9.1: Brown's 14 grammatical morphemes and their order of acquisition.

Morphemes	Examples
Present progressive	-ing
Prepositions	in, on
Plural (regular)	-s, -es, etc.
Past-irregular	came, ran, etc.
Possessive	-'s
Uncontracted copula	is, am, are, (as in: she *is* pretty)
Articles	a, the
Past regular	-d, -ed, -/t/
Third person regular	-s, -/z/, etc. (as in: 'she ru*ns*')
Third person irregular	does, has (as in: 'they do' vs. 'she d*oes*')
Uncontracted auxiliary	is, am, are (as in: 'they are running')
Contracted copula	-'s, -'m, -'re (as in: 'she*'s* pretty)
Contracted auxiliary	-'s, -'m, -'re (as in: 'they*'re* running')

From JE McLean and LK Snyder-McLean (1978) A Transactional Approach to Early Language Training. Columbus, OH: Merrill.

regarded as emerging and could be encouraged next. Opportunities can be provided later to encourage use of morphemes that do not occur or cannot be elicited. If a targeted morpheme does not emerge after practice, check to see whether the child comprehends the underlying concepts. You might find that your practice sessions are more successful if you precede each session with a game in which the meaning of the target morpheme is demonstrated.

You do not need to attempt to teach all 14 of the morphemes that are included in Appendix F, nor should the order in which they are presented in Appendix F be strictly followed. Rather, select one which will best help the child to communicate more effectively. Alternatively, select a morpheme that is already emerging. This would include any morpheme that is used only occasionally. You can record the morphemes that the child is using, or those that appear to be emerging, in the summary assessment sheet for morphemes that is included in Appendix C.

Information on the morphemes currently used by the child may be obtained from language samples and reports from parents, other carers or teachers. These methods involve obtaining information about the child's speech by tape or video-recording the child during a play session (see Appendix A) or by asking parents or other carers to record the child's utterances over a set time period such as one day a week. You may wish to use the sample observational record form for recording two- or three-word utterances that is included in Appendix D for this purpose.

Structured assessment of morphemes

As opportunities to use all the morphemes do not always occur naturally, it is helpful to try to elicit them during a planned activity. You may find that the child is able to use certain morphemes even though they were not evident in your observational records. In the following discussion, suggestions are made for activities that will provide the child with an opportunity to use some of the 14 morphemes identified by Brown (1973; see Appendix F and the summary assessment sheet for English morphemes in Appendix C). Since not all the morphemes readily lend themselves to such elicitation, only those that can be expected to appear early in the child's development will be covered here. These include the present progressive '-ing', as in 'running'; prepositions such as 'in' and 'on'; the possessive '-'s' as in 'Mary's shoes' and the past irregular such as 'fell' and 'sat'.

Present progressive ('-ing')

Will the child use '-ing' (the present progressive tense) with verbs to convey continuous action? Select 10 actions. Mime each action, then ask the child 'What am I doing?' If necessary prompt with 'I'm eat . . .'. Suggested actions could include: eating, drinking, clapping, brushing, driving, sleeping, reading, walking, hitting, drawing, painting. Does the child use '-ing' appropriately?

If the child uses '-ing' in 90% of the responses, then this morpheme has been acquired. If '-ing' is not used at the required level, you will need to provide more practice in this skill. If '-ing' is not used at all, model the answer and encourage the child to imitate you. Then demonstrate at least three of the actions again and ask 'What am I doing?' Does the child use '-ing' after modelling?

If yes, you can conclude that more practice is likely to be helpful. If no, then the child may not yet be ready to extend his or her language in this way.

Suggestions for encouraging use of the present progressive ('-ing')

Collect some simple pictures of actions, such as a boy jumping, a woman kissing a baby, a dog running and a girl eating an ice-cream. If the child's normal response when asked 'tell me what is happening' is to say 'boy jump', then model and prompt the response 'boy jumping', using the C-I-C strategy. If the child says 'kiss baby', you should encourage use of 'kissing baby' and so on. You could also use action games, with the adult miming actions and then asking 'what am I doing?' Alternatively, use dolls or soft toys to demonstrate the actions in a game. Take turns with the child to model an action and then ask 'what's doll doing?' or 'tell me what Teddy is doing'. The binary choice strategy of asking, for example, 'is the boy swimming or jumping?' may also be useful in the beginning because it provides the child with cues about how to answer.

The morpheme 'in'

Will the child use 'in' to define the location of an object? Provide the child with five opportunities to answer 'where is the ball?' using 'in' plus 'there', or 'in' plus a labelling word. You will need to collect five small containers such as a cup, box, shoe, bag and a toy car or truck as well as a small ball. Let the child watch you hide the ball in one of the five containers. Ask 'where's the ball?' Try not to let the child substitute a pointing or other gestural response by making sure both hands are out of sight, either folded or held. Alternatively, close your eyes and say 'tell me where . . .' Repeat the task with each of the containers. Does the child use 'in' appropriately?

If 'in' is used in four out of five of the responses, then you can assume that this morpheme has been acquired. If it is not used at the required level, you will need to devise some games to encourage this skill.

If the child did not use 'in', model the answer 'in the bag' or 'in the shoe' and encourage imitation as you repeat the five tasks. Does the child use 'in' after modelling?

If yes, you can conclude that this skill is emerging and some practice can be given in the use of the morpheme. If no, the child is probably not yet ready to learn to use this morpheme.

Suggestions for encouraging use of 'in'

Collect an assortment of pictures showing items inside a variety of containers. Show them to the child and label each picture, for example, 'juice in a cup', 'Daddy in his bed', 'bottle in her mouth', 'baby in the pram', 'bird in a nest'. If you use the C-I-C strategy, the child has the opportunity to learn the response needed to answer a question such as 'where's the baby?' with 'in pram' or 'in the pram'.

During normal daily activities, ask the child where common household objects belong, for example, in the bath or cupboard or bin. Once again, use the C-I-C or a binary choice strategy.

The morpheme 'on'

Will the child use 'on' to define the location of an object? Prepare five pairs of objects, which can be arranged so that one is supported on top of the other; for example, a doll or yourself with a hat on, a spoon balancing on a cup, a toy car on a box, a doll on a toy chair/table and a ball on a book. Ask 'where's X?' If necessary, encourage the child by asking 'tell me where'. Each answer should be 'on X' or 'on there'. Does the child use 'on' appropriately?

If the child uses 'on' in four out of five responses you can assume that this morpheme has been acquired. If not, you will need to plan more games to practise this skill. To find out whether the child will use 'on' after training, repeat the five tasks but model the answer in each case, and encourage the child to imitate you. Does the child use 'on' after modelling?

If yes, you can conclude that the child will benefit from training in the use of this morpheme. If no, it is probably not yet time to help the child in this way.

Suggestion for practising use of 'on'

Tell the child that you are going to put an object, such as a car, 'on' various things and you want him or her to say where it is. You could even put the child 'on' suitable things or you could demonstrate 'on table', 'on chair', 'on ball', using a doll or other object. Remember to use the C-I-C or binary choice strategies in these activities.

Once the child has learned the rules of the game, you should change roles. Let the child try to trick you by putting an object 'on' something unexpected. Look for opportunities during the day to practise use of this word.

The plural (-s)

Will the child indicate plurality by adding a final '-s' to object labels? Collect a shoe-box or drawstring bag and put several similar or identical objects in it. Hand the child the box or bag and say 'Look. What's in here?' The answer should be 'X-s' as in 'cows', 'keys' or 'spoons'. Repeat this for five different objects. Some appropriate items to use include spoons, cups, cars, balls and blocks. Does the child add the final '-s' to the object labels?

If the plural '-s' is used in four out of five instances then the child has acquired its use. However, if the plural '-s' is not used at the required level, the child will need more practice. If there is no evidence of usage of the plural '-s', you should repeat the task, but model the appropriate answer and encourage imitation. Does the child use the plural '-s' after training?

If yes, then you can conclude that he or she will probably benefit from more practice.

Remember to provide some opportunities for the child to understand the concept of plurality before you introduce a model of the morpheme for imitation. This will help him or her learn to use it appropriately.

Suggestions for encouraging use of the regular plural ('-s')

Assemble multiple copies of items, such as pencils, blocks, buttons and a box. The adult and child could take turns to tell each other to 'put the buttons in the box' and so on. Or you could collect pairs of pictures, one of each pair showing a single object, the other showing several examples of the same object. Give the child one of the pair and keep the other. Label 'car', 'cars'; 'apple', 'apples'; 'cat', 'cats'. Once again, use the C-I-C or binary choice strategies.

It is a good idea to avoid irregular plural forms (such as sheep and feet) when the child is learning this morpheme. Example of irregular forms can be acquired later.

Past irregular

Will the child demonstrate use of the past tense of irregular action words such as broke, fell, ran, sat, blew? Demonstrate a series of actions such as those listed below using dolls, cars, animals or any toy that moves or changes. Afterwards ask 'what happened?' or 'what did I do?' or 'what did dolly do?' The child should reply using the past irregular tense if he or she is able to mark with words the time aspect of the event.

The following are some possible action sequences:

Fell: a doll walks and then falls down.

Ran: a doll runs.

Sat: show doll sitting on a chair, then remove the chair.

Blew: blow out a match or candle or blow a light object like a feather.

Broke: show a sharp pencil point, then break it or break a twig in half.

Does the child comment on the events using the past tense of an irregular verb? If the child used the past irregular in four out of five responses you can assume that he or she is able to represent past tense in this manner. If not, more opportunities to practise may be needed. Repeat your demonstrations but model the correct answers and encourage the child to imitate them. Does the child use the past irregular after modelling?

If yes, then the child will probably profit from more encouragement in using this form. If no, then the child is probably not yet ready to learn to express the past irregular verb form.

Suggestions for encouraging use of the past irregular form of action words

Play a series of games with objects that provide opportunities for use of past irregular verb forms. Model the form and encourage the child to imitate. Use a series of picture cards that demonstrate these action sequences, such as Jack and Jill, Humpty Dumpty. Ask 'what happened?', then 'what happened next?'

The possessive (-'s)

Will the child indicate possession by using '-'s' with labelling words? Select items that are known to belong to five members of the family or playmates, such as bags, shoes, hats or toys. Ask 'whose is this?' 'who owns this?' or 'to whom does this belong?' Does the child indicate possession with '-'s?'

If the child used the possessive '-'s' in four out of five instances, he or she has this skill. If it is used inconsistently, more practice is needed. If there is no evidence of use of '-'s', repeat the tasks, but model the answer each time and encourage the child to imitate. For example, point to the child's pants/dress/chair and ask 'whose is this?' and answer '[Tom]'s pants/dress/chair'. Does the child use a possessive '-'s' after modelling?

If yes, you should provide more practice. If not, the child is probably not yet ready to learn to use this speech form.

Suggestions for encouraging the possessive ('-'s')

Have paper dolls or pictures of a boy and girl and let the child sort out pictures of clothes which belong to each. As the clothes are sorted, use the C-I-C or binary choice strategy to elicit the correct response. You should label each item as 'boy's X' or 'girl's X', allowing the child a chance to sort or dress the doll when the possessive marker is used appropriately.

Alternatively, select a colourful picture of a dog (or another animal) and as you point to the body parts, label 'dog's tail', 'dog's nose' and so on. Encourage the child to imitate. Once again, the C-I-C and binary choice strategies can be used.

Other morphemes

The remaining morphemes (items 7 to 14 in Appendix F) have not been discussed in detail here because they are usually acquired later, when the child has more advanced language skills. However, they may also be encouraged through games that involve objects and pictures, or at appropriate times during normal daily activities.

Children who are slow in acquiring the early morphemes sometimes do not attend to speech closely enough to perceive small sounds like '-s', '-ing' or '-ed' when they are embedded in a longer utterance. It may be helpful to include some activities that will help the child learn to listen more carefully to the speech that is heard as part of a teaching programme. Games like 'Simon Says' can help a child learn to listen. Similarly, any activity that includes an action that is contingent on hearing a morpheme can be used. For example, give the child a page with drawings of balloons. Let the child colour in a balloon when a morpheme that you are currently practising is heard. For example:

Dog running	colour a balloon
Dog run	do not colour a balloon

Other possible games include Bingo, where the child puts a coloured counter on a card each time the target morpheme is heard. A post-box game can also be used in which the child 'posts' a counter each time the target morpheme is heard. Activities like these will help the child attend to the morphemes that are embedded in speech.

It is important to remember that morphemes are often acquired very slowly, because children probably need to develop an understanding of the underlying concepts before they can be expected to use morphemes correctly. When providing activities to encourage the use of particular morphemes, it is a good idea to begin the session with some games that demonstrate the meaning of the morpheme that you want to teach. In normal language development in English-speaking children, the pattern of acquisition occurs in the following sequence, in terms of the child's mean length of utterance (MLU).

MLU	Morphemes acquired
2.0 to 2.5	-ing; in; on
2.5 to 3.0	past irregular; possessive (-'s); uncontracted copula
3.0 to 3.7	articles; regular past; third person regular; third person irregular uncontracted
3.7 to 4.5	auxiliary; contracted copula; contracted progressive auxiliary.

Once children have learned to use grammatical morphemes they are able to convey more complex meanings such as number and tense. They will continue to refine these messages, with the addition of other forms and constructions from the adult grammatical system, until they have acquired the range of skills that are present in the speech of mature language users.

Summary

There is some evidence that children who have been delayed in producing first words will show further delay in combining words into simple phrases and sentences. This chapter suggested ways for assessing the language and communication skills of children who are using single words and for encouraging them to combine words according to the 10 two-word rules. This development represents an important step towards learning to express meaning in more complex phrases and sentences.

By the time that children have acquired the principal grammatical morphemes of their language community, it may be said that the skills that contribute to becoming a competent language user have been mastered. Once this stage is reached your task should be to ensure that opportunities to use language skills appropriately are provided with peers as well as adult partners. In this way, the child will learn that talking is worthwhile, both as a social tool and as a means for making things happen.

Once children begin to produce three- or four-word utterances, you will need to consider one additional aspect of their language: pragmatics or the communicative intentions that are expressed through actions, sounds and words. This aspect of language should be monitored throughout the language acquisition process since communicative intentions will be evident from the time that children first begin to use their actions and vocalisations to communicate with their carers. This aspect of communication is considered in the next chapter.

Chapter 10
Communicative Intentions

Children with delayed language seem to use words initially in two ways: to label or name objects or events that interest them and to answer questions that are directed to them. They often initiate conversations less frequently than their non-delayed peers and are slow to use language in other ways, such as giving information or asking questions. So once children have begun to combine words into simple sentences, you should check to see how they are using their language and to ensure that they are acquiring the range of communicative intentions or pragmatic functions that is evident in the speech of children who are developing normally. This chapter is concerned, therefore, with the way children use language, or what they are doing when they communicate to attract attention, get information, protest, ask for assistance and so on.

This component of language was considered in Chapter 2 as one of the four main elements of a child's language system. It is usually the first aspect of language to be observed in young infants, when they learn to attract attention or convey some other meaning, intentionally, through facial expression, actions and sounds.

Current evidence suggests that, in the early stages of development, children express eight main types of intention in their communicative acts. The first three functions (to indicate, obtain objects or services and regulate) usually appear early and are expressed through a variety of actions, gestures and sounds. With increasing competence, children begin to combine words into simple sentences and it is at this stage that they learn to use words in more varied ways; to initiate, obtain and give information, discover new words and answer questions. The eight categories of intention expressed by children learning to talk are outlined below:

- To indicate the existence of people, objects or events; for example, 'look at . . .' or 'there [and pointing]'. This skill provides the child with a means of introducing a topic of conversation with another person. It can be called learning 'to refer' or 'to predicate' and involves the child engaging another person in joint activity by directing his or her attention to some topic nominated by the child.

- To obtain desired objects or services; for example, 'want . . .' or '[give] me . . .'. This skill has been described as 'instrumental'. With it, the child is able to use an adult as a means to achieve some desired objective, such as winding up a clockwork train or reaching to get a toy that is out of reach.
- To regulate other people's actions, including:

protest	'stop'
rejection	'no', 'don't', and
requesting attention	'look at me'

This is an important skill for children to learn since they are now able to influence the behaviour of others. To some extent they can now control what happens to themselves.

- To initiate, maintain or terminate social interaction, including: greetings ('hi', 'hello'); taking turns in a conversation ('yes', 'me too'); farewells ('bye', 'see you').
- These skills are critical for children. They must acquire the strategies needed to take part in social exchanges with other people since it is through such interactions that much of their learning will occur.
- To obtain information by asking questions, such as 'where . . .?', 'what . . .?', 'who . . .?', 'how . . .?' 'why . . .?' Learning to ask questions is another important skill that is usually acquired after children have begun to use longer sentences of four words or more. Initially, children use intonation alone to ask questions, as in 'my drink?' Later they will begin to use words such as 'where', 'when', 'why' and so on.
- To discover new words as in 'what is this?', 'what's this?' and 'what is . . . called?' This is a special form of questioning. When children learn to ask questions of this type, they are demonstrating metalinguistic awareness or an understanding of language as a system of signs and symbols. Again, this skill is probably acquired after they have begun to produce more complex sentence forms.
- To give information such as 'that's a . . .' as well as to request it. Children who use this function are well advanced in their communication development.
- To answer questions such as 'yes, I want one'. This is an important use of language because children need to be able to respond appropriately to questions directed to them. When they can use language in this way they are demonstrating acquisition of some of the most important elements of language, including knowledge of the rules involved in: taking turns with a partner in a dyadic exchange (eye

contact, proximity, waiting for a turn, responding at the correct time); recognising the meaning intended by a speaker in asking a question; understanding that an appropriate response should be produced; keeping to the topic.

Learning to use language in these different ways is an important aspect of learning to talk. So when working with a child who has problems with language, you should check to see whether he or she is using words to express these functions. Children's use of these pragmatic functions can be checked at any point in language development, although the more complex skills of asking and answering questions, discovering new words and giving information are usually acquired later, after basic syntax skills have been learned. If the child does not appear to be able to use language in each of these ways, particularly if he or she has progressed through the five language stages described earlier in the book, you should devise situations in which expression of these communicative intentions can be practised.

You can assess a child's use of communicative intentions by unstructured observational procedures, such as were described in earlier chapters, or by setting up structured tasks designed to elicit use of the language functions that you expect the child to be able to express. Procedures for assessing the child's use of communicative intentions are outlined in the following section of this chapter. Strategies are then described that can be used to help a child expand the range of intentions that he or she is able to communicate.

Suggested assessment activities

Check whether your child has the skills needed to express the range of communicative intentions that have been observed in children learning to talk. To do this, you can use an unstructured or informal approach. However, opportunities to watch children express these types of meanings do not usually occur very often, so you may find it more satisfactory to use the ideas for structured assessment that are described below.

Unstructured observation of communicative intentions

Observe the child in a natural setting to find out if any of the communicative intentions listed earlier are being used. If necessary, ask the child's parents, or other familiar adults if the child is expressing any of these meanings. A check list, including a description of the eight communicative intentions that you should expect to observe, is included in the summary assessment sheets in Appendix C.

Structured assessment of communicative intentions

Since the expression of communicative intentions is totally under the child's control it can be very difficult to devise situations in which these behaviours will be elicited. Suggestions for structured situations that may trigger two of these behaviours in a child are presented here. The remaining six types involve behaviours that are difficult to elicit. If you decide to use the suggested assessment tasks you need to be aware that a child may fail to respond appropriately because he or she does not want to comply rather than because these ways of using language have not been learned.

Here are some suggestions for eliciting the production of the first two of the intentionally communicative acts listed earlier. For each task, note whether the child used an action, gesture, sound or word to communicate an intention.

- To indicate the existence of people, objects or events. Can the child show you things that are of particular interest? Can the child use pointing, gesturing, or a specific sound or word to attract your attention, or the attention of others, to look at something of interest? Will the child attempt to indicate something to an adult? Sit down with the child at a table. While you are preparing to play a game, accidentally push an object off the table. Ignore the incident. Does the child draw your attention to the fallen object? If yes, how does the child communicate? By action, gesture, sound or word? At the end of an activity, pack everything you have used into a box and, by accident, leave one item out. Does the child draw your attention to the forgotten object? If so, how does the child communicate? Is it by action, gesture, sound, word? If the child responds appropriately in either situation, you may conclude that he or she knows how to indicate something to another person.

- To obtain objects or services. Can the child demonstrate an appropriate skill to obtain something that he or she wants, using another person to obtain the object or service? Will the child attempt to obtain the assistance of an adult to get something that he or she wants? Collect four small objects or toys that will interest a child. Put each one into a clear container with a lid that the child will have difficultly in opening without help. Put the four containers in front of the child. Help the child to open the first container and get the toy. Now indicate that he or she can open the remaining containers. When the child has difficulty with the second container, offer to help. When you have helped to open the second container, indicate that he or she should get the other two toys out of their containers. This time do not offer to help unless the child produces an action, gesture, sound or word to obtain assistance. Does the child try to obtain your help? If so, how does the child communicate? Is it by action, gesture, sound, or word? Put four gold stars or other attractive stamps onto four small squares of paper or cardboard. Put each square into a container with a lid that is difficult to open. Follow the same procedure as in the previous task. Tell the child that he or she can take the stars/stamps home. Does the child try to obtain your help? If so, how does the child communicate? Is it by action, gesture, sound, word? If the child responds appropriately in either situation, you may conclude that he or she knows how to obtain help from another person.

Once you have collected information or structured assessment about the child's use of language to express intentions, you can decide whether it is necessary to provide experiences that will encourage more effective use of these skills. For example, if the child is only able to attract attention or reject help by screaming or stamping, teach a more conventional and appropriate way of expressing this meaning – for example calling out 'look', 'come here', 'help me', or shaking the head and saying 'no'. In the following section, suggestions are made for games and other activities that can be used to help a child communicate these and other meanings more effectively. As in earlier chapters, suggestions are made for activities that can be carried out in planned games and in naturally-occurring daily situations.

Suggestions for encouraging communicative intent

Your primary objective here is to help the child acquire skills that can be used to influence and control aspects of the environment: for example, to gain attention and satisfy current needs. Your immediate goal is to help the child learn to use conventional actions, gestures or words and intonation patterns to convey a message. Initially, the child may need to learn to communicate by using non-verbal means such as gestures or physical movements. Later, appropriate words can be substituted for these more primitive and less explicit ways of communicating. Many of the activities described in earlier chapters can be used here, provided they involve the child in taking an active role as initiator or leader in the task.

Learning to indicate the existence of people, objects or events

Many children point and say 'there' to indicate to you that they have seen something of interest. Such behaviour often occurs when you are both looking at a book. Watch to see if your child uses a word or gesture to indicate. If you do not see this type of behaviour, model appropriate actions and words and encourage the child to imitate you and show you interesting things. Watch for suitable situations and respond when the child tries to direct your attention. During daily activities, show your interest in what the child is doing and encourage him or her to show you what is happening; for example, the picture she has painted or the road he has built. Listen to what you are told and respond appropriately. Your aim is to help the child learn that it is worthwhile to get adults to look at things that are interesting. Remember that the child's earliest attempts to indicate will be expressed through actions such as tugging your arm or pointing. Once the child can convey meaning in these ways, you should encourage use of appropriate words, such as 'look', 'see' and 'there'. Use the C-I-C strategy described in Chapter 8. Later you can encourage the child to use two words as a way to indicate something, such as 'Mum' plus 'look', or 'look' plus 'ball'.

Learning to obtain desired objects or services

Once the child is using words to indicate, he or she should also learn to use words to obtain objects or help. Watch to find out which strategies the child is currently using for these purposes. Look for opportunities to model appropriate words and encourage imitation. For example, if the child can say an appropriate word for food or drink, you should ask 'what do you want?' and expect an answer that will eventually take the form 'I want some milk' or 'I would like a banana'. If the child does not yet know the right words to use to ask for help or an object, give an appropriate model. Say 'do you want an apple or a banana?' or 'do you want some milk or apple juice?' This is helpful because it gives the child an opportunity to hear a model of appropriate words which can then be imitated. You can then model 'Matthew wants an apple?' or 'I want a banana' using the C-I-C strategy. You will need to continue to model such words for the child to imitate until he or she can say them spontaneously. Once the child can say appropriate words you should prompt their use by saying 'you ask'.

The steps involved in learning to obtain or ask for objects and services may be summarised as:

* Learning to use word labels spontaneously; use the C-I-C strategy for teaching this;
* Learning to answer a question that has two options (a binary choice) and gives the child a model of the appropriate words; for example:

| Adult | 'Do you want an apple or a banana?' |
| Child | 'Banana.' |

| Adult' | 'Would you like to go on the swing or the slide?' |
| Child | 'Slide.' |

Learning to ask for something spontaneously or following a prompt such as 'you ask'

The child will initially only use one word to ask for things. As the length of his or her utterances extends, so the length of requests will extend, possibly in the following sequence: 'juice', 'want juice', 'me juice', 'I want juice' or 'me juice please', 'can I have juice, please?' Note that, initially, the child is not expected to use words like 'please' and 'thank you'. These words do not convey any useful information and are taught later, when the child is able to produce sentences longer than three or four words.

Learning to regulate other people's actions

Learning to regulate the actions of others involves two main skills: learning to protest and reject, and learning to request attention from another person. Most children acquire these skills fairly easily but some children experience difficulties in learning to express these meanings intentionally.

Most children learn to say 'no' or 'don't' without any difficulty. However, children who are having problems learning to talk sometimes fail to begin to use these words and may not even learn to protest or reject by other means, such as by crying, or turning away to avoid something they do not want. You should observe the child carefully and find out whether he or she is expressing protest or rejection by using actions, sounds or words. If the child does not appear to be expressing these meanings in any form you may need to devise situations in which they can be learned.

If protest and rejections appear to be expressed through actions or sounds but the child is not using any consistent gestures or words, you may need to teach some. Look for suitable opportunities to model the expression of these meanings through gestures or words. If necessary, set up a game in which the child can learn to communicate in this way. For example, while playing on a tricycle, stop the tricycle and hold it. Encourage the child to push you away and say 'no'. Model the word when you interfere and stop the game. Once the child says 'no' or pushes you away, let the game continue. If the child is playing with a stuffed toy, a toy car, or building with blocks, get in the way or pretend to take the toy or some of the blocks. Model 'no' or 'don't' and encourage imitation. Once you have observed the child expressing protest or rejection using words and actions spontaneously then you will know that this language function has been acquired.

Learning to request attention

Children usually learn to attract attention to themselves at an early age. In a busy family, this is an important skill for a child to acquire. Many children learn to call 'Mummy' to get attention and later will call out 'look at me' to ensure that mother looks when they are jumping, climbing or doing something interesting. Watch to see if your child is using actions or sounds to attract attention. If the child is only using actions, you could teach him or her to call out, using the name of an adult or words like 'look' or 'watch me'. Sometimes greeting words like 'hi' or 'hello' can be used in this way.

Learning to initiate, maintain or terminate social interaction

The skills of initiating, maintaining or terminating a social exchange are best learned at appropriate times during the day. For example, the child can learn the appropriate words of greeting and parting when arriving and leaving kindergarten or a friend's house. Social contact with a partner is usually achieved through use of devices such as naming the partner ('hello Jason!') together with physical proximity and eye contact during conversation. You should look for naturally occurring opportunities to encourage a child to use these behaviours appropriately.

Learning to obtain information by asking questions

Children initially learn to obtain information by using a rising intonation with a single word. Only later will a simple sentence be used for this purpose. For example, learning to ask questions usually follows the sequence:

'Daddy?'
'Daddy go work?'

Much, much later, the child will use a 'wh-' question form, complete the verb and invert it:

'Where Daddy go?' or
'Me can go?' or
'Can I go?'

Another early question form is 'what?', with utterances such as 'what(s) that?' or 'what (does that) boy do?' 'What', 'who' and 'where' forms are closely associated with the child's development of an interest in the environment. It is only later, when concepts about cause, manner and time have been developed, that the child will use question forms like 'why', 'how' and 'when'.

Games that involve turn-taking are a good way to teach children to ask and answer questions. The games need to be organised so that the child can take both roles, asking and answering questions. The adult should initially take the questioner role, to model it for the child. Subsequently, the adult and child can change roles so that the child can ask questions of the adult. Once the rules of the game are learned, these games can be played with small groups of children with all the group taking turns to ask as well as answer questions. Lotto games are a good means for practising these skills. Here are some other ideas:

- 'Where' questions can be encouraged in a hiding game, with the child taking turns to hide an object and asking 'where . . . gone?' after the other person has modelled this behaviour several times. Alternatively the child could play a matching card game in a small group. The child can learn to ask 'where . . . ?' rather than the more complicated question form 'who has . . . ?' to obtain the card that will make a pair.
- 'What' questions can be practised using labelling (or naming) and action words that the child already uses. A series of objects or pictures could be used in a turn-taking game to ask 'what('s) that?' or 'what(s the) boy doing?' Begin by asking the questions, then change roles with the child who can take the questioner's role. Similar games can be devised to help the child learn to use the other question forms: why, who, how and when.

Use of the remaining three communicative intentions, to discover new words, to give information and to answer questions can be taught within activities similar to those that were described in earlier parts of this chapter.

Summary

Learning to use language in a variety of ways is a very important part of learning to talk. A child may learn to comprehend and say words correctly in terms of their meaning or the semantic aspect of language and can learn to combine words into sentences that are correct in terms of grammatical rules or syntax and morphology. However, these skills are relatively useless if the child cannot use these words and sentences to influence events. This is the pragmatic aspect of language and represents as important a facet of a language system as the other aspects (semantics, syntax, morphology and phonology) that were considered in Chapter 1.

This concludes Part 2 of the book. The remaining chapters are concerned with some of the more general issues in language acquisition, such as increasing intelligibility, use of signs to supplement speech, working with children in groups and working with children from language backgrounds other than English. These topics often need to be considered when efforts are made to help children who are experiencing difficulties to become more competent language users.

Part 3
Issues in Implementation

The final chapters of the book explore a number of practical issues associated with the provision of language development experiences for children experiencing delays and difficulties. Phonological aspects of development are addressed first by Christine Hardman, a speech pathologist with wide experience in helping children with phonological difficulties and in advising parents how they can help their children. The use of signs to supplement or complement pre-linguistic or relatively unintelligible attempts to communicate are also examined. Issues are then considered that are associated with the implementation of language strategies in a range of specific contexts that are becoming increasingly common in the daily experiences of young children. These include situations where children are gathered in groups, as in preschools, nursery schools or other early childhood education settings. They also include situations where professionals advise and guide parents about the development of their children as in early intervention programmes and other services that provide support for parents concerned about the development of their children.

The last issue to be addressed in this set of chapters arises from experiences gained by the writers during the operation of a parent-based language programme, where many of the families seeking support and guidance about their child's language development came from language backgrounds other than English, the major language of the community in which the language programme operated. Questions arising from the needs of this group of parents are considered in the final chapter of the book.

Chapter 11
Phonological Development and Intelligibility

CHRISTINE A. HARDMAN, SPEECH PATHOLOGIST

Most children begin life by 'telling' us just how they are feeling, through a whimper or a lusty yell. The skill of making sounds has begun and between the earliest cry of hunger or pain and the most complicated spoken word there is often a lengthy, sometimes bumpy, path of development and refinement. This chapter is concerned with this development. It begins with a review of the early development of phonological skills and then provides suggestions about ways to promote children's sound-making in the early stages of learning to talk.

Phonological development

The earliest recognisable sounds of communication are varied cries representing a variety of needs or emotions. As babies become more involved with the world and begin to enjoy the noises that they can make, the sounds become more gurgling or vowel-like, as in 'ah' and 'oo'. Care-givers will often find this very pleasurable, spending much time gurgling and cooing in response. These early sounds need little effort to produce and the movements of the tongue and lips are small. Later the sounds become more complicated, such as 'bubub' or raspberries and growls involving much finer movements of the lips, tongue or palate. It is hard to believe that a simple 'raspberry' sound requires very tight lips closed around the tongue, with a strong force of air being pushed against it.

Vocal production then usually flourishes with a wide variety of sounds beginning to appear. Starting with one sound at a time, such as 'bu', the baby progresses to strings of sounds as in 'bubbubbub', eventually incorporating a variety of sounds within the one string that might sound like 'bubbawidzee'. These sounds often seem to be produced for the baby's own enjoyment and it is common for parents to tell of 'little Jake lying in his cot for ages and ages just talking to himself'. Lips, tongue and palate are all now given plenty of useful practice, with greater need for control as speed of use increases. However, as yet, no meaning or intent can be said to be occurring.

The next step on the ladder of sound development usually involves linking sounds with actions or situations. Lip smacking or 'm' may begin as part of a meal-time routine, encouraged and modelled by care-givers. Similarly, sounds emerge such as 'br' when pushing a toy car or 'pa' during games involving smacking the bath water. The use of these sounds progresses to the point where infants are able to relate the sounds to specific actions or situations. At this stage they may begin to use their vocalising more specifically to ask for something or to give information, as when the child says 'br' and points out of doors, telling you there was the sound of a car outside, or when the child smacks his or her lips together to indicate that he or she is hungry and would like something to eat.

During this time there is frequently a lot of 'sound practice', with infants babbling for minutes at a time. These noises often sound very 'adult-like' and are beginning to include phonetic characteristics of the child's home language, such as English, Arabic or Cantonese. There are rises and falls in intonation reflecting those heard in the speech of care-givers. On picking up a toy telephone, a child may now consistently say 'eh-oh', linking the approximation of a sound he or she has often heard with an associated action. Singing nursery rhymes or songs now becomes a fun game, with imitated sounds being linked to familiar music and rhythms. Meaning behind the sounds is limited, but connections are being made between these sounds and their referents. More information on this stage of development is included in Chapter 7, in the discussion of the pre-verbal skills of performatives and protowords.

By the time children begin to attempt real words, they have generally been making a wide variety of sounds that, in English, include using the tongue:

- at the front of the mouth (t, d, n);
- in the middle of the mouth (l);
- at the back of the mouth (k, g);
- with lips tightly sealed (p, b);
- with lips lightly sealed (m);
- with lips rounded (w).

At this stage, children will also have produced sounds requiring 'pops' of air as in 't', 'd', 'k', 'g', 'p', 'b', and will have attempted sounds requiring a steady air flow such as 's', 'f' and 'sh'. Sounds requiring air to be directed through the nose rather than the mouth will also have been used, including 'm' and 'n'. Infants will have practised putting sounds at the beginning of syllables, such as 'bu', in the middle as in 'bubbu' and even at the end of syllables, as in 'bubbub'.

As infants experiment with sounds in words, some mistakes are expected. Examples of such frequently occurring 'errors' and common sound patterns associated with the production of early attempts are set out in Table 11.1.

The period in which errors such as those listed in Table 11.1 can be expected may last well into the time when first word combinations occur. A lisp, where the 's' is made with the tongue between the teeth, may be acceptable for a small child using single words. Such errors may last well into the period of first words and even simple sentences. Some children will still be making acceptable 'mistakes' for 's', such as 'think' for 'sink', even after they have begun to put in a marker to indicate plurals, as in 'carth' for 'cars'. Later on, when sentences have become more mature and vocabulary more varied, this will often have righted itself with a clear 's' being produced. Examples of the sounds you would expect to hear as children pass through the developmental stages proposed by Brown (1973) are set out in Table 11.2.

Risk factors associated with the development of phonological skills

For the development of sounds to occur according to plan, muscles of the jaw, lips, tongue, palate and even the lungs need to be functioning reasonably well. Difficulty in coordinating movements or in holding muscles 'tight' may not make a noticeable difference during the produc-

Table 11.1: Examples of common sound patterns in early language

Common sound patterns	Examples
Omission of final consonants in words	'book' → 'boo', 'eat' → 'ee'
Substitution of a similar sound type	'sheep' → 'seep'
Substitution of earlier for later developing sounds	'car' → 'tar', 'rabbit' → 'wabbit'
Lisp with tongue between the teeth	'suck' → 'thuck'
Consonant-blend reduction	'snake' → 'nake', 'climb' → 'cimb'
Omission of unstressed syllables	'blanket' → 'bat'
Reduplication (complete or partial) of syllables	'cuddle' → 'kukoo'

Adapted from Rahmani (1987) and Shriberg and Kwiatkowski (1986)

Table 11.2: Sounds expected in terms of expressive language structures (Brown's morphemes) and language stage

Sounds expected(approx. 75% accuracy word level)	Language structures; Brown's (1973) morphemes	Language stage Brown (1973)
h, ŋ (sing), p, m, w, b, n, a, t, y, k, g, ʒ(vision)	present progressive '-ing' plural ('-s') possessive ('-s')	2–3
f	articles (a, the) regular past tense	4–5
Note: other sounds may be attempted, such as 's', but accuracy is not necessarily expected at this stage.	third person regular third person irregular uncontracted auxiliary (he is hopping) contracted copula (he's tall) contracted auxiliary (he's hopping)	

Source: Kilminster and Laird (1983); Brown (1973)

tion of the earlier sounds that require less effort to produce. However, a child's difficulties in these areas may become increasingly apparent as the sounds to be produced become more complex. This may be of particular relevance for some children with problems in muscle coordination, such as those with Down syndrome (Selikowitz, 1990).

Equally, for satisfactory progress to occur children need to be able to hear sounds in their environment as well as the sounds that they themselves make. Without adequate hearing, this environmental input and self-feedback is missed, with the possibility that sound-making may become slow or stop altogether. Some children are known to be at particular risk of a reduction in hearing due to fluid build-up in the middle ear (glue ear). This group includes children with Down syndrome (Selikowitz, 1990), children whose parents smoke (Haggard, 1995) and children with enlarged adenoids (Silman and Silverman, 1991). The presence of sensory-neural or 'nerve' hearing losses may also need to be investigated should sound development fail to progress.

The general health of an infant may also play a part in sound development. An unwell, listless baby may not have developed the interest or even have the energy to produce sound, requiring its energy levels to be used for the more important purposes of supporting life.

Encouraging the development of appropriate speech sounds

The types and amount of sound that children hear are important for the development of their own sound output. As Chapter 4 suggested, talking to a baby is crucial, even at an early age, as it provides the building blocks for the child's future development. It is vital for the baby to hear speech sounds and intonation patterns. A baby left to play alone, quietly in the cot, for hours may easily miss out on those building blocks needed for the growth of sounds. On the other hand, if a baby is not very responsive to the noises his or her parents make, there is a risk that the parents will become discouraged and that sound play will lose its appeal. Perseverance is recommended and will generally prove worthwhile.

It can be seen that, for young children, the production of speech sounds and the developments that can be expected at each stage are complicated. However, by monitoring what your child is doing, and providing appropriate sound models, you may be able to facilitate progress. If you are concerned about any aspect of the child's speech, follow your intuition. Organise an assessment with an appropriate professional, such as a speech pathologist, as early as possible. In doing this, you may be able to minimise any long-term difficulties. In the mean-time, the most important thing to remember is that most children learn skills more naturally through play and general life experience. It is not necessary for parents to become a 'teacher' with structured lessons or tasks. Parents or care-givers talking to and generally interacting with their children throughout the day can provide plenty of opportunities for encouraging sound development. In many cases, they do not even realise that this encouragement is happening. Here are some suggestions for helping a child to develop effective sound-making skills.

- Try to remember that sound-making should be enjoyable and interactive. The more fun a baby has listening to sounds and making sounds, the more sounds he or she will want to make. Getting a giggle from a parent by making a raspberry may certainly encourage many more raspberries to be blown. A dad imitating his 'brilliant' child's use of his 'name' will certainly help to encourage that child to say it over and over. A cycle of mutual enjoyment will be the result.
- Secondly, remember that face-to-face contact between infant and carer allows the infant to see and hear the sounds being made. Video records of parents interacting with their babies (Trevarthen, 1979) have shown that infants will practise a face shape such as lip-rounding while carefully inspecting a parent's face during sound play. This will happen well before the children actually start to say the particular sound in question.

Assessing early sounds

Table 11.3 provides an outline of the stages of sound development in infancy. By listening to your infant's vocalisations, writing them down and checking against this chart, you will be able to determine a starting place to begin practising and encouraging sounds with the baby. For example, if the baby is starting to make a few different sounds, such as gurgles and squeals, you could make silly sounds by filling your cheeks with air and 'popping' them, or by making raspberries. Once the baby starts to eat solids, it is a good idea to try to leave the spoon in the baby's mouth until he or she closes their lips on it. You can also begin to encourage the baby to drink from a cup. Both of these activities encourage development of muscle coordination and strength.

Assessing early word skills

As with the suggestions made for checking your baby's early sounds, the easiest way to monitor early word production is by listing the child's spontaneous 'words'. Spell the words as they sounded when the child produced them. You need this information in order to check that the child is able to make the sounds appropriate to his/her level of sound development.

Make a list of the words you hear the infant using. Look at the list you have made and identify the sounds that the child is using. You can use the checklist in Appendix G to record these sounds or circle the sounds in Table 11.4. With this information, you will be able to answer the following questions:

- Does the child attempt a wide variety of sound types?
- Does the child attempt sounds in all positions within the mouth?
- Does the child use sounds at the beginning of words/end of words/middle of words?
- If the child is not attempting a particular sound, will he or she use it in imitation?

Refer to Table 11.1 for more examples of common sound patterns in children's early language.

If your child is spontaneously producing the types of sounds that are appropriate for his or her current language level as defined in Brown's (1973) stages (see Table 11.2), you will not need to give any extra practice. If the sounds are only produced in imitation, more opportunities to practise may be required. If the child does not produce the sounds at all, more specific help may be needed.

Suggestions for practising sounds that are not being used

Describe to the child how the missing sounds are made. Table 11.5 has some suggestions about ways of describing sounds to children. Model them. If necessary you may like to let the child touch your face as you

Table 11.3: Checklist for assessing and practising early sounds

Behaviour to check	Yes/no	Suggested activities for care-givers
Does the infant suck from a bottle or nipple? If yes: are the baby's lips sealed well?	Y/N	If you answered 'no' to any of the questions, or if you have any concerns about feeding, talk to an appropriate professional, such as a nursery nurse, infant health sister, paediatric unit in hospitals.
Is the baby sucking strongly?	Y/N	
Does the baby take a long time to feed?	Y/N	
Is the baby irritable during feeding?	Y/N	
Does the infant make a few sounds such as gurgles, varied cries and occasional squeaks?	Y/N	Make lots of 'small talk'. Say 'hello, you've woken up. Time to get up, then. Off we go. Into your pram.' Have lots of face-to-face time, while you talk. Make silly noises, sing-song noises or make faces and noises to your baby, such as 'ooh-ooh', 'ah-ah' and raspberries, lip smacks, cheek pops. Have fun and try not to be discouraged by the lack of response.
Has the infant started solid foods?	Y/N	Leave the spoon in the baby's mouth until he or she closes on it. Encourage chewing and munching on a variety of toys, fingers, then food. Some gagging on lumps is to be expected. Encourage food play to help build tolerance to different textures and sensations. Encourage drinking from a cup, even before the baby can reliably hold the cup. This encourages a more mature suck and swallow pattern, increasing coordination and strength. Ask for help if you are unsure.
Is the infant making more sounds, such as raspberries, growls, coughs, lip pops, tongue clicks or kisses?	Y/N	Try to copy the child's sounds. Remember to leave time for the child to 'talk back' to you. Encourage the sound that the child is not yet making.

Table 11.3: contd.

Behaviour to check	Yes/no	Suggested activities for care-givers
Is he or she making vowel sounds such as 'ah' and 'ooh' or consonants like 'b', 'm', 'n', 't' and 'd'?	Y/N	
Is the infant mainly using tongue sounds like 'la-la', 't', 'd' and 'n'?	Y/N	Encourage lip sounds and actions such as lip popping, lip smaking, 'm', 'p', 'b', lip rounding and kissing. Encourage lips together when playing or sitting. Check that lips are closed when swallowing or eating off a spoon.
Is the infant mainly using lips sound and actions?	Y/N	Encourage tongue clicks, 'la-la', 't', 'd', 'n', sticking tongue out.
Is the infant using long, complicated strings of sounds in what seems like conversation?	Y/N	Encourage 'conversations'. talking to your child and leaving spaces for the baby to talk back to you. See Chapter 7 for examples of sounds to link to particular actions or words. See Chapter 8 for ideas to encourage development of real words.

Table 11.4: Earlier developing sounds and their position within the mouth

Common sound types	Position in the mouth		
	Front	Middle	Back
Pop	p b	t d	k g
Flow	f	s ʒ(vision)	h
Nasal	m	n	y ŋ (sing)
Glide	w		

make the sound. You may also like to give a gestural cue, such as a fist popping open for 'p', 'b', 't' and 'd' or a slow sweep of the hand for 'm'. This will help the child see as well as hear the sound you are making.

Encourage the child to imitate your model. Reward any efforts with praise or a turn in a favourite game. For example, if the child says 'p' five times after you have modelled it, reward with:

- praise or cuddles;
- stickers, stars or stamps;
- throwing a ball at a set of skittles.

Table 11.5: Describing sounds to children

Sound	Description	Association
p	Put your lips together and pop (whisper)	p-p-p: the 'boat sound' My Putt Putt Boat
b	Put your lips together and pop (loud sound)	b-b-b: the 'bouncing ball sound' My Bouncing Ball
t	Put your tongue up behind your teeth and pop (whisper)	t-t-t: the 'dripping tap sound' Mr Tap
d	Put your tongue up behind your teeth and pop (loud sound)	d-d-d: the 'hammer sound' Mr Hammer
k	Put the back of your tongue up (pretend to cough or growl) Tilting the child's head slightly back and having them hold the front of their tongue down with a finger may help.	k-k-k: 'kookaburra sound' Mr Kookaburra
ch	Push your lips around and blow (whisper; a quick sound)	ch-ch-ch: the 'train sound'
m	Put your lips together and hum (feel the vibration by putting your finger on the side of your nose)	m-m-m: the 'humming sound'
l	Put your tongue behind your top teeth (long sound)	la-la-la: the 'singing sound'
h	Puff	h-h-h: the 'panting dog sound'
w	Move your lips around then back, from a kiss to a smile	w-w-w
g	Put the back of your tongue up (loud sound)	g-g-g: the 'drinking sound'
f	Bite your bottom lip and blow (whisper)	f-f-f: the 'fly spray sound' Mr Flyspray
v	Bite your bottom lip and blow (loud sound)	v-v-v: the 'plane sound' Mr Plane
s	Put your teeth together, smile and blow	s-s-s: the 'snake sound' Mr Snake
z	Push your lips around and blow (loud sound)	z-z-z: the 'bee sound' Mr Bee
sh	Push your lips around and blow (whisper: long sound)	sh-sh-sh: the 'be quiet sound'
r	Put you tongue up to the top of the middle part of your mouth (sliding back from 'l' may help)	r-r-r: the 'car starting sound'

Animal sounds or environmental noises may be useful to describe the required sound, as in 'p' for blowing out a candle and 's' like a snake.

When the child is consistently able to say the target sound that has been practised, you can try using it in simple words.

Suggestions for practising sounds in words

As previously noted, it is acceptable for some 'mistakes' to be made in words in the early stages of learning to talk. When such mistakes are made, you can:

* Accept the child's attempts to say a word. Repeat it correctly, slightly emphasising the incorrect sound. For example:

  Child: 'Dere du'
  Adult: 'Yes, there is a duck. Duck. The duck says quack quack. Duck.'

* Set up a box of familiar items that have the missing or mispronounced sound in the name. For example, Jason is missing the end sounds in simple words. Items in the box might include: ball, soap, sock, cup, book, sheep, block. Take turns at 'finding' the toys and naming them. If correct, either spontaneously or in imitation, reward the child, model the correct word or describe it. For example:

  Child: 'Sheep'
  Adult: 'Hey, that was fantastic. It is a sheep. You were very clever to remember the "p" sound at the end.'

  If the child was incorrect, reward, model and describe. For example:

  Child: 'Shee'
  Adult: 'Good try. It is a sheep. Sheep. It has a sound at the end, too. Sheep.'

* You may also use your hands to show how sounds are being used or not used in words. For example, if the child is missing the beginning sound in a one-syllable word like 'ball' put your closed fists side-by-side at eye level. Open each in turn to represent the first and second parts of the word, as in

  'b'   'all'
  open one fist   open second fist

  By opening only one hand at a time, you can describe which part is actually being missed. For example:

| (b)– | 'all' |
| keep fist closed | open fist |

Say: 'I could hear the last part. I wonder what happened to the "b" at the beginning.'

| 'b' | 'all' |
| open one fist | open second fist |

- Look through books or magazines together to find pictures of things which have the sound you want to practise. Model and describe the word. Encourage the child to say the word, rewarding and describing the practice sound as necessary. Cut out the pictures and either paste them in a scrapbook or put them in a 'treasure bag' for later practice.
- At the supermarket, find as many items as possible that include the practice sound. Encourage the child to say the word as the items go in the shopping trolley and again when they are unpacked. Naming things may also be practised at meal-times, bath-time and in any joint activity during the day.
- Put three or four objects on a tray or bench. Ask the child to name the objects and then close their eyes. Take away one object and ask the child to name what is missing.
- Hide several pictures or objects that have your practice sound in their names. The child has to find an object, put it in a 'sound spot' such as a box or basket and name it. Again, praise, modelling and description are required from the adult.

Listening to similar sounds

If the child is using short sentences regularly, does he or she notice the difference between pairs of words that sound similar? The ability to discriminate is necessary for the child to be successful in recognising and reproducing sounds in words correctly. You can check this skill by setting up a game using a variety of toys and pictures that have similar sounding names or associated noises, such as:

- shoe, moo (cow), two;
- cat, mat, bat, hat;
- doll, ball;
- key, tea, bee, pea;
- mouse, house;
- train, crane.

Ask the child for each object by name. Does the child identify the correct object when requested during this activity? If not, will the child do it if you repeat the word, emphasising the initial sound?

Difficulties in identifying the difference between two similar sounds may be due to difficulties in actually perceiving the sounds. These may be caused by mild hearing loss such as that associated with 'glue ear'. It may also be that the child can hear the two sounds but does not recognise that they are different. This is called a problem in 'auditory perception'. In the former situation, a hearing test and tympanometry with appropriate medical follow-up would be recommended. In the latter instance, activities can be planned to improve the child's listening skills. For example, you could use two boxes to represent two practice sounds such as 'b' and 'm'. Ask the child to place objects beginning with these sounds into the appropriate box. If the child does this correctly, praise and reward the child. If he or she produces an incorrect solution, praise the attempt, model the sound and describe the method of making the sound. Then help the child to put the object into the correct box.

Summary

This chapter has introduced the path of sound-making from birth to the use of words and early sentences. This is not always an easy progression. Sound-making is complicated by 'mistakes' that may be stress-inducing for care-givers, but which are actually regarded as acceptable. By monitoring areas of concern, it is possible to determine the significance of sounds being used relative to developing language and, if necessary, to provide opportunities to maximise the child's sound skills. This will further encourage growth towards effective communication.

Chapter 12
Signing: a Stepping Stone to Speech

Earlier chapters demonstrated that learning to talk is one of the most complex tasks to be faced by children during the early years of their development. However, for some children, the process of acquiring and using spoken language is particularly long and difficult. A small number of these children can hear words but are not able to make much sense of them. A few have difficulty in developing the skills needed to use words, with the result that they are unable to communicate their meaning to other people. Others begin to develop expressive language skills but are unable to produce words clearly enough for a listener to understand what they are trying to say. An augmentative method of communication, such as the use of natural gestures, facial expressions or manual signs, may assist such children to begin to communicate more effectively.

There is general agreement (Bloomberg and Johnson, 1991; Dice, 1994; McConkey and Price, 1986; MacKay and Dunn, 1989; Schaeffer, 1980) that the introduction of signing to supplement or replace other means of communication may be helpful for some children in the early stages of language acquisition. In particular, it may assist children who are at risk of, or are already experiencing problems in understanding and using language. Gestures provide a visual prop to assist in the comprehension of messages (Martinsen and Smith, 1989). In the same way, signing can supplement, and in some cases replace, other, more primitive forms of communication. For example, a child who has learned to ask for a drink by pulling your arm can be taught an appropriate sign to replace the pulling action.

In many day-to-day conversations with children, parents use gestures to emphasise what is being said. For example, Mummy says 'get the book; it's somewhere over there' while pointing in the general direction of the missing item, or describes the giant as 'huge', with arms reaching high. Such gestures create a visual picture that adds to the impact of spoken words. This situation also occurs when young children begin to convey their own messages. For example, Denny looks up at Daddy after completing his puzzle, smiles and claps his hands. The message is: 'I've finished, aren't I clever?' Claire comes up and tugs Mummy's skirt and pulls her to the fridge. The message is: 'I want something to eat or drink.' Babies can ask for another turn in a game well before they have the words, by putting their hands out to Daddy to play 'Round and Round the Garden' again, by pulling his hands for another turn of 'Row, Row, Row your Boat', or wiggling their fingers to say 'I'd like to sing Twinkle, Twinkle Little Star.' Sometimes an object is used, as when Azim fetched a cup to tell you that he wanted a drink, or your bag when it was time to go home. Often a sound is included in these communicative acts which will continue to be used until the child is able to produce recognisable words to convey meaning.

This chapter is concerned with the use of augmentative means, particularly manual signs, to supplement speech for children experiencing problems in either expressing and/or understanding language. The reasons why signs are used to help some children learn to talk are considered and suggestions are made for deciding which children may benefit from learning to understand and use signs. Procedures are described for deciding when such signs should be introduced, which signs should be used, and how they should be taught.

Why introduce signs?

There are many reasons why the introduction of signs can be a positive step in helping children to develop early communication skills. For example, as suggested earlier, the use of gestures or hands in conjunction with speech is a natural part of everyday language. It adds to the message that is given, allowing what is said to be both heard and seen. Congruent use of both spoken words and signs to teach an initial vocabulary to children who are known to be at risk of difficulties in learning to talk is likely to be more effective than the use of spoken words alone. Children remember the speech sounds associated with a particular entity, such as 'drink' but also remember the visual image of the hand movement that is consistently paired with a word. Some children, including many with severe learning difficulties, perform cognitive tasks more effectively when presented with material in a visual or concrete mode, rather than a purely auditory mode. The likelihood of recall is enhanced when information is accessed through more than one sense. In this way, the augmentation of speech, through the use of manual signs and other aids, supports language learning and enhances the cognitive level at which the child is able to function.

At a more practical level, the speed at which adults speak is often too fast for children to hear and process the message being sent. In this situation, comprehension is enhanced if speech is supplemented with gestures or other aids that reinforce the message being conveyed. When using a gesture or sign in conjunction with speech it is common for the speaker to slow down, either to recall a specific sign, to add emphasis, or to ensure that the listener has seen and attended to the whole message. This pause allows more time for the information being sent to be received and understood. It also helps to reduce any overload that may occur when well-intentioned care-givers talk too much when interacting with their child.

By using a gesture or sign, eye contact can be encouraged with those children for whom lack of attention and poor eye contact is an additional part of their communication difficulty. For example, the rapid movement of two fingers away from the face, as in the Auslan or Makaton gesture for 'look', often seems to encourage the child to turn to look at the speaker, rather than just attend to the spoken word alone. If a child is looking away from a speaker's face, using the hands to gain attention and draw gaze back into a face-to-face position encourages the eye contact necessary for effective interaction. A physical prompt to respond can be given in the form of shaping the child's hands to form a sign.

Signs can be particularly helpful in developing children's understanding of words for things that have no concrete referent, such as 'come', 'give' and 'put'. For these types of words, a sign provides a physical cue or prompt that helps to give meaning to these otherwise abstract words.

Specific gestures, signs and other forms of augmentative communication provide a simple means for a child to get a message across with more accuracy than just tugging or pointing. Listeners will be more likely to understand these messages if the child's speech is difficult to understand, or if speech has not yet become the child's preferred method of communication. By being able to communicate with others, the child is less likely to become frustrated and more likely to try to communicate again.

Who could benefit from signing?

Children who might benefit from the introduction of signs as a supplement to speech include those who:

- Are known to be at risk of significant delays or difficulties in understanding or using spoken language. This group could include children with Down syndrome, or those with general developmental delays and moderate to severe learning difficulties;
- Children who continue to demonstrate marked difficulties in producing understandable speech despite previous involvement in other language development services or programmes.

The initial aim of signing is to provide a greater opportunity for children to understand spoken language. Therefore, although some consideration should be given to the child's fine motor control when deciding whether or not to introduce signs, this may not initially be a major factor to consider. When a child begins to use signs, an approximation of the desired hand movement is generally acceptable, provided it conveys the required message. Fine tuning of movements can always be done later. However, when children seem to be physically unable to produce even simple hand movements, an alternative augmentative system should be considered. This might involve the use of real objects, photographs, drawings, picture symbols or pictographs, small line drawings that represent specific concepts such as COMPIC (Anderson, Bloomberg, Dunne, Jones and Snelleman, 1986), Rebus (Clark, Davies and Wood-cock, 1974) or Bliss symbols (McNaughton, 1975) and other electronic (voice-output) or non-electronic (communication board) systems (see Bloomberg and Johnson, 1991 and Jones and Cregan, 1986).

When should signing be introduced?

Parents and other carers begin to teach spoken language to their children from the moment they are born, gurgling, singing, talking and playing with them. Language teaching occurs all the time, with parents frequently unaware of the importance of all of these activities. Once an infant or child has been identified as being at risk of significant disruption in his or her language growth, additional gestures or signs can be introduced by care-givers to supplement their speech and maximise the impact of the messages the child is receiving. Sometimes this process may begin soon after birth. In other cases, speech is not augmented until much later, when the child has not begun to talk as expected. By introducing signs to the child as early as possible, parents maximise the possibility of the child understanding the signs and using them communicatively. If imitation does not occur, an assisted method of teaching can be introduced. This process will be considered in a later section of this chapter.

What meanings should be initially selected for signing?

Each child is an individual, with his or her own particular likes, needs and wants. Initially, when selecting a vocabulary of signs to introduce to a child, it is a good idea to include signs for specific needs. Children's main interests are often associated with food and favourite toys or activities, so if Joshua's favourite food is cheese, you could begin by using a sign for 'cheese'. If the child loves to listen to tape-recorded songs, introduce a sign for 'music'. At this stage, the names of objects and activities are often the most frequently used signs. Other common signs are for meanings for which there are no concrete referents, such as 'gone' and 'more'. These signs are often easily recognisable. Examples of such iconic signs include: two fingers touching the mouth for 'food' and a cupped hand tipped towards the mouth for 'drink' (see examples of frequently used signs, Figure 12.1). Other simple commands such as 'give', 'look', 'sit' or 'point' could also be introduced to assist in the child's understanding of what he or she is being asked to do.

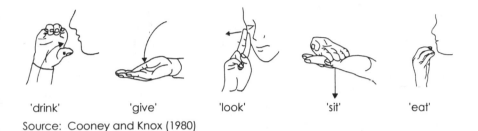

'drink'   'give'   'look'   'sit'   'eat'

Source: Cooney and Knox (1980)

Figure 12.1: Examples of single commands

Which augmentative system should be used?

A number of issues should be considered when selecting an augmentative communication system for a child. You need to take into account the child's particular needs and skills. For example

- Is the system likely to be temporary, as a support until the child's oral language skills become adequate. Is its main purpose to encourage comprehension and communication? Is it likely to become the child's main method of communication, in the short or long term?
- Is the child physically capable of using the proposed system? Does he or she have adequate control of fine motor movements to make hand signs? Are the signs sufficiently iconic to be understood by relative strangers? Is the system portable? Can it be easily learned by the child? Is there a financial consideration?
- How likely is it that those people in direct contact with the child will learn and use the system? What, if any, system is used in the preschool, school or other setting or situation in which the child is likely to be involved?

Whichever system you decide to use, you will need to monitor it to ensure that it continues to meet the needs of the child. In particular, you will need to check that the vocabulary continues to be adequate for the child's expressive and receptive needs. You will also need to continue to monitor whether or not an additional or alternative system should be included in the child's communication options.

If you decide to use a manual sign system, some useful sources of information include Jeanes, Reynolds and Coleman (1993), Johnson (1989), Miles (1988), Paget, Gorman and Paget (1976) and Walker and Cooney (1984).

How are signs taught?

You can initially introduce signs to a child as part of your natural language. This will involve always pairing a gesture or sign with the spoken word. Whenever the word is uttered, the gesture or sign is used at the same time. You do not need to pair every word in a sentence with a sign, but only the key words. For example, for the sentence 'Let's go in the car', you would only sign 'car' or 'go car'. 'Give me the book' would have signs paired to the words 'give' and 'book'.

It is very important that the signs used are linked, as often as possible, to the actual object or activity which they represent. This is essential in building up the child's understanding of what is being said and signed. Teaching words and signs without linking can result in the child being able to 'perform' a sign without necessarily understanding its meaning or using it in a communicative way. It is also important to give the child opportunities to use a sign if he or she is able. Questions like 'Do you want a drink?' only require the child to respond 'yes' or 'no', whilst questions such as 'What do you want?' or even 'Do you want a drink or a sandwich?' give the child much more scope to use those signs that have been learned.

Sometimes learning by imitation is not enough. If the child does not attempt to use signs after significant parental or carer usage, some assistance may be needed. To do this, you should take the child's hands and help make the required sign while saying the word at the same time. This process is called 'shaping'. Such assistance may be particularly useful for children with severe difficulties and delays because it will help to avoid repeated failure. Children respond positively to the experience of success, even though the actual attempt by the child to sign was assisted rather than unaided. It is crucial that the child looks at both the speaker and the sign as it is being made, so try to keep your hands close to your face while signing as a way of encouraging face-to-face interaction. As has already been suggested, this also encourages eye contact and improved attention to the speaker.

Remember that the more people who are involved with introducing signs to a child, and the more fun that is had doing it, the greater is the chance that the child will develop the use of signs as a supplement to his or her own growing language skills. When a child begins to use some signs, it is a good idea to prepare a 'Diary' or 'These are my words' book. This should include drawings or photographs of the signs that the child uses and the way that they are made. The book should also include pictures of the objects or actions to which the signs refer. Those inter-acting with the child can refer to this book to check on current vocabu-lary and the exact signs being used. This is particularly useful when the child's signs are not always clear. From the child's point of view, the most important point is that messages are being received and understood. Any procedure that clarifies the meaning of a vocalisation or hand move-ment for a familiar or unfamiliar listener should be used. These supports can be abandoned as the child's skills in communication increase. Some useful tips to follow when you begin to introduce signs to a child include:

- Before signing a word, make sure the child is watching you.
- Always say the word as you sign it.
- Encourage the child to sign as you would encourage speech. For example, 'tell me . . .'
- Use the sign each time you say the word.
- Only introduce one or two new signs at a time.
- Before expecting the child to use a sign, make sure you give plenty of opportunities for him or her to learn what it means.
- Expect the child to sign, just as you would expect speech.
- Accept any approximation of a sign, but as the child becomes more capable, expect and encourage the clearest sign that the child is able to produce.

Summary

The development of comprehensible spoken language is the ultimate goal for almost all children. The use of signs is one way to help achieve more effective communication for children experiencing difficulties in the early stages. Evidence suggests that signs may facilitate, and will certainly not interfere with, the child's acquisition of language and, in particular, of intelligible speech. Signs can help children to experience the benefits and fun of communication. They should be accepted as a useful tool for children who are struggling to acquire effective language skills.

Chapter 13
Working with Children in Groups

Many of the ideas suggested in this book for encouraging the development of early language skills have focused on individual children and their specific skills. Strategies have been described for pinpointing a child's current language level, selecting appropriate objectives, such as specific actions, gestures, sounds or words, choosing activities and materials that will give opportunities to practise the new skills, and checking on progress.

Many of the situations described in earlier chapters for implementing effective teaching strategies involved settings where an adult spent time alone with the child, working through selected activities. However, all these tasks can be carried out in a variety of contexts. A parent may help a child at home, during special play times or routine daily activities with siblings. However, for many reasons, parents are not always able to help their own children learn new skills. Some children learn more quickly when they are helped by another adult, therapist, teacher or nursery aide, rather than a parent. Teachers and other carers working in the early childhood field are sometimes the first to recognise that a child is experiencing difficulties in learning to talk. For some children the playgroup, preschool, nursery school or other early childhood setting is an ideal context in which to learn new language skills. Such children respond to situations where they can watch, imitate and learn from their peers. This chapter is concerned with the strategies that can be used by teachers, therapists and others to implement language objectives for an individual child in a context that involves groups of children.

There are a number of advantages associated with the implementation of language objectives for an individual child in contexts that involve other children. For example, you can ensure:

- generalisation of emerging language skills. Early childhood programmes usually provide a variety of activities for the child to participate in. When teaching new language skills, it is important to provide opportunities for the child to practise the skills in a variety of

147

situations. This ensures generalisation of the skill: that the child is able to use the new skill in contexts other than that in which it was first learned;

- that the child has opportunities to imitate appropriate language models provided by other children in the group;
- that the child has opportunities to practise newly acquired language skills during interaction with peers and other adults.

The most important point to remember when helping a child with language difficulties within a group context is that you must have a very clear idea of your goals for each child. You can then ensure that he or she has opportunities to hear appropriate language modelled by other children, and to use those actions, sounds or words that have been selected for practice. You can also take steps to see that adults who have contact with the child are aware of your language objectives and help in their implementation.

In this chapter we will consider three types of group situations that can be used for encouraging and practising language:

- informal or naturally occurring routines;
- structured or planned group activities;
- unstructured group play.

Informal or naturally occurring routines

Many opportunities for encouraging language occur naturally during the day, as part of the familiar sequence of events that fill the timetable of a busy early childhood programme. Think about the routines that recur each day, as the children arrive, put away their bag, coat, hat, choose an activity and settle to play. Later, there are the relatively fixed times for eating, toileting, sleeping and going home. During the day, children frequently spend time playing with building blocks, with dolls, or painting, running and jumping, singing and listening to music or a story.

In Chapter 3, the idea of 'scripts' was introduced as a way of explaining children's concepts or mental schema for the familiar events that comprise their daily timetable at playgroup, preschool or other early childhood programme. Children make sense of the daily events of their lives by learning the scripts, or the actions and language associated with these events. If you are working in an early childhood programme and need to identify specific language objectives for the children in your group, one option is to identify the language component of the scripts associated with different activities in your programme. You can then plan ways to encourage the children to acquire these language skills. You should begin by observing your daily programme to identify the scripts, or routines, followed by the children in your group. Some activities have clearly defined expectations about what each child involved in a particular activity must do and say. Puzzles, art and craft and painting are probably examples of these types of activity. Others, such as outside play, dressing up, or imaginative play, are less structured, with more freedom for the children to act spontaneously and follow their own interests. Newly enrolled children must learn how to behave in the different activities they encounter. They need to learn the pattern of the daily routines so that they can follow the rules of the programme and behave as expected, both in terms of their actions and language. For example, during story time they must sit quietly, not wriggle, listen, watch the teacher and the book, be ready to answer any questions that are asked. You will need to look for language objectives that can be practised during these routine activities. You should also be aware that some of the children may be helped by the introduction of signs to support their communicative attempts (see Chapter 12). If any children have learned to use signs or consistent gestures you will need to find out which words have been learned and how the signs or gestures are performed.

Morning break-time provides an example of a daily routine that can be structured to provide children with opportunities to practise language skills. Each child in the group can be asked 'What do you want?' and then encouraged to answer by saying or signing that he or she wants a drink or some fruit. You should vary your expectations for each child according to his or her language level. For example, initially you may only expect a child to look at your face before being given something to eat or drink. Gradually, this expectation can be changed as the child learns to say 'milk' or 'juice' when prompted. Use the binary choice or the C-I-C strategies to provide a model of the words to be used. Eventually, the child will learn to ask 'Can I have a drink, please?' or 'May I have an apple?'.

Here is a list of the objectives that you can use for children asking for their juice and fruit. It gives you some idea of the stages in learning to ask. Remember to prompt the children at each stage, asking first 'What do you want?' pausing to give time to respond and then, if there is no reply, using a binary choice such as 'Do you want juice or some apple?' or the C-I-C strategy with 'What do you want?' 'Say milk.' 'What do you want?'.

Sequence of objectives for learning to ask

Asking for a drink:
'j' or 'd' (an appropriate sign could be used here)
'juice' or 'drink'
'I drink' or 'Lorie drink'

'I juice' or 'I have juice'
'Can I have juice?'
'Can I have orange juice?'
'May I have some orange juice, please?'

Asking for fruit:
'e' (use a sign here)
'eat'
'I eat' or 'apple'
'I eat apple' or 'I eat fruit'
'Can I have apple?'
'May I have some apple, please?'

With plenty of practice, children will gradually improve from saying simply 'juice' or 'I want juice' to asking properly, using a complete sentence. They can use these skills many times during the day, at home as well as at school. This is a good way for children to begin to learn to ask for things. Think about other daily routines where a similar procedure can be followed.

The strategy described above for learning to ask can be useful in many other group situations. For example, if children are learning to match objects to pictures, each child can be encouraged to say or sign something at an appropriate level while doing the task. A child who is not yet talking might be able to make an appropriate sound, such as 'br'mm', to accompany the car that is being matched to a picture. A more competent child might be encouraged to label the car or make a simple sentence about it, like 'Daddy's car' or 'My daddy has a car too', as part of the object-picture matching game. In a group activity such as building with blocks, one child could be encouraged to say 'er-er' while moving a heavy block into place, while another might be encouraged to label the object being built or talk about it in some way, as in 'boat', 'my boat' or 'boat go fast'. Other situations where this approach can be used include water and sand play areas, dough table and, in fact, any activity where children are engaged in a shared task that is supervised by an adult who can give encouragement to ask for objects or assistance.

Some of the best opportunities for practising language occur during the telling and retelling of familiar stories, particularly where a story involves repetitive use of language. These situations are useful because the children do not have to think of something to say. They only need to remember their part in the story, or listen to what the other children are saying. For example, when traditional stories like 'The Three Bears', 'The Three Billy Goats Gruff' or 'The Three Little Pigs' are recounted, the different parts can be acted out by the children. When the script requires the child to say 'Who's been sleeping in my bed?' some children may only be able to say 'my bed', while others can say the whole sentence. Simple puppets can be useful in assisting children with their parts. These familiar 'scripted' stories provide a very effective opportunity for practising language.

Much of the language that children use is learned in situations that involve familiar scripts, such as those described above. For example, many children, even those who cannot talk, know what to do when they greet and leave people, either smiling or waving and saying 'Hi', 'Hello' or 'Bye'. When they go to a birthday party, they know to say 'Happy Birthday' when they arrive with a present for the birthday child. They know that they will be expected to play games, eat, help blow out the candles on the cake and sing the 'Happy Birthday' song before they go home. When they go to bed, they know that they will say 'Ni Ni' or 'Goodnight' to everyone, get into bed, that the light will be turned off, and that they will go to sleep. So look for activities in which there are opportunities for the child to use language in a routine situation and make sure that the child joins in. Many of these opportunities arise when adults and children are in a group together during daily activities. Home or shopping corner, and even a table with a telephone, provide excellent opportunities for encouraging children to use familiar scripts, so try to include these when planning opportunities to practise your language objectives.

Structured or planned group activities

Children often learn useful speech from listening to other children modelling appropriate words and you can take advantage of this in many situations. For example, singing games such as 'Here we go Round the Mulberry Bush' provide children with clear actions to perform, such as dancing in a circle, and words to sing. All these singing games give the children instructions about what to do and, more important, what to say. Regular greeting and goodbye songs and routines with the whole group also provide similar opportunities. These are very useful situations for children who lack confidence to begin to join in.

Group games using the 'surprise' bag mentioned in Chapter 7 can also be used here. You might like to play using different foods (apple, cup cake), clothing and personal items (hat, shoe, brush) or household equipment (doll's house bed, chair, table). The child can be encouraged to talk about his or her chosen object, such as its colour, function, size and texture.

Board games that can be played at a table or on the floor are useful sources of opportunities for practising language. A lotto game, using pictures of objects (car, hammer and cup), animals (dog, bear, cow) and events (shopping, a party, bath-time) and cards with sets of matching pictures, can provide good opportunities for talking, with less competent children learning to imitate their more competent friends in the game. Two children can take charge of the cards and ask the question 'Who has . . . ?' A more able child can model such language for the child whose speech is difficult to understand. The other children in the game have to say 'my turn', 'I do', 'me' or perhaps label their cards, when it is their turn. Such games are good for language learning because they provide many opportunities for each child both to hear and say useful words and sentences. Each child has an opportunity to say 'my turn' or 'me' several times to fill the card, and may also have opportunities to label pictures on the cards or ask 'Who has this?' Simple 'Snap' games and picture dominoes are also useful.

The advantage of using group activities is the chance they provide for each child to talk according to his or her current capability. The games themselves should be enjoyable. In addition, the children learn that talking is worthwhile because speech makes something happen in the game. There are opportunities to practise taking turns and to learn language modelled by more competent children.

Unstructured group play

As noted in Chapter 3, some of the most valuable situations for children to acquire language are associated with those activities and contexts within an early childhood programme that allow children to explore and use materials and equipment freely, to pretend and to simply interact informally with other children and adults. Examples of these situations include:

- materials and equipment: playing with Lego, dough, sand, water;
- pretend games: dolls' corner, dressing up, going shopping;
- informal games: chasing, hide and seek, jumping together, talking.

Children can be encouraged to practise emerging language skills during these informal games by an adult prompting and modelling targeted sounds, actions and words, such as 'roll', 'cut', 'splash', 'dolly sick', 'Teddy eat', 'jump', 'me too', 'now'. If possible, encourage the child to join in such games with other more competent children who can act as conversational partners in the activity. You may need to join in the game during the early stages, but should try to withdraw as soon as the children are able to continue the activity without support.

One of the major problems that limit the effectiveness of language development programmes carried out with children in one-to-one settings, as with a special teacher, therapist or other professional, concerns generalisation, or the need for the child to learn to use newly acquired skills in other settings, outside the classroom or clinic where the teaching has taken place. One of the most important functions of children's informal games is to provide opportunities for children to generalise new skills, to begin to communicate spontaneously in natural situations, with peers and other adults. Indeed, it can be argued that, in order to be confident that your language activities have been successful, you need to observe the child using newly learned skills in informal games with peers, or in contexts other than those in which they were acquired. Early childhood settings provide ideal contexts for this to occur.

Finally, it is worth noting that, for most children, language objectives are achieved most quickly if they are shared between home and the child's playgroup, preschool or other early childhood programme. The selection of language objectives, their implementation and the monitoring of progress can be shared across home and other settings, with parents and teachers, therapists or other interested adults contributing to the child's progress.

Summary

When planning a language programme for a child, remember that new language skills can be practised in structured or semi-structured one-to-one activities, as discussed in Part 2 of this book (Chapters 6 to 10). However, if you have an opportunity to help a child in a context that involves groups of children, you should remember that your goals can be implemented in:

- naturally occurring routines and situations;
- structured or planned group activities;
- unstructured group play.

The most effective learning will occur when opportunities for talking occur in many different situations during the day. So make sure that you take advantage of all possible occasions for practising new language skills. The most important aspect is to ensure that you expect from each child only what he or she is capable of at his or her particular level of development.

Chapter 14
Working with Parents: A Model Support Project

In the second part of this book, a set of procedures was described for encouraging early language skills in young children who are experiencing difficulties or delays in learning to talk. These ideas have been developed within the context of a community-based language programme that was set up in Sydney in 1979. The principal aim of the programme, known as the Laurel House Early Language Project, is to stimulate early language skills in young children with delayed language, or at risk of such delay, by teaching their parents how to encourage early language and communication skills in their children. The procedures followed in the project are based on the assumption that language is a product of meaningful interaction between a child and familiar adults and older children (McLean and Snyder-McLean, 1978). This view of language development underlies the ideas presented in earlier parts of this book. In this chapter, the procedures followed in the daily operation of the project are described. Case studies are used to illustrate the types of problems presented by children attending the programme and the way in which individual programmes are organised and implemented for children and their families.

About the language programme

The Laurel House Early Language Project is an individual early intervention service for children aged two to five years who are at risk of, or experiencing difficulties in, the early stages of communication and language development. It is available to any parent who is concerned about problems being experienced by a child in learning to communicate. The programme is funded through annual submission-based grants from the New South Wales Department of Community Services (DCS). There are no fees. It is located at Laurel House, a DCS assessment centre for children with developmental or learning difficulties and their families. The programme is staffed by a qualified early childhood language teacher with specific training and experience both in language development and with children with special learning needs. It is administered by consumers through a management committee.

Children are accepted into the programme from around the age of two, but priority is given to children who are three years and six months or older and to those not yet at school who are receiving no other services. Children can be referred to the programme by any agency, including an early intervention teacher, preschool teacher, speech pathologist or directly, by parents. The programme is available to all families, regardless of cultural or linguistic background. Where necessary, the procedures followed are adjusted in accordance with the needs of each family.

How is the programme organised?

There are three stages in a child's language programme:

- Stage 1 involves a parent or carer and child attending 12 weekly sessions of about 45 minutes with the language teacher. At these meetings, the child is assessed and, with the help of parent or carer, an individual plan is developed. Suggested games and activities are written into a Parent Language Book for the parent, carer and other family members to do at home. It is anticipated that these activities will help the child begin to develop new skills in communication. After these 12 weekly visits, the second stage in the language programme begins.

- Stage 2 gives parent and child an opportunity to continue to improve their communication skills but with less frequent contact with the language teacher. The language teacher continues to monitor the child's progress for a further three months through visits at three- to four-weekly intervals. After this period, the assessment is repeated and progress is reviewed. By this time, the parent or carer should have learned how to communicate more successfully with the child. They should also have learned how to help the child develop better language and communication skills. On completion of Stage 2 (approximately six months after entering the programme), discussions are held about the need for continued involvement in the programme. Alternative forms of assistance may now be more appropriate. The language teacher has information about services in the region served by the project and will refer the family directly to other agencies as necessary.

- Stage 3 provides an option of check-up visits at approximately 12-weekly intervals until the child moves on to other services or the parent and teacher feel that there is no further need for support from the programme.

How does the programme operate?

Initial assessment

On entry to the programme, the child's language development status is determined using a mixture of formal and informal assessments which include:

- Sequenced Inventory of Communication Development (SICD) (Hedrick, Prather and Tobin, 1984). This is a standardised test of expressive and receptive language skills in children from birth to five years of age.
- Child Language Development: Learning to Talk assessments. These procedures are described in Part 2 of this book (Chapters 5 to 10). Examples of forms used to record assessment data are included in Appendix C (summary assessment sheets).
- Language sampling. This provides a measure of the child's stage of language development as measured by the typical length of the child's sentences or the mean length of utterance (MLU). The language sample is taken with a parent or carer playing with the child. Through this approach, information about the child's receptive and expressive language, pragmatic development and play skills is obtained from those who are most familiar with the child. The procedures followed in recording information are described in Appendix A.
- Parent inventory. This is based on the parent inventory used by Horstmeier and MacDonald (1978). Information is sought about the current communication skills of the child, preferred activities, any specific needs perceived by parents and any areas of particular concern. Parents and carers are asked to observe the child in a series of structured and naturally occurring situations as a means of obtaining information about selected communicative behaviours. This information provides the language teacher with useful background information on the child at home. It also gives useful data about the child's interests and skills and these are used in selecting activities and language objectives. A copy of this inventory is included in Appendix H.

From the start, parents or carers are actively involved in the programme. For example, infants and young children are often very difficult to test, so early items on the SICD include information derived from reports of the child's competencies by a parent or carer. It should be noted that, while information relating to the development of articulation is recorded, there is no formal assessment or targeting of these skills within the programme.

Setting up an individual child's programme

Once initial assessments are complete, and this usually takes more than one visit to the language teacher, results are collated and a 'starting off' point is identified. During discussions with parent or carer and child, initial targets for practice are selected and a range of situations are planned within which suggested activities can be implemented. The proposed activities are modelled by the teacher with the parent and child together. No formal goals are set. Rather, aims are stated in the form of desirable outcomes. For example, it might be suggested to Mirtha's mother that she could 'encourage greater use of single words, both object labels and action words during normal daily activities, when looking at books and while playing with Mirtha'. This process is outlined in Chapter 8. This approach ensures that both parent and child feel no pressure to 'perform' by a set time. It also allows the language teacher to change or modify the targets if they prove to be inappropriate or if progress is more rapid than initially expected.

A list of words and suggested activities in which the words could be practised is compiled in consultation with the mother. This information is recorded in a book for Mirtha's mother to use at home. In addition, written information on the stages of early language development, suggestions for appropriate adult language, and ways to encourage play are shared with the parent. Copies of these resources are included in Appendix H.

The weekly session with the language teacher

A typical 45-minute session involves informal reporting on the week's progress at home by the parent, revision of activities previously suggested and introduction and practice of new activities or language targets. The parent and child usually engage in a series of activities with the teacher, which may include:

- role play and role exchange in a turn-taking setting, such as a tea party, bathing a doll, block/car/ball play;
- modification of adult language models to a level commensurate with the child's, with a discrepancy sufficiently challenging to ensure progress towards the next level;
- review of parental use of expansion, extension, commenting, binary choice and home rules;
- discussion of the implementation of new activities and strategies at home.

No formal sequence is followed during weekly sessions. Two or more of the activities listed above might be carried out concurrently. For example, while playing with blocks, the parent might comment on aspects of what happened at home during the week, or the teacher might introduce the concept of binary choice, modelling its use during the game. At all times, the emphasis is on activities and situations that are compatible with the child's abilities and interests, both intellectual and physical, and on the parent's available time. The aim is to ensure that parent and child progress at a rate that is comfortable for them. Although the initial activities and targets are suggested by the teacher, parents are encouraged to become actively involved in choosing activities and situations in which they feel comfortable and which are important to the family as a whole. By the end of Stage 1 they should be capable of selecting new language objectives and recognising appropriate situations for practising these tasks.

For children with mild learning disabilities and developmental delays, particular attention is given to the development of listening skills. Once the children begin to understand the 'rules of the game', parents are encouraged always to expect at least a minimum level of communicative behaviour in particular situations, such as a rule that they should 'encourage Dominic to answer the question: "Do you want toast or a biscuit?" before he gets something to eat.' The use of natural gestures and signs is also discussed with some parents, particularly those whose children are at a pre-verbal level. Provided their motor development allows it, these children are introduced to simple signs or gestures such as 'more', 'drink', 'eat', 'sit' to assist their communication (see also Chapter 12). Parents are also free to discuss their feelings about any aspects of the child's disability and development, ask questions, and make comments on any aspects related to the programme and its effects at home. The notion of partnership is emphasised with the parent as the 'expert' on the child and the home environment and the teacher with the background in language development.

Parents attending with their children are encouraged to share the programme and activities with other members of the family, and to invite other family members to attend sessions if they wish. If siblings attend the sessions, they are included in the activities as much as possible. Parents are encouraged to let interested older siblings and other family members such as grandparents assist at home. This ensures that appropriate communication skills and methods are encouraged in all members of the child's family, increasing the opportunities for the child to generalise skills across a range of people and situations.

Language development strategies

Play is the principal medium used for encouraging and practising communication. Considerable care is taken to encourage turn-taking and joint attention. Strategies such as modelling, prompting, commenting, visual and verbal cuing are described and modelled for parents. The concepts of extension and expansion of children's utterances are introduced and the importance of following the child's interest and lead is encouraged and modelled during sessions (see Chapter 4).

Toys and materials used in the programme are, as far as possible, readily available at home or relatively inexpensive to buy. Parents are also encouraged to use everyday resources from home, but there is a small collection of books available for parents to borrow and this ensures that the children have access to a variety of books at an appropriate level. The teacher encourages and guides the parents in choosing books for their children.

Case studies

The case studies set out below illustrate how individual families' programmes are organised.

Study No. 1

Anna, aged two years and nine months, was referred to the programme by a psychologist at Laurel House after having been assessed as having a developmental disability in the lower moderate range, with a severe delay in language development.

Initial assessment of preliminary skills (Programme Level 1) indicated that Anna was not yet consistently attending to an object or activity for at least five seconds, taking turns, imitating actions, or playing appropriately with objects; she mouthed any objects given to her. An occupational therapy report indicated that she had difficulty releasing her grasp of an object. Eye contact with others was brief and only occurred when a familiar song was sung.

During language sampling, Anna failed to attend to any of the toys or books presented by her mother. However, she cooperated when her mother placed a doll in her arms and helped her to pat it. She also allowed her mother to cover her face with a cloth to play Peek-a-boo.

On the parent inventory (Appendix H) it was reported that Anna responded to music. She sometimes used 'a-a' to protest when an object she was mouthing was removed. In the observation tasks, she failed to respond to requests to identify named objects or play appropriately with familiar toys. Her mother was keen for her to learn to make better eye contact.

It was agreed that initial targets for Anna would include encouragement to make eye contact with an adult to request repetition of a familiar song or action game. The songs 'Row, Row, Row your Boat' and 'If you're happy and you know it' were chosen, as both involved physical contact for Anna. At the conclusion of the song, Anna was consistently asked 'more?' as she was physically assisted to sign 'more'. Any eye contact or appropriate body movement was rewarded with praise and repetition of the game.

To assist development of motor imitation and turn-taking, Anna was physically assisted to take turns banging a toy drum with her hand and hitting a xylophone with a stick placed in her hand. Verbal prompts such as 'Mama's turn', 'Anna's turn' were used as appropriate, along with performative sounds 'boom boom' (drum) and 'la la' (xylophone) to accompany the actions. (At this stage, Anna was not expected to vocalise.) Anna's motor imitation attempts and response to 'Anna's turn' were rewarded with physical and verbal approval and repetition of the game. As her competence increased, further turn-taking activities were introduced, such as rolling a ball, stacking blocks, 'posting' objects in a box.

The game of 'Peek-a-boo', played with a cloth, was chosen to encourage both eye contact and turn-taking. In turn, the questions 'where's Mama?', 'where's Anna?' were asked. Anna was physically assisted, if necessary, to remove the cloth in response to 'ah'. As the cloth was removed the adult attempted to make eye contact with Anna while saying 'boo'. Any eye contact or attempt to remove the cloth was rewarded as above. 'Mama's turn' and 'Anna's turn' were used to encourage the concept of taking turns in a game.

As Anna's eye contact developed, recognition of familiar objects was added to her targets. The first objects chosen were a shoe, a ball and a cup. One was hidden under a cloth and the adult asked 'Where's . . .?' while directing Anna's attention to the cloth. As she looked towards the cloth, it was raised to the accompaniment of 'ah' and the object's name was said and signed. Anna was then assisted to touch the object – 'Anna get . . .'. The action was repeated several times for each object.

To assist further development of eye contact and motor imitation, Anna was encouraged to look in a mirror and helped to do simple actions, such as 'touch your nose' and 'pat your tummy', as well as to follow simple action songs such as 'Roly Poly'. Where possible, these activities were incorporated into normal daily activities such as nappy-change time, bath-time, dressing and meal-times. Her mother also set aside short periods (five to 10 minutes) during the day when opportunities arose. Anna's sister and brother were also encouraged to play with her informally when she approached them. Her family was urged to use these ideas with activities of their own choosing.

Because of her overall delay, Anna's progress was slow. However, at the end of six months she was responding to her name, 'Mama's turn', and 'Anna's turn' in play with all activities introduced. She was beginning to use actions to request routines such as 'Peek-a-boo' and 'Row, Row,

Row your Boat'. She would pick up an object and post it on request. She was also using simple sounds and words such as 'ah' (as in 'ah boo' in a game) and 'Mama' to request attention.

Study No. 2

Mirtha was a three-year-old girl with Down syndrome. She had an overall developmental delay in the upper-moderate range and a moderate delay in language development. Her mother heard about the Laurel House project through a friend and contacted the teacher about her need for assistance to help her daughter in the area of communication.

Initial assessment indicated that Mirtha was at the 'first words' level (Programme Level 3). In a language sample she used, either spontaneously or in imitation, a number of performatives like 'num num', 'sh', as well as a variety of single words including people labels ('Mum'), object labels ('cup', 'baby', 'shoe', 'car', 'ball'), location words ('there'), modifiers ('more') and socially useful words ('gone', 'bye'); see Appendix D, first words list. A number of these words were recognisable only in context, lacking either the initial or final consonant. She also used natural gestures to indicate several actions.

On the parent inventory, Mirtha's mother reported that her daughter was able to follow directions, name approximately 20 objects or people and that she understood the use of a variety of objects. However, both she and the child were becoming frustrated at Mirtha's inability or refusal to express her wants verbally at times, and her own inability to understand Mirtha. Although a speech pathology assessment was not available, it was noted that Mirtha still tended to drool and had difficulty moving her tongue about, suggesting poorly developed oral muscle tone.

Following discussion, it was agreed that Mirtha should be encouraged to use single words, both object and action labels, to obtain her wants during routine daily activities, during play and when looking at books (see Chapter 8). As a number of her words sounded the same, such as 'ba' for ball, bath and baby, it was also agreed that signing would be introduced to assist Mirtha to make her message clearer (see Chapter 12). Signs were also introduced for new action labels, like 'drink', 'eat' and 'toilet' so that she could indicate her needs more easily. Information about talking to children and encouraging play were given to Mirtha's mother and discussed (see Appendix H).

New words and signs were introduced in play with Mirtha's favourite Teddy involving normal daily routines such as breakfast, bath-time and dressing. A list of appropriate words was compiled and agreed upon. Mirtha gradually learned new words and signs and the 'rules' of the game, such as telling Teddy to 'drink', requesting 'pour' before being allowed to pour Teddy some tea and choosing to 'wash' Teddy's arm or tummy. As she began to understand the new words, signs and rules, the child was required to use them to obtain what she wanted and to give information at home during daily routines and when reading books. To assist her with learning the new words and signs, games such as the 'surprise' bag (Chapter 8) were introduced. Mirtha really enjoyed this as it gave her the opportunity to choose something from the bag and involved anticipation and unstructured play with the objects. Books with good clear pictures of people, objects and actions were lent to her mother to supplement the family's own collection of books and to give Mirtha the opportunity to use her new words in a variety of situations.

When Mirtha was able to sign or say words clearly, the C-I-C Procedure (Chapter 8) was introduced for these words and she was encouraged to use her words to initiate conversations as well as to respond. As Mirtha was already, by now, using some single words, her mother was encouraged to use appropriate two-word responses that included Mirtha's own single word when she and her daughter were talking together (see Chapter 9).

All ideas and illustrations of new signs were included in Mirtha's 'Language Book' at each session. As Mirtha attended preschool, her mother took her 'language book' to preschool each week so the teachers there could supplement her language programme in their activities. The language teacher also contacted the preschool teacher to discuss their programme so language appropriate to her needs could be introduced and encouraged.

At the end of six months, Mirtha's vocabulary had increased significantly. She was using a combination of words and signs for a variety of communicative purposes. With the assistance of signs, many of her words, previously intelligible only in context, became clear and she discontinued using signs for them. She was also starting to put two words together using sentences that included a combination of words only and words plus a sign. Both Mirtha's and her mother's frustration had disappeared and they were now enjoying their time together.

Study No. 3

Dominic, aged four years, was referred to the programme by his preschool teacher. Although he could speak in sentences, he was not playing or communicating as well as his peers. He was also beginning to exhibit a number of unacceptable behaviours.

Initial assessment was undertaken using the SICD (1984), language sampling and the parent inventory. Results on the SICD indicated that both his receptive and expressive language behaviours were delayed by approximately 16 months. It was noted that he had particular difficulty with tasks requiring listening, discrimination of speech sounds and following directions, although hearing tests had revealed no difficulties. In the language sample, approximately 80% of his utterances were intelligible, with half of them comprising one or two words and his longest intelligible utterance containing five morphemes. His MLU of intelligible utterances was 2.4. He used the early English morphemes '-ing', 'in', 'on', the plural 's', articles 'a' and 'the', and contractible copula '-'s' (as in 'I'm hungry') regularly (see Table 9.1 for examples of Brown's 14 English Morphemes). He also used the 10 language rules used in early sentences (see Chapter 9 for a discussion of these rules).

It was decided that the best way to assist Dominic at this stage would be to encourage him to extend his current use of syntactic rules and morphemes to longer utterances and in a variety of situations. This would be done by attracting his attention and listening skills and giving him opportunities to practise listening and following two-part instructions. At the same time, his parents would be given ideas to assist them in developing appropriate communication strategies, such as expansion of his utterances, commenting and prompting (see Appendix H). As Dominic particularly enjoyed playing with his Lego, he would be given opportunities to talk about what he was building. During these games, his parents would comment on his play using simple sentences, encouraging him to tell them more about what he was doing. At meal-times, and during family outings such as shopping trips, Dominic would be encouraged to talk about what he saw and what they did, using sentences of at least three or four words.

To facilitate listening, attending and following directions, Dominic's family would make sure he was listening before giving information or instructions. If necessary, his parents would remind him 'Are you listening?' This would happen during daily routines, when asking for food and drink at meal-times, and in structured play with simple board games such as lotto and dominoes. Other situations where language objectives could be encouraged included listening games such as 'Simon Says' and 'I went shopping and I bought . . .', using visual props such as collections of objects and pictures for food, clothes and toys. At story time, Dominic would be encouraged to 'tell' a familiar story with the assistance of the pictures.

At preschool, his teachers assisted by encouraging Dominic to play in small groups of children who could provide good language models while playing with dough, cutting and pasting, and participating in construction play with blocks. When possible, his teachers commented about what the boy was doing, using strategies similar to those used by his family.

As Dominic's listening skills and his confidence in talking with his peers improved, new morphemes were introduced to him. The first to be tried was the uncontracted copula as in 'It is a big tower.' It was initially presented in adults' comments and then by encouraging him to imitate others, such as at snack-time, saying 'I am hungry'. By the end of six months, his MLU had increased to 2.8 and his longest utterance to eight morphemes. He was asking a variety of 'wh-' questions, as in 'Where's the blue block?' and 'What's that boy doing?' Use of all morphemes heard in the initial language sample had increased and he had added several others. As Dominic's ability to communicate effectively increased, the incidence of inappropriate behaviours declined dramatically both at home and at preschool.

Links with other agencies

When children attend a preschool, day care centre or any other early intervention or therapy programme, telephone contact is made with other professionals working with a particular family and current language targets are discussed. Where possible, these are then incorporated into the other services being received by families. This ensures that suggestions made by the language teacher are compatible with those from other services. Reports are also written to other agencies with whom the children are involved, as required. All ideas and suggestions to the parents are recorded in a Language Book at each session and the parents are encouraged to take their book to preschool or day care with the child. Teachers and others working with the child are invited to contact the language teacher at any time for information, for support, or to share information.

Working with families from language backgrounds other than English

The Laurel House project is located in an area of Sydney that has a high incidence of families whose first language is not English. Such families have a variety of first languages including Arabic, various Chinese and other Asian languages, and a number of European languages. Experience with these families suggests that the children are learning the rules of communication rather than rules relating to a specific language during play sessions with the language teacher. If communication with carers is difficult as a result of language barriers between the teacher and families, assistance is sought. Professional interpreters are used for initial assessment and the first programme session, when required, to ensure that the parents understand the principles and procedures involved.

Although the language teacher works in English, parents are encouraged to use the language they feel most comfortable with when practising language-related activities with their children. Signing is used to assist the child and parent to move between the two languages when appropriate (see also Chapter 15). Experience suggests that many parents have already made the decision to use English as the primary means of communication with their child before they enter the programme, although in some cases the children themselves seem to have made that choice. Reports by the parents suggest that children from families where English is not the home language show improvement in both understanding and use of their home language as well as English, as a result of involvement in the language programme.

Because of the individualised nature of the programme and sensitivity to cultural attitudes, parents whose main language is not English are able to feel comfortable with the daily implementation of programme targets in the language they choose. Coincidentally, a number of mothers from non-English speaking backgrounds have thanked the language teacher for helping them to improve their own command of English!

Assessment of progress

The child's progress is routinely assessed after six months in the programme. As with initial assessment, these results are shared with the parents, providing opportunities for both parents and teacher to comment on the results, make future suggestions, and discuss needs. Ongoing contact for the next 12 months is discussed and agreed on along with suggestions, if appropriate, for referrals to other early intervention or therapy services. At the same time, the parents are asked to evaluate the programme in terms of their needs. Their responses typically indicate that the programme has increased their knowledge and understanding of how to encourage language development. It has also given them skills to share this information with other family members and guide them in assisting the children.

Although parents are free to leave the programme at any time before the end of Stage 1 and Stage 2, very few have chosen to do this. Reasons for leaving the programme early are usually associated with the family moving too far away to travel on a weekly basis or as a result of entry into preschool or another early childhood programme that provides a wider range of support services. In both instances, all possible information is provided to help in the children's transition to the new situation.

As well as being involved in their children's individual programmes, parents are also invited to join the community advisory group through which funding is received. This group advises and assists the teacher with the overall needs and expectations of families, thus ensuring that the programme remains relevant to families' needs and that policies and procedures are in accordance with the requirements of the New South Wales Disability Services Act (1993).

Evaluation of programme impact

Overall, results obtained from these assessments indicate consistent gains in both receptive and expressive language for most children, although progress depends on the degree of the child's delay, the nature of his or her disability and the parents' ability to follow through on activities and ideas suggested during the sessions. Table 14.1 includes details of changes in receptive and expressive language skills achieved by 13 children (10 male, three female) in the slow learner, mild and moderate learning disability ranges who completed Stages 1 and 2 of the programme in 1995. Stage 1 comprised 12 weekly visits and Stage 2 involved contact at three- or four-weekly intervals for a further three months. The children were aged from 25 to 59 months at entry to the programme (median age 35 months). When first assessed on the SICD, their receptive language ages ranged from under 16 months to 32 months (median 24 months) and expressive language ages ranged from 12 months to 36 months (median 20 months). Results on the SICD show that all the children made some gains over the six-month intervention period of Stages 1 and 2. In considering the SICD scores reported in Table 14.1, it should be noted that children's receptive and expressive language ages on the SICD are calculated in terms of four-month increments, from birth to 48 months. As a result, the test is not particularly sensitive to the relatively small changes in communicative skills that may occur over an intervention period of six months. Note that the 1979 version of the SICD was used in calculating these results.

Data set out in Table 14.1 show that all the children recorded increases in language skills of at least four months over the six-month intervention period. The greatest change recorded was in the receptive language of a boy aged 53 months at the start of the programme (Child L). When assessed prior to entry to the programme on the Griffiths Mental Development Scales (GMDS) (Griffiths, 1984) the boy was reported to be in the upper range of mild developmental delay, with mild delay in both receptive and expressive language skills. Child L's receptive language score, initially only 28 months, increased by 16 months to 44 months over the study period. His expressive skills, initially less delayed at 36 months, increased by only four months to 40 months. In contrast, a three-year-old child assessed at the upper end of the severe developmental delay level on the GMDS prior to entry to the programme, with severe language delay (Child H) gained only four months in both receptive and expressive language ages over the intervention period. While this level of change could be described as modest, it is worth noting that the child's overall development was slow, with receptive language skills 12 months behind chronological age at the time of entry to the programme, and expressive skills even more

Table 14.1: Age at entry, sex, level of developmental and language delay and pre- and post-test SICD and MLU results for 13 children attending the Laurel House Early Language Project in 1995

Child	Sex	Entry age in months	Developmental delay on entry*		SICD score R: receptive E: expressive		MLU	
			Overall	Language	Pre	Post	Pre	Post
A	M	25	low – average	mid –mild	R16 E12	R28 E24	1	2.1
B	M	25	upper – mild	severe	R16 E12	R28 E24	1	1.2
C**	F	29	mixed – difficult behaviour	severe	R>16 E>16	R20 E N/A	0	1
D	M	30	lower – mild	upper – moderate	R16 E12	R28 E24	1.03	1.8
E	M	31	mild-moderate	severe	R16 E12	R24 E16	1	1
F	M	32	mild	moderate – severe	R20 E16	R28 E20	0	1
G	F	35	upper –severe	mid –mild	R28 E28	R32 E32	1.3	2.3
H	M	36	slow learner	severe	R24 E>16	R28 E20	1	1
I	F	38	lower – mild	moderate – severe	R24–28 E20	R28–32 E28	1.3	2.3
J	M	38	upper – mild	moderate	R32 E24	R36 E28	1.81	2.03
K**	M	43	upper – mild	mid – moderate	R32 E28	R36 E36	1.3	>2
L	M	53	upper –mild	mid – mild	R28 E36	R44 E40	2.4	3.2
M	M	59	mid – mild	lower – moderate	R32 E>32	R36 E36	2.03	2.68

* Developmental status as assessed on the Griffiths Mental Development Scales and similar measures.
** Children from language backgrounds other than English.

delayed, at less than 16 months. In this case, the rate of H's receptive language development remained unchanged over the period in the programme but the rate of expressive skill development increased.

More typical of the changes observed in children participating in the programme are those reported for two two-year-old boys (Child A and Child B). Child A was described as 'low average' on the GMDS with mild delay in both receptive and expressive language skills, while Child B, described as 'upper mild' in developmental delay on the GMDS, was reported to be severely delayed in language skills. Both boys showed gains of 12 months on both receptive and expressive language skills over the time in the programme. The MLU (mean length of utterance) of both boys at the start of the programme was one word. When retested after six months, Child A's MLU had increased to just over two words while Child B had increased slightly to 1.2 words. Subsequent testing should show further consolidation in these emerging skills. Increased parental knowledge about the process of language development, coupled with greater confidence about strategies for encouraging language, should ensure that gains achieved as a result of participation in the programme are maintained until the children are able to access other appropriate services, such as those provided for children of school age.

No recent data are available on the maintenance of the gains achieved by the 13 children included in Table 14.1 after the six-month programme. However, data reported in an earlier study including children in the programme (Price and Bochner, 1988) indicated that, although this rate of progress was generally not maintained except for children who had reached the two-to-three word utterance stage, increased intelligibility and MLU were evident for 90% of the children.

Summary

The individualised nature of the Laurel House Early Language Project, along with sensitivity to different family structures, needs and management styles, ensures that the parents develop their skills in such a way that they are able to take a more active, informed role in encouraging their children's language development. Issues associated with implementing the programme with families from language backgrounds that are other than English are considered in the next chapter.

Chapter 15
Working with Children from Non-English Language Backgrounds

Helping children with communication difficulties whose home language is different from the major national language presents a double dilemma for the teacher or therapist. Firstly, there is the question of adequate assessment of the stage of the child's communication development. Then it is necessary to decide which language the family and professionals should use in assisting the child.

Current research on language development in children from bilingual backgrounds suggests that the more skilled they are in their home language, the better able they are to learn a second language (Ramsey, 1987). The importance of the social context of language is also recognised (Salinger, 1988; Duncan, 1989). Makin, Campbell and Jones Diaz (1995) discuss the importance of recognising and preserving children's cultural and linguistic diversity, while at the same time assisting them to become effective communicators in the English language, which they encounter once they enter a playgroup, preschool or other early childhood programme. Makin *et al.* document the benefits for the child's language, literacy and cognitive development of providing early instruction in the home language within these non-home settings. Makin (1992) demonstrates the social and motivational benefits to children in both formal and informal early childhood settings when periods of home language support are provided on a regular basis. This is particularly desirable for children who are also experiencing delays in the development of their home language (Duncan, 1989).

It is important to remember that children who are having difficulty developing communication skills in their first language will inevitably experience difficulties acquiring a second language. However these difficulties may not be as great as their performance in the new language initially suggests. For example, children entering a non-familiar language environment for the first time often spend a silent period as they attempt to master the linguistic aspects of the second language environment (Krashen, 1982). Their apparent difficulties in developing the second language may result from social and emotional factors, such

171

as fitting into an environment that is culturally and linguistically different, rather than to problems with the new language. Before deciding to intervene and help children from a different language background it is important to determine, first, whether the child is experiencing difficulties in the home language or whether his or her current problems stem principally from unfamiliarity with the new linguistic environment.

In assessing the language development of children from linguistically different backgrounds, you need to consider the extent to which the child is competent in both home and the major community language (Santos de Barons and Barona, 1991). Where children have family members, such as older siblings, who are linguistically competent in the dominant community language, or who have had regular exposure to the dominant language through preschool or other forms of out-of-home care, they may have developed skills in both.

Whatever the language that is being learned, the stages that children pass through in the acquisition of their first language are the same as those described by Bates (1976), Bloom (1970), Brown (1973) and Halliday (1975)(see Chapter 2). Moreover, observation suggests that, in the early stages, their pragmatic development is also fairly similar (Duncan, 1989). It is only later that children become aware of the differences that distinguish one culture or social group from others and begin to adjust their ways of communicating in response to these differences. As children's skills increase, efforts need to be made to provide assessment and learning conditions that encourage meaningful interaction in activities that are both developmentally and culturally appropriate.

Assessment

How then, should the assessment of communication development in children from linguistically different backgrounds be approached? There are several options, depending on the extent to which the child is familiar with the major community language, as well as available personnel and resources. Whether or not you decide to carry out an assessment of the child's competence in English, you will need an assessment of the child's competence in his or her home language.

Where qualified, competent speakers of the child's home language are available, they can undertake assessment tasks with the children. What form this assessment takes will depend, in part, on the availability of culturally appropriate resources. For example, qualified interpreters can assist in obtaining reports from parents and care-givers on the children's language competence at home. They can also assist in the administration of both structured and unstructured assessment tasks. When trained interpreters are not available, other members of the family circle may be able to provide assistance as interpreters. However, this is not recommended unless suggested by the family, because it may not be culturally appropriate. A carer in the child's nursery school, preschool or child-care centre who is familiar with the child's usual communication strategies may be able to assist with the assessment, or provide useful observational data. If possible, the person who is to take primary responsibility for assisting the child in developing new language skills should be present during any assessments, and if appropriate, be part of the assessment process. This will enable him or her to observe the child's interaction strategies and will also provide useful information for later programming.

When no support from interpreters or family members is available, you will need to rely on your own observation of the child (Duncan, 1989; Mills, 1993). Reliable information can be obtained about the child's understanding of basic concepts by using appropriate materials and careful observation over a range of situations, including play and familiar routines. While there may be differences in the combination of sounds used by children from different language backgrounds, the activities in which they are engaged when they make these sounds provide clues to their meaning or significance. For example, while eating or feeding a baby, an English-speaking child may accompany the action with 'yum yum' while a Cantonese speaker may say 'oum'. Whatever the sound combination that is heard, the parent or carer will soon confirm whether the sound is specific to the activity and whether it is regularly used by members of their language community.

For children who are already using words, you may need to ask somebody familiar with the child's home language – either a parent, teacher or classroom aide – to translate the child's words for you. Any sound combination regularly used in a specific context should be checked with a person who is familiar with the child's home language. For example, a child whose family speaks Arabic at home may regularly use 'ana' when approaching other children or an adult. An Arabic speaker may confirm that the child is saying 'me'. Further observation may confirm that the child is using the word 'me' to draw attention to something of interest or to request permission to join in an activity.

A tape or video-recorder may be useful in observing a child engaged in a naturally occurring or structured assessment situation. However, make sure you have the family's permission to record the session and to listen to or view the taped material as this may not be culturally acceptable to some families. Parents, even if their command of the community language is limited, are usually happy to assist, if asked, by indicating whether the child's utterances include real words or phrases. It is also important, here, not to neglect the child's use of gesture to communicate. Communicative gestures vary between languages, so it is important to check the meaning of any gestures used with a person who is familiar with the child's language background. As with monolingual children, it is important to make every effort to obtain accurate and relevant information from a variety of sources.

Implementing a programme

Once you have completed your assessment, you will be able to provide useful opportunities for learning, provided you adhere to a few simple procedures. For example:

- Respect linguistic and cultural differences, both in choice of play materials, approach to play and involvement in family routines.
- When working with families, allow the parents to choose which language they will use at home. Although current research (Duncan, 1989; Makin, Campbell and Jones Diaz, 1995) supports the use of the family's home language, some will prefer to use the major national language used by most other children at the preschool or nursery centre.
- If you are working in a preschool, nursery school or child-care centre, you will probably use the language dominant at the centre. However, you must ensure that the family is aware of the language you are using. They need to have clear knowledge of the form of language used by teachers with children for requests and instructions. They also need to know any relevant vocabulary, as well as any signs or gestures. If necessary, seek the assistance of a competent speaker of the family's language to pass this information on to them. If there is a member of staff in your centre who speaks the child's home language, this may be the most appropriate person to act as the primary assistant for the child. Involvement of other children with the same home language in routine activities and play may also help the child. The suggestions for working with groups of children in Chapter 13 would be appropriate when implementing language objectives for children who do not speak English at home.
- For children at the pre-verbal stage, while there are variations in performative sounds and gestures used by people from different language backgrounds, many are similar and actual functional play with objects, such as pretending to drink, rocking a baby, pushing a car, stacking blocks, is not culturally dependent.
- For those who are using early words, or who are ready to practise them, it may be helpful to follow an agreed or standard signing system in conjunction with both the home and national language. The sign will remain the same, regardless of the language used, providing both a consistent referent and a bridge between the two languages. If you suspect that the child is having difficulties in language acquisition, it may be useful to initiate the use of agreed signs even before the child starts to use words. Chapter 12 on signing

sets out further suggestions on when and how to begin such a programme.

Summary

This chapter has considered some of the issues that arise when teachers, therapists and others encounter a child whose home language is not English and who is experiencing problems in communication. In helping such a child, you should remember that the basic processes underlying the development of early communication are universal. However, to ensure that any linguistic differences are overcome you will need to use strategies that are culturally sensitive. You will also need to take care that these strategies are modelled in such a way that parents and care-givers feel both involved and comfortable with the procedures that you are implementing.

References

Anderson, K., Bloomberg, K., Dunne, L., Jones, P. and Snelleman, J. (1986). Computer pictographs for communication (COMPIC). North Balwyn, Victoria: Compic Development Association.

Austin, J.L. (1962). How to Do Things With Words. Oxford: Clarendon Press.

Barrett, M. (1995). Early lexical development. In P. Fletcher and B. MacWhinney (Eds) The Handbook of Child Language, 362–92. Oxford: Blackwell.

Bates, E. (1976). Language and Context: The Acquisition of Pragmatics. New York: Academic Press.

Bates, E., Bretherton, I, and Snyder, L. (1988). From First Words to Grammar: Individual Differences and Dissociable Mechanisms. Cambridge: Cambridge University Press.

Bates, E., Dale, P.S. and Thal, D. (1995). Individual differences and their implications for theories of language development. In P. Fletcher and B. McWhinney (Eds) The Handbook of Child Language, 96–51. Oxford: Blackwell.

Bates, E. and Snyder, L. (1987). The cognitive hypothesis in language development. In U. Uzgiris and J.M. Hunt (Eds) Infant Performance and Experience: New Findings with the Ordinal Scales, 168–204. Urbana, IL: University of Illinios Press.

Benedict, H. (1979). Early lexical development: comprehension and production. Journal of Child Language, 6, 183–200.

Bernstein, B. (1961). Social structure, language and learning. Educational Research, 3, 163–76.

Bever, T.G. (1970). The cognitive basis for linguistic structures. In J.R. Hayes (Ed.) Cognition and the Development of Language, 279–362. New York: Wiley.

Bloom, B.S. (1964). Stability and Change in Human Characteristics. New York: Wiley.

Bloom, L. (1970). Language Development: Form and Function in Emerging Grammars. Cambridge, MA: MIT Press.

Bloomberg, K. and Johnson, H. (1991). Communication Without Speech: A Guide for Parents and Teachers. Hawthorn, Victoria: Australian Council for Educational Research.

Bochner, S. (1986). Development in the vocalisation of handicapped infants in a hospital setting. Australian and New Zealand Journal of Developmental Disabilities, 12(1), 55–63.

Bochner, S., Price, P. and Salamon, L. (1988). Learning to talk: A programme for helping language-delayed children acquire early comminication skill. North Ryde: Macquarie University.

Brown, R. (1973). A First Language: The Early Stages. Cambridge, MA: Harvard University Press.

Bruner, J.S. (1976). From communication to language – a psychological perspective. Cognition, 3(3), 255–87.

Bruner, J.S. (1983). Child's talk: Learning to Use Language. New York: Norton.

Bruner, J.S. and Sherwood, V. (1976). Peekaboo and the learning of role structures. In J.S. Bruner, A. Jolly and K. Sylva (Eds) Play: Its role in development and evolution, 277–85. Harmondsworth: Penguin.

Bushnell, L.W.R., Sai, F. and Mullin, J.T. (1989). Neonatal recognition of the mother's face. British Journal of Developmental Psychology, 7, 3–15.

Cattell, R. (1980). Child Language: Theories and 'The Real World'. In T. Le and M. McCausland (Eds), Proceedings of the Conference on Child Language Development, 7–10 September, 1–22. Launceston, Tasmania: Launceston Teachers' Centre.

Chazan, M., Laing, A. and Jackson, S. (1971). Just Before School: Schools Council Research and Development Project in Compensatory Education. Oxford: Blackwell.

Chomsky, N. (1986). Knowledge of Language: Its Nature, Origin and Use. New York: Praeger.

Clark, C., Davies, C. and Woodcock, R. (1974). Standard Rebus Glossary. Pine Circles, MN: American Guidance Service.

Conti-Ramsden, G. (1994). Language interaction with atypical language learners. In C. Gallaway and B. Richards (Eds) Input and Interaction in Language Acquisition, 183–96. Cambridge: Cambridge University Press.

Cooney, A. and Knox, G. (1980) Sign it and say it: A manual of New South Wales (Australasian) signs for use with the Revised Makaton Vocabulary. Stockton: Stockton Hospital Welfare Association.

Cromer, R.F. (1991). Language and Thought in Normal and Handicapped Children. Oxford: Blackwell.

DeCaspar, A.J. and Fifer, W.P. (1980). Of human bonding: Newborns prefer their mothers' voices. Science, 208, 1174–6.

Dice, K. (1994). Selection of initial vocabularies for use in manual sign language programs. In K. Linfoot (Ed.) Communication Strategies for People with Developmental Disabilities: Issues from Theory to Practice, 85–123. Sydney: MacLennan and Petty.

Dore, J. (1975). Holophrases, speech acts and language universals. Journal of Child Language, 2, 21–40.

Dore, J. (1978). Conditions for the acquisition of speech acts. In I. Markova (Ed.) The Social Context of Language, 87–111. Chichester: Wiley.

Duncan, D. M. (Ed.) (1989). Working with Bilingual Language Disability: Therapy in Practice. London: Chapman & Hall.

Fletcher, P. and MacWhinney B. (Eds) (1995). The Handbook of Child Language. Oxford: Blackwell.

Fraiberg, S., Smith, M. and Adelson, E. (1969). An educational program for blind infants. Journal of Special Education, 3(2), 121–39.

Gallaway, C. and Richards, B.J. (Eds) (1994). Input and Interaction in Language Acquisition. Cambridge: Cambridge University Press.

Garcia, E.E. and De Haven, E.D. (1974). Use of operant techniques in the establishment and generalisation of language. A review and analysis. American Journal of Mental Deficiency, 79(2), 169–78.

Gardner, R.A. and Gardner, B.T. (Eds) (1989). Teaching Sign Language to Chimpanzees. Albany: State University of New York Press.

Goldbart, J. (1988). Re-examining the development of early communication. In J.

Coupe and J. Goldbart (Eds) Communication Before Speech: Normal Development and Impaired Communication, 19–30. New York: Croom Helm.

Gray, B.B. and Ryan, B.P. (1973). A Language Program for the Non-Language Child. Champaign, IL: Research Press.

Greenfield, P.M. and Smith, J.H. (1976). The Structure of Communication in Early Language Development. New York: Academic Press.

Griffths, R. (1984). The Abilities of Young Children: A Comprehensive System of Mental Measurement for the First Eight Years of Life (rev. ed.). High Wycombe, Bucks: The Test Agency.

Haggard, M. (1995). Risk factors for Otitis Media: Where next? Keynote address, Australasian Conductive Deafness Association Inc., Second National Conference, Melbourne, September 28–30.

Halliday, M.A.K. (1975). Learning How to Mean: Explorations in the Development of Language. London: Edward Arnold.

Hayden, A.H. and Dimitriev, V. (1975). The multidisciplinary preschool program for Down's Syndrome children at the University of Washington model preschool center. In B. Friedlander, G. Sherritt and G. Kirk (Eds). Exceptional Infant, 3. New York: Brunner/Mazel.

Hedrick, D.L., Prather, E.M. and Tobin, A.R. (1984). Sequenced Inventory of Communication Development (SICD) (rev. ed.). Seattle: University of Washington Press.

Horstmeier, D.S. and MacDonald, J.D. (1978). Ready, Set, Go, Talk to Me: Individualised Programs for Use in Therapy, Home, and Classroom. Columbus: Merrill.

Howe, C.J. (1993). Language Learning: A Special Case for Developmental Psychology? Hove: Erlbaum.

Hunt, J. McV. (1961). Intelligence and Experience. New York: Ronald Press.

Hutt, S.J., Tyler, S., Hutt, C. and Christopherson, H. (1989). Play, Exploration and Learning: A Natural History of the Pre-school. London: Routledge.

Ingram, D. (1978). Sensori-Motor Intelligence and Language Development. In A. Locke (Ed.) Action, Gesture and Symbol: The Emergence of Language, 261–90. London: Academic Press.

Ingram, D. (1989). First Language Acquisition: Method, description and explanation. Cambridge: Cambridge University Press.

Jeanes, R.G., Reynolds, B. and Coleman, B.C. (Eds) (1993). Dictionary of Australasian Signs. Melbourne: Victorian School for Deaf Children.

Johnson, T. (1989). A Dictionary of the Sign Language of the Australian Deaf Community: Auslan. Petersham, NSW: Deafness Resources Australia.

Jones, P.R. and Cregan, A. (1986). Sign and Symbol Communication for Mentally Handicapped People. London: Croom Helm.

Kaye, K. (1982). The Mental and Social Life of Babies. Chicago: University of Chicago Press.

Kent, L.R. (1974). Language Acquisition Program for the Severely Retarded. Champaign, IL: Research Press.

Kent, R.D. and Miolo, G. (1995). Phonetic abilities in the first year of life. In P. Fletcher and B. MacWhinney (Eds) The Handbook of Child Language, 303–34. Oxford: Blackwell.

Kiernan, C. and Reid, B. (1987). The Pre-verbal Communication Schedule (PVCS). Windsor: NFER/Nelson.

Kilminster, M.G.E. and Laird, E.M. (1983). Articulation development in children aged three to nine years. Australian Journal of Human Communication Disorders, 6(1), 23–30.

Knobloch, H., Stevens, F. and Malone, A.F. (1980). Manual of Developmental Diagnosis: The Administration and Interpretation of the Revised Gesell and Amatruda Developmental and Neurological Examination. Haggerstown, MD: Harper & Row.

Krashen, S.D. (1982). Principles and Practice in Second Language Acquisition. Oxford: Pergamon.

Lipsitt, L.P. (1977). The study of sensory and learning process of the newborn. Clinics in Perinatology, 4, 163–86.

Locke, J.L. (1993). The Child's Path to Spoken Language. Cambridge, MA: Harvard University Press.

Locke, J.L. (1995). Development of the capacity for spoken language. In P. Fletcher and B. MacWhinney (Eds) The Handbook of Child Language, 278–302. Oxford: Blackwell

MacKay, G. and Dunn, W. (1989). Early Communicative Skills. London: Routledge.

Makin, L. (1992). Supporting children's home languages in mainstream educational programs. Australian Review of Applied Linguistics, 15(1), 71–84.

Makin, L., Campbell, J. and Jones Diaz, C. (1995). One Childhood Many Languages: Guidelines for Early Childhood Educators in Australia. Pymble NSW: Harper Educational.

Mandler, J.M. and Johnson, N.S. (1977). Remembrance of things parsed: story structure and recall. Cognitive Psychology, 9(1), 111–51.

Martinsen, H. and Smith, L. (1989). Studies of vocalization and gesture in the transition to speech. In S. von Tezchner, L.S. Siegel and L. Smith (Eds) The Social and Cognitive Aspects of Normal and Atypical Language Development, 51–68. New York: Springer-Verlag.

McCarthy, D. (1954). Language development in children. In L. Carmichael (Ed) Manual of Child Psychology, 492–630. New York: John Wiley.

McConkey, R. and Price, P. (1986). Let's Talk: Learning Language in Everyday Settings. London: Souvenir Press.

McLean, J. and Snyder-Mclean, L. (1978). A Transactional Approach to Early Language Training. Columbus, OH: Merrill.

McNaughton, S. (1975). Teaching Guidelines – Blissymbolics Communication. Fareham, MA: Farleys.

McNeill, D. (1970). The Acquisition of Language: The Study of Developmental Linguistics. New York: Harper & Row.

Miles, D. (1988). British Sign Language. London: BBC Books.

Mills, J. (1993). Monolingual teachers assessing bilingual children. In R. Mills and J. Mills (Eds) Bilingualism in the Primary School, 59–85. London: Routledge.

Mowrer, O.H. (1960). Learning Theory and Symbolic Processes. New York: John Wiley.

Nelson, K. (1973). Structure and strategy in learning to talk. Monographs of the Society for Research in Child Development, 38, No. 149.

Nelson, K. (Ed.) (1986). Event Knowledge: Structure and Function in Development. Hillsdale, NJ: Erlbaum.

Nelson, K. (Ed.) (1989). Narratives from the Crib. Cambridge, MA: Harvard University Press.

Nelson, K. and Gruendel, J.M. (1979). At morning it's lunchtime: a scriptal view of children's dialogues. Discourse Processes, 2, 73–94.

Nice, M. (1925). Length of sentences as a criterion of child's progress in speech. Journal of Educational Psychology, 16, 370–9.

Paget, R., Gorman, P. and Paget, G. (1976). The Paget–Gorman Sign System (sixth edition). Headington: Paget–Gorman Society.

Patterson, F. (1978). The gestures of a gorilla: Sign language acquisition in another pongid species. Brain and Language, 5, 72–97.

Piaget, J. (1962). The Language and Thought of the Child. London: Routledge & Kegan Paul.

Pieterse, M. (1988). The Down syndrome program at Macquarie University: A model early intervention program. In M. Pieterse, S. Bochner and S. Bettison (Eds) Early Intervention for Children with Disabilities: The Australian Experience. Sydney: Special Education Centre, Macquarie University.

Porter, R.A., Makin, J.W., Davis, L.B. and Christenson K.M. (1992). Breast-fed infants response to olfactory cues from their own mother and unfamiliar lactating females. Infant Behaviour and Development, 15, 85–94.

Premack, D. (1976). Intelligence in Ape and Man. Hillsdale, NJ: Erlbaum.

Price, P. (in press). Parent-child interaction and language intervention. In M. Beveridge, G. Conti-Ramsden and I. Lender (Eds) Language and Communication in Mentally Handicapped People, 185–221. London: Chapman & Hall.

Price, P. and Bochner, S. (1988). The handicapped child and early language intervention programs. In M. Pieterse, S.E. Bochner and S. Bettison (Eds) (1988). Early Intervention for Children with Disabilities: The Australian Experience, 147–54. Sydney; Macquarie University Special Education Centre.

Rahmani, M. (1987). Consonance. Canberra: National Library of Australia.

Ramsey, P. (1987). Teaching and Learning in a Diverse World. New York: Teachers College Press.

Ratner, N. and Bruner, J.S. (1978). Games, social exchange and the acquisition of language. Journal of Child Language, 5(3), 391–401.

Salinger, T.S. (1988). Language Arts and Literacy for Young Children. Columbus: Merrill.

Santos de Barons, M. and Barona, A. (1991). The assessment of culturally and linguistically different preschoolers. Early Childhood Research Quarterly, 6, 363–76.

Savage-Rumbaugh, E.S. (1986). Ape Language: From Conditioned Response to Symbol. New York: Columbia University Press.

Schaeffer, B. (1980). Spontaneous language through signed speech. In R. L. Schiefelbusch (Ed.) Nonspeech Language and Communication: Analysis and Intervention, 421–46. Baltimore: University Park Press.

Schaffer, H.R. (1989). Language development in context. In S. von Tetzchner, L.S. Siegel and L. Smith (Eds) The Social and Cognitive Aspects of Normal and Atypical Language Development, 1–22. New York: Springer-Verlag.

Searle, J.R. (1969). Speech Acts: An Essay in the Philosophy of Language. London: Cambridge University Press.

Selikowitz, M. (1990). Down Syndrome, the Facts. New York: Oxford Medical Publications.

Shatz, M. (1987). Bootstrapping operations in child language. In K. Nelson and A. Vankleech (Eds) Children's Language, 16. Hillsdale, NJ: Erlbaum.

Shriberg, L.D. and Kwiatkowski, J. (1986). Natural Process Analysis: A Procedure for Phonological Analysis of Continuous Speech Samples. New York: Macmillan.

Silman, S. and Silverman, C.A. (1991). Auditory Diagnosis: Principles and Applications. San Diego: Academic Press.

Skinner, B.F. (1957). Verbal Behaviour. New York: Appleton-Century-Crofts.

Slater, A. (1989). Visual memory and perception in early infancy. In A. Slater and G. Bremner (Eds) Infant Development, 43–71. London: Erlbaum.

Snow, C. (1994). Beginning from baby talk: Twenty years of research. In C. Gallaway and B. Richards (Eds) Input and Interaction in Language Acquisition, 3–12. Cambridge: Cambridge University Press.

Snow, C.E. (1995). Issues in the study of input: Finetuning, universality, individual and developmental differences, and necessary causes. In P. Fletcher and B. MacWhinney (Eds) The Handbook of Child Language, 180–93. Oxford: Blackwell.

Snyder, L.K., Lovitt, J.C. and Smith, J.O. (1975). Language training for the severely retarded: Five years of behaviour analysis research. Exceptional Children, 42, 7–15.

Stageberg, N.C. (1971). An Introductory English Grammar (second edition). New York: Holt, Rinehart & Winston.

Stern, W. (1924). Psychology of Early Childhood up to the Sixth Year of Age. New York: Holt.

Stremel, K. and Waryas, C. (1974). A Behavioural-Psycholinguistic Approach to Language Training. In L. McReynolds (Ed.) Developing Systematic Procedures for Training Children's Language. ASHA Monographs No.18.

Sylva, K., Bruner, J. and Genova, P. (1976). The role of play in the problem-solving of children 3-5 years old. In J. Bruner, A. Jolly and K. Sylva (Eds) Play: Its Role in Development and Evolution, 244–57. Harmondsworth: Penguin.

Sylva, K., Roy, C. and Painter, M. (1980). Childwatching in Playgroup and Nursery School. London: Grant McIntyre.

Terrace, H.S. (1981). A report to an academy. Annals of the New York Academy of Sciences, 364, 94–114.

Trevarthen, C. (1979). Communication and co-operation in early infancy: A description of early intersubjectivity. In M. Bullowa (Ed) Before Speech: The Beginning of Interpersonal Communication, 321–49. Cambridge: Cambridge University Press.

Uzgiris, I. and Hunt, J.McV. (1975). Assessment in Infancy: Ordinal Scales of Psychological Development. Urbana, IL: University of Illinois Press.

Vygotsky, L.S. (1978). Mind in Society. The Development of Higher Psychological Processes. Cambridge, MA: Harvard University Press

Vygostky, L.S. (1986). Thought and Language. Cambridge, MA: Harvard University Press.

Walker, M. and Cooney, A. (1984). Line Drawings for use with the Revised Makaton Vocabulary: Makaton Australia. Newcastle: University of Newcastle, Special Education Centre.

Wells, G. (1985). Language Development in the Preschool Years. Cambridge: Cambridge University Press.

Werner, H. and Kaplan, B. (1963). Symbol Formation: an Organismic-Developmental Approach to Language and the Expression of Thought. New York: Wiley.

Winitz, H. (1969). Articulatory Acquisition and Behaviour. New York: Appleton-Century-Crofts.

Appendix A
Taking a Language Sample

A language sample gives useful information on how a child is communicating as much as on the appropriateness of your language. This information is particularly useful for children who are just starting to talk.

To take a language sample, you should:

- Set up a situation where you can play with the child using toys or books that you know he or she enjoys. Once you begin to play with the materials, try to say nothing for the first few minutes. Play alongside the child at first, in parallel play mode, following the child's lead rather than directing his or her activity. This will give the child an opportunity to demonstrate his or her communication skills without prompting from you. After a few minutes, you can begin to play more interactively. Follow the child's lead and talk with the child about what you are doing.
- Record your play together for five to ten minutes using video or audio-tape.
- Transcribe your language sample using the following guidelines:
  - Listen or watch the tape and write down every utterance made by both you and the child. An utterance need not be a complete sentence. If there is a longish pause, write the next words said as a new utterance.
  - Use a new line for each utterance.
  - Write the child's and adult's utterances in different colours.
  - Note whether any utterance was accompanied by a meaningful sign (S) or gesture (G).

Be sure to write down exactly what was said or seen, not what you expected to hear or see. Sometimes your child's speech may not be clear. Write what was said and put the correct form of the word afterwards in brackets. If the child only makes sounds, try to record these. Below are two examples recorded while a parent and child were reading a book together:

Example 1:
Adult: 'that's a car'
Child: 'car'
Adult: 'push car'
Child: 'br'mm br'mm' (+G)

Example 2
Child: 'drink' (+S)
Adult: 'drink milk'
Child: (drinking sound)
Adult: 'all gone?'
Child: 'all gone' (+G)

Analyse your language sample to gain information about your own language and that of the child. This could include calculation of the ratio of adult–child utterances and the mean length of utterance (MLU) of the child.

Ratio of adult: child utterances

Count the number of utterances spoken by you and the number spoken by the child. If the ratio is more than 2:1 (if there were twice as many utterances by the adult when compared with those of the child) then you are probably talking too much and not giving the child enough opportunity to speak. For example:

Total child utterances:51
Total adult utterances:107 ratio 2:1 (acceptable)
Total adult utterances:150 ratio 3:1 (too many words)

Calculating your MLU and the MLU of the child

To calculate an MLU, count the number of words spoken and divide this by the number of utterances spoken. Do not include signs or gestures here. Calculate the MLU separately for both adult and child. If your MLU is more than a couple of words longer than that of the child, take care to keep your utterances short and simple. For example:

Child MLU: 1.3
Adult MLU: 3.1 (acceptable)
Adult MLU: 5.6 (too many words)

If the child is using a number of signs, sounds and gestures, you may wish to keep a record of the number used during the language sample.

You will expect this number to reduce as more intelligible words are uttered. Keep a record of:

- the total number of signs;
- the total number of sounds;
- the total number of gestures.

If the child uses a mixture of intelligible and unintelligible words, it may be useful also to calculate an MLU for intelligible utterances. This is done by dividing the total number of intelligible words by the total number of utterances, as in the following example:

Total number of intelligible words: 39

Total number of utterances: 32

MLU (intelligible):   1.2

Appendix B
Data Collection

Regular data collection may only be useful for some people. It involves the use by a parent or teacher of simple procedures to record the day-to-day progress of the child with regard to his or her set objectives. Recording the child's progress on a regular basis can tell you accurately whether he or she is learning. Progress may be slow but having a record to show that change is taking place may help to prevent parents and teachers from becoming discouraged.

To collect data and monitor a child's progress you will need data collection sheets suited to the task the child is learning. The following two Data Collection Sheets, Format 1 and Format 2, are examples of suitable forms to record your observations of the child. Similar examples are included in Horstmeier and MacDonald (1978). Each of the two sheets has space to record the following information:

- child's name;
- competency level;
- activity;
- materials needed;
- specific instructions;
- the next step in the programme;
- space for 10 target items and a record of how the child performed over five sessions. One sheet can be used each week, with information recorded from up to five sessions of language practice within a week.

The sheets come in two formats to cover the range of language tasks encompassed in a language programme:

Format 1:   yes/no

This is used when it is necessary only to ascertain whether the child can or cannot perform the required task. For example, does the child:

- look at objects with an adult;
- take turns during a game with a ball;
- take part in functional play with soft toys or cars;
- imitate an action when it is accompanied by a sound.

Format 2:   C-I-C

This is used when the task involves use of expressive language by the child. For example:

Practice level	Specific activity
single word	to label
two words	to use action words

The list of practice targets is usually made up of some easy items to give the child confidence and a number of new items. A decision about when to change the items is generally made on the basis of how quickly the child learns and whether he or she is using items learned in the everyday environment. As a general rule an item will be dropped when a child has completed it successfully for at least three sessions in a row. An item may also be dropped because it is deemed inappropriate if a child has made no progress after two weeks.

The two data collection sheets provide a means for you to compile a useful record of a child's progress throughout the programme. It is important to remember, however, that if any of the people working with the child find recording data difficult it is more important to provide practice opportunities for the child than to record information about the progress on specific language objectives.

Figure B1: Data Collection Sheet, Format 1

Name _____
Activity _____

Competence level _____
Materials needed _____

Activity	Date:			Date:			Date:			Date:		
	Yes	No	Comment	Yes	No	Comment	Yes	No	Comment	Yes	No	Comment
Total												
	Total			Total			Total			Total		

Taking the next step _____

Source: Horstmeier and MacDonald (1978)

Figure B2: Data Collection Sheet, Format 2

Name _____

Activity _____

Competence level _____

Materials needed _____

| Activity | Date: | | | | Date: | | | | Date: | | | | Date: | | | |
	C1	I	C2	Comment	C1	I	C2	Comment	C1	I	C2	Comment	C1	I	C2	Comment
Total																

Taking the next step _____

Source: Horstmeier and MacDonald (1978)

Appendix C
Summary Assessment Sheets

Level 1

Preliminary skills: looking together

Child's name _____ Date _____

Criterion: child is involved in joint attention with adult for at least five seconds.

Procedure: engage child in activity that should attract his or her attention. Encourage the child to look.

Materials: pop-up toy; toy car in bag; picture book or pull-along toy; bell in box; glove puppet; simple pictures.

Scoring child's response: yes = 1; no = 0.

Looking together tasks	Child's response	Comment	Alternative tasks
pop-up toy			pull-along toy
toy in bag			bell in box
finger play			puppet talks to child
picture book			simple pictures
Total			

Pass: three out of four tasks

Emerging: if only one or two tasks are passed, give more practice.

Not yet ready: if no tasks are passed, you should encourage eye contact and tracking or following a moving object.

Figure C1: Preliminary skills: looking together

Preliminary skills: taking turns and imitation

Child's name _____ Date _____

Criterion: child takes a turn or imitates an action or sound in an activity with an adult.

Procedure: adult introduces game and invites child to participate, saying 'do this' or 'your turn', 'my turn'.

Materials: cloth, can, five blocks or toy and cloth, small bean bag, peg board.

Scoring child's response: yes = 1; no = 0.
Note: accept sound-word approximations

Turn-taking and imitation tasks	Child's response	Did child need training to pass item?	Alternative tasks
Turn-taking: push car			throw bean bag
build block tower			take pegs off board
Imitation: clap hands			hit drum
hit table			tap head
rub tummy			wave fingers
drop toy			stamp foot
Total			

Pass: three out of four tasks, including at least two imitation tasks.

Emerging: if two or more tasks are passed, give more practice.

Not yet ready: if only one task is passed, give more practice in turn-taking and imitation activities.

Figure C2: Preliminary skills: taking turns and imitation

Preliminary skills: appropriate play

Child's name _____ Date _____

Criterion: child plays appropriately with objects, either functionally or imaginatively.

Procedure: present items to child. If necessary, say 'Look, you play' or 'What can you do with this/these?'

Materials: car, hairbrush, teapot and cup, book or animal, bowl and spoon, paper and crayon.

Scoring child's response: yes = 1; no = 0.

Appropriate play tasks	Child's response	Did the child need training?	Alternative tasks
toy car			toy animal
hairbrush			cup
teapot			bowl and spoon
book			paper and crayon
Total			

Pass: three out of four tasks.

Emerging: if one or two tasks are passed with or without training, give more practice.

Not yet ready: if no tasks are passed, give more practice in looking together and/or turn-taking and imitation skills.

Figure C3: Preliminary skills: appropriate play

Level 2

Performatives

Child's name_____ Date_____

Criterion: child produces performative sounds during play.

Procedure: introduce a game, make an appropriate sound during the game and encourage the child to imitate you.

Materials: model cars or aeroplanes, model animals or doll and tea-set, musical instruments.

Performative tasks	Child's response	Did the child need prompt to pass?	Alternative tasks
Peek-a-boo			Ring-a-Ring-o'-Roses
model cars			tea-set and doll
model animals			musical instruments
Total			

Pass: if the child passes two out of three tasks, go to the next level in the programme (level 3).

Emerging: if only one task is passed, give more practice.

Not yet ready: if no tasks are passed, go back to imitation and turn-taking skills in the previous level in the programme (level 1).

Figure C4: Performatives

Level 3

First words

Child's name _____ Date _____

Criterion: child produces single words during play.

Procedure: introduce a game, model appropriate words and encourage child to talk.

Materials: large cloth or paper bag, small familiar toys as listed or simple picture book.

Scoring child's response: yes = 1; no = 0.

First words tasks	Child's response	Did the child need a prompt to pass?	Alternative tasks
Spontaneous: ball			shoe
car			doll
cup			hat
spoon			key
Imitated: bell			train
bird			comb
bath			cow
truck			pig
Total			

Pass: if the child passes three out of four tasks in both spontaneous and imitated speech, go to the next chapter on early sentences (level 4).

Emerging: if one or two tasks are passed in either mode, give more practice.

Not yet ready: if no tasks are passed in either mode, go back to the previous level in the programme (level 2).

Note: developmentally appropriate single syllable words may be substituted for both spontaneous and imitated speech for children whose first language is not English. For ideas on choosing words starting with appropriate consonant sounds, see Chapter 11 on phonological development.

Figure C5: First words

Level 4

Early sentences

Child's name _____ Date _____

Early sentence rules	No. of instances observed	percentage use
agent+action		
action+object		
agent+object		
modifier (possession) +object		
modifier (recurrence) +object		
modifier (attribution) +object		
agent/object+location		
action+location		
negation+any word		
introducer+any word		
Total		

Figure C6: Early sentences

Level 5

Communicative intentions

Child's name _____ Date _____

Communicative intention	Example	No. of instances observed	Mode
to indicate			
to obtain desired objects or services			

to regulate actions
   protest
   reject
   request attention			

to initiate, maintain or terminate social interaction			
to obtain information by asking questions			
to discover new words			
to give information			
to answer questions			

Mode: Action (A)
     Gesture (G)
     Sign (S)
     Word (W)			

Figure C7: Communicative intentions

English morphemes

Child's name _____ Date _____

Morpheme	Specific form	No. instances observed	Percentage use
present progressive	-ing		
preposition	in		
preposition	on		
plural (regular)	-s, -es, etc.		
past (irregular)	came, ran, etc.		
possessive	-'s		
uncontracted copula	is, am, are, as in 'is it blue'		
articles	a, the		
past regular	-d, -ed, -/t/		
third person regular	-s, -/z/, etc. as in 'she runs'		
third person irregular	does, has, as in 'they do' vs 'she does'		
uncontracted auxiliary	is, am, are, as in 'is she running?'		
contracted copula	-'s, -'m, -'re, as in 'it's blue'		
contracted auxiliary	-'s, -m, 're, as in 'they're running'		
Total			

MLU	Morphemes acquired
2.0 to 2.5	-ing, in, on, plurals
2.5 to 3.0	past irregular, possessive 's', uncontracted copula
3.0 to 3.7	articles, regular past, third person regular
3.7 to 4.5	third person irregular, uncontracted auxiliary, contracted copula, contracted progressive auxiliary

Figure C8: English morphemes

Appendix D
Observation Record Forms

Child's name _____ Date _____

Gesture (describe physical action or gesture)	Meaning	Date first used

Figure D1: Analysis of gestures

Child's name _____ Date _____

Spontaneous = S; Imitation = I

Word	S	I	Date first used	To whom?	What was going on?	What was the child trying to say?	Was the word used again frequently?

Figure D2: Single words

Child's name _____   Date _____

Phrase	Date first used	To whom?	What was going on?	What was the child trying to say?	Was the phrase used again frequently?

Figure D3: Two, three or more word phrases

Child's name —————————————   Date —————————

Communication mode: Sound = S; Gesture = G; Word = W; Phrase = P

Sound Gesture Word Phrase	Date first used	To whom?	What was going on?	What was the child trying to say?	Was this used again often?

Figure D4: Sounds, gestures, words or phrases

Appendix E
First Words List

Child's name _____   Date _____

Speech mode: spontaneous (S), imitation (I)

People	S-I	Objects	S-I	Location	S-I	Action	S-I	Modifiers	S-I	Socially useful	S-I
Family		banana		up		kiss		more		bye-bye	
Mummy		apple		down		sleep		my		hi	
Daddy		orange		there		want		mine		hello	
baby		bickie		here		wash		your		no	
		lolly		in		eat		big		please	
		cup		out		drink		little		thanks	
		spoon		on		sit		hot		ta	
		nose		off		down		wet		ni-night	
		eye				fall		yuk		goodnight	
child's		comb				comb		that			
name		shoe				brush		this			
Teachers		sock				gone		a			
		chair				all-gone					
		bath				go					
Carers		bed				stop					
		door				throw					
		key									
		ball									

Figure E1: First words list

202

Child's name _____   Date _____

Speech mode: spontaneous (S), imitation (I)

People	S-I	Objects	S-I	Location	S-I	Action	S-I	Modifiers	S-I	Socially useful	S-I
Pets		Teddy				do					
		dolly				open					
		dog				come					
		book				look					
		bike				point					
		bus				jump					
Soft		car				help					
toys		clock									
		light									
Pronouns		T.V.									
me		tree									
I											
you											
mine											

Figure E1: continued

Child's name _____   Date _____

Speech mode: spontaneous (S), imitation (I)

People	S-I	Objects	S-I	Location	S-I	Action	S-I	Modifiers	S-I	Socially useful	S-I

Figure E2: First words list – record form

Appendix F
Brown's 14 Grammatical Morphemes and their Order of Acquisition

Order of acquisition	Morphemes	Specific form(s)
1	Present progressive	-ing
2–3	Prepositions	in, on
4	Plural (regular)	-s, -es, etc.
5	Past irregular	came, ran, etc.
6	Possessive	-'s
7	Uncontracted copula	is, am, are (as in: she *is* pretty)
8	Articles	a, the
9	Past regular	-d, -ed, -/t/
10	Third person regular	-s, -/z/, etc. (as in: 'she runs')
11	Third person irregular	does, has (as in: 'they do' versus 'she does')
12	Uncontracted auxiliary	is, am, are (as in: 'they are running')
13	Contracted copula	-'s, -'m, -'re (for example 'she's pretty')
14	Contracted auxiliary	-'s, -'m, -'re (for example 'they're running')

From McLean and L.K. Snyder-McLean (1978).

Appendix G
Articulation Development and Australian Norms

Age at which 75% accuracy is expected
Age (years, months)

3	h	ŋ	p	m	w	b	n	d	t	j	k	g	ʒ
3.6	f											
4	l	ʃ	tʃ									
4.6	s	z	dʒ									
5	r											
6	v											
8	ð											
8.6	θ											

Phonetic symbol	Key words Initial	Medial	Final
h	hat	behind	
ŋ		singer	wing
p	pie	happy	top
m	me	coming	some
w	wet	hour	
b	be	cubby	rub
n	no	funny	when
d	do	muddy	said
t	tie	letter	cat
j	you	beyond	
k	key	pocket	like
g	go	bigger	leg
ʒ		measure	
f	fun	coffee	laugh
l	leg	follow	ball
ʃ	she	pushing	wash
tʃ	chin	kitchen	watch

s	see	pussy	mess
z	zoo	easy	hose
dʒ	jump	magic	edge
r	run	borrow	
v	vest	ever	stove
ð	this	other	smooth
θ	thumb	nothing	both

Source: Kilminster and Laird (1983).

Appendix H
Resources for Use in a Parent-based Programme

The materials included here were developed for use with parents in the early language project described in Chapter 14. The procedures followed in the project have been described in Part 2 of this book and were derived, in part, on the ideas for language intervention described by Horstmeier and MacDonald (1978). The four resources set out below include:

- *Stages in Learning to Talk.* This provides a description of children's behaviour as they acquire language. It is given to parents at the first meeting with the language teacher as a source of information about the sequence of skills that are expected to emerge as children learn to talk.
- *Talking to Children.* This reviews some of the ways in which adults can assist children to begin to communicate more effectively. Ideas for communicating with infants and young children at the pre-linguistic stage are identified and strategies are suggested to use when interacting with young children who are learning to talk.
- *Encouraging Play.* This is an introduction to the concept of play and to the ways in which adults can interact with their children to develop appropriate play skills and, at the same time, encourage early language.
- The *Parent Inventory.* This provides a list of questions designed to elicit basic information about the child and his or her current language skills at home. Information is also sought about parents' main concerns and expectations for the child. Parents are also asked to complete some simple observation tasks based on the type of activities that are included at each stage of the language programme. The Inventory was developed from the *Oliver,* a parent information form associated with Horstmeier and MacDonald (1978).

Stages in Learning to Talk

Pre-programme stage: uncontrolled vocalising

Initially infants' vocalising is largely triggered by physical events. They cry because of hunger or pain. Soon they learn to vocalise for their own entertainment with squeals and shouts when alone in the cot. The sounds produced at such times are often interpreted as meaningful by care-givers, but there is no evidence that babies produce the sounds consciously, to cause an effect on a listener.

Stage 1: preliminary skills: looking together, turn-taking, imitation and appropriate play

As infants develop, they acquire increasingly complex sets of behaviour for exploring their environment, learning about objects and people, and playing. Initially they mostly put objects in their mouth, but gradually they learn to bang, throw or wave them. These strategies become increasingly complex. They learn to put small objects inside larger ones, or to bang two objects together to create an interesting effect. Some of these actions are learned by accident while others are learned during play sessions with familiar adults, in games involving looking together, imitation and turn-taking.

Stage 2: pre-verbal skills: performatives and protowords

Performatives

Early play routines often include a sound within a set of actions, such as 'ee-ee' to accompany a pop-up toy or 'oops' when the doll falls off the table. These consistent sounds associated with actions are called performatives.

Many early sounds appear to be imitations of interesting noises heard by the child, such as 'tick tick' (clock), 'toot toot' (bus or car), or a tongue click (horse). Other sounds reflect familiar speech patterns such as lip-smacking for preferred food, humming when tired and ready for bed, or 'oh oh' when someone falls over.

Protowords

The earliest signs of language appear when the infant begins to combine contact with objects and interactions with adults in one event. For example, the infant has watched entranced as a wind-up car turned circles for some time and has also often watched Daddy wind up a toy to activate it. The signs of early language appear when the child attempts to attract the father's attention to wind the toy by using a consistent gesture or sound. These early consistent word-like sounds are called 'protowords'.

Some children create their own word-like sounds for particular experiences. These are used consistently with familiar adults, who understand the meaning of the sounds. Normally such protowords are abandoned as the child learns to use more conventional word forms, as when 'car' replaces 'brmm brmm' or 'bottle' is used instead of a sucking noise.

Stage 3: first words

Children's first words are usually associated with experiences that have a high level of interest for them. For example, they often label things that move or change ('gone'), make a noise ('car') and are colourful ('balloon'). Words are used first to draw the attention of an adult to events of high interest ('plane', 'bird'). Later, they use words in other ways; for example, to reject an invitation ('no' to avoid a bath) or to obtain objects or services ('ball' to get a ball or to play with it in a game). Most first words are labels for objects and people, although a range of other words are also acquired to represent actions ('ride'), states ('wet'), attributes ('big') and other meanings ('bye', 'more').

Stage 4: combining words – putting two words together and early sentences

Current evidence suggests that once children have about 30 or more words of various types, they begin to combine them into simple sentences. The way they sequence these words directly reflects their experiences or perception of the world. Initially they use single words to represent a variety of meanings: for example, 'drink' can mean a glass of milk or the act of drinking. Later, more explicit action words are acquired, such as 'want' and 'go'. These are eventually paired with labels to make simple sentences like 'want drink', 'go car' and 'Mummy car', or phrases like 'my car' and 'big ball'.

After children have learned to combine two words to express a variety of meaning, they begin to string more words together to produce longer sentences, such as:

'me want' + 'want drink' = 'me want drink'

'go car' + 'Mummy car' = 'go Mummy car'

At this stage children start to express more detailed information by adding words for colour, size, possession and so on, as in 'me go big red car', 'want blue ball'.

When the child has achieved these skills, it may be claimed that the basic elements of the language system have been acquired.

Stage 5: extending meaning: using English morphemes

Once children are using three- and four-word sentences you will observe them beginning to use parts of our adult grammar system to indicate, for example, plurals, present and past tense, as in words such as 'cars', 'running', 'goed' (went) and 'fell'. By this stage, they have mastered the most difficult tasks in learning to talk. Future progress will involve learning more words, more complex grammar and more sophisticated use of language skills.

Table H1: A summary of the stages in learning to talk

Pre-linguistic stage	Early vocalising: parents attach meaning to infant sounds that are not yet intentional
Stage 1	Preliminary skills • looking together • turn-taking and imitation • appropriate play
Stage 2	Pre-verbal skills • performatives ('br'mm', 'quack-quack') • protowords (word-like vocalisations)
Stage 3	First words ('dog', 'Mum', 'car')

Stage 4	Combining words • putting two words together ('Daddy car', 'dog gone') • early sentences ('boy fall down', 'cat go there')
Stage 5	Extending meaning • adding English morphemes, (plural 's' as in 'dogs')

Talking to Children

Communication begins in infancy, long before the child is able to produce first words. This stage is crucial because it is the period when all the necessary skills that proceed language are established. This is the time when mothers respond to the child as if the signals were meaningful; for example, while feeding, changing or soothing a crying child. Through this process the child learns that he or she can cause things to happen.

As the child's repertoire of actions and sounds increases, the responsive adult will begin to join in the child's 'game'. Sounds made by the child are imitated back by the mother or carer, introducing the earliest form of turn-taking. Mothers will poke out their tongues, shake their heads and imitate the child's gestures. They will follow the child's gaze and pointed finger, and then pass the toy to the child, or move the mobile as if in response to a request to do so. Soon the child seems to make the gesture or sound intentionally, and once this happens, the interaction that is occurring can be called truly communicative. When the baby puts up his or her arms to be lifted out of the cot, mothers say 'up'. Soon the baby learns to signal that he or she wants to be lifted out, and as sounds develop, will make appropriate gestures and approximations to the word 'up' to say 'take me out of here!'

These early 'games', in the context of the baby and carer's shared interactions in everyday routines, become the basis for all later language learning. The carer is responsive to the child's needs, and to early attempts to communicate. As the child becomes more competent, gestures turn into sounds, and babbling sounds become more specific. Gradually, the carer extends what is expected of the child, waiting for a sound to be made with the gesture before lifting the infant from the cot. The adult's aim is to involve the child in conversation, to provide a context or meaning for the gestures and early sounds. This process can be described as providing 'scaffolding'. It assists the child to move from an immature to a more mature level of communication. What children can do today in co-operation, tomorrow they will be able to do on their own.

Responding to the child

The most important factor in facilitating language acquisition is the responsiveness of the mother or carer to the child. This continues to be of paramount importance at all stages of the child's development.

The 'responsiveness' idea suggests that the purpose of adult speech is to involve the child in conversation, because it is only through participation in language experiences that the child learns all facets of the language system. The adult provides a conversational framework which allows for the child's lack of skills. As a result, the child is able to take part in meaningful interaction with another person. Through these experiences the child gradually learns the various skills needed for effective use of language. Until these skills are acquired, the adult partner has to sustain the conversation by encouraging the child to respond or, in some instances, by taking the child's turn. The importance of involving children in conversation about topics of shared interest and activity cannot be overstated.

The practical implications of engaging children in conversation are tied in with what was learned earlier about needing a reason to communicate. If the child is not motivated to communicate, no learning will take place. The key to successful interaction with young children is to follow their lead. Language experiences and interaction with language partners need to be concerned with the topic or activity in which the child is currently interested. The partner needs to keep the conversation going, allowing each person to take turns in talking. The longer the topic is maintained, with both partners taking a turn to say something, the more opportunities the child has for participating in a conversation, while also receiving feedback and responses to his or her communicative acts. The adult should also take care to encourage conversations initiated by the child by responding in a manner which encourages continued talking. If new topics are constantly being introduced by the adult, the child has fewer opportunities for feedback.

Respond to the child. Follow his or her lead in play or during routine daily activities. Talk about things that are taking place in the here and now, things that interest and involve the child. Encourage participation, giving plenty of opportunity for turn-taking. Allow plenty of time to respond. Sometimes adults are too quick to jump in with another comment, not realising that the child needed more time to work out what to say. Making a reply means finding the right words and putting them in the right order. These are skills adults take for granted, but they are hard work when you are first acquiring them. Talk about what the child is doing, respond to what he or she is trying to say, even if all the sounds and words are not quite correct. Children play an active role in their language learning and you need to encourage them.

Conversation skills

The complexity of the skills needed to take part in conversations was referred to earlier. This process begins in earliest infancy, when you interpret the baby's early sounds and actions. Adults must take both roles in the interaction until the time when the infant can take a turn, saying 'mumumum', waiting for the mother to echo the sound before saying it again; or pointing to the teddy bear and waiting for the mother to pass it. Children need so much assistance from a caring adult who is also a competent communicative partner because the skills involved in conversation are so complicated and difficult to master. They require constant opportunities to practise, in a wide variety of contexts, with plenty of encouragement and feed back. The skills involved in conversation include:

- listening to the sounds of the message
- understanding the meaning
- thinking about how they want to respond
- selecting the right gesture, sounds or words to reply
- taking turns at the appropriate moment – not interrupting
- checking to see if their message has been understood

The whole process is repeated again and again, with the child gradually becoming increasingly competent in selecting the correct gestures, sounds, words or word combinations to convey a message. They also begin to learn when to wait and listen and when to speak and take their turn, how to initiate and obtain the attention of the person they want to communicate with, to share the messages which are becoming an increasingly important part of social interaction.

Helping slow, non-initiating children

The importance of 'responsiveness' has been a recurring theme in the discussion on how adults interact with young children. But what happens if you have a child who is passive and rarely initiates any activity or sound? This is a very difficult situation for a parent or carer and often the lack of response from the child can lead to the adult 'giving up' and in fact spending less time with their child. In this situation the carer needs to use all the ingenuity that can be mustered to try to get a reaction from the child. As with very young infants, take both roles in the interaction when carrying out the daily routines of dressing, bathing, feeding and so on. Talk about the immediate situation. Attract the child's attention to noisy toys, coloured mobiles, moving leaves, trains going by, and the myriad of things we take for granted in our daily lives.

Respond enthusiastically to any reaction the child makes. Repeat the sound or gesture, and tell the child how clever he or she is for making it.

Familiar routines and nursery rhymes can be used over and over, with the adult taking all roles, while involving the child as much as possible, until finally the child will make a response. The most important qualities in this situation are perseverance and patience, and faith that your efforts will be rewarded by an increasingly interactive, communicative partner. The less a child responds or talks, the more opportunity and encouragement is needed. Initiate interaction in every situation, then react to any response the child makes. This will help the child to take the first step, which, once achieved, will be followed by an increased willingness to join in and take a turn. This will eventually lead to the child attracting your attention with a message he or she wishes to share.

With children who have a very short attention span, the problem is compounded but the response is the same. There is also the added necessity to change the topic or stimulating event more frequently, and ensure that the consequences of any participation are very rewarding. Be very alert to any appropriate behaviour, and acknowledge and encourage any participation.

Strategies

There are many strategies that can be used in interacting with young language-learning children. There is no clear guideline about when any particular strategy is appropriate, but they will all have a place in your interactions with young language-learners.

Directives or commands

Research has shown that too many commands reduce the child's opportunity to choose the topic and to talk about what is of interest. This may be worth remembering as you recall how important it is to be responsive to the child. However, there are situations where directives are needed to attract the child's attention, and to encourage participation in a game or activity. This may be particularly true for slower, more passive children, or those with difficult behaviours. A balance is needed, and using an enthusiastic tone of voice will help.

Questions

Questions are a great way of engaging the attention of a child. However, if used too frequently they will limit the child's capacity to follow his or her own interests. Some questions restrict the type of answer that is appropriate, such as questions that can only be answered by a 'Yes' or

'No', or a single word, as in 'Are you hot?' or 'Do you want an apple or a banana?' Open-ended questions give the child more scope to express what he/she thinks or wants; for example, 'What shall we do now?' and 'What will we eat?' Remember to give the child time to respond.

Comments

Comments give you a chance to respond to what the child is doing or saying. They also allow the child to take another turn as you negotiate the topic or game together. This strategy will encourage the child to talk about what he or she is thinking or doing, and allows you to use simple phrases and sentences to talk about what you are doing together. For example:

'Teddy's having a bath'
'We're going shopping'

Modelling

The strategy of modelling can help provide the child with the language needed to extend his or her talk about the things that are of interest. This can be done as you comment and take turns in any interaction that takes place, in a game or a routine daily activity.

For example: 'Lucy's going to bed'

Acknowledge what the child is saying

This is an important part of being responsive to the child. It encourages him or her to make the effort to keep taking a turn in the interaction. A lot of effort goes into saying the things that make up a conversation, so be sure you acknowledge everything that is said. This makes the child feel that his or her contribution is valued and that you are interested in it. It also allows the child to take another turn after you have acknowledged what was said last time. For example:

Child: 'Tree'   Adult: 'It is a big tree'
Child: 'Train go'   Adult: 'The train is going fast'

Expansions

Expansions are statements that provide a little bit more information than was contained in the child's statement. They allow the child to hear new words that can gradually be included in utterances, as he or she becomes able to use more words together. For example:

Child:	'Bear's eating'
Adult:	'Bear's eating toast'
Child:	'Eating toast'

Child:	'Boy ball'
Adult:	'Boy's kicking the ball'
Child:	'Yes, boy kick ball'

The expansion acknowledges what the child has already said, and extends it a little bit further, providing a model for the child's next turn, or for use in a later conversation.

Corrections

Learning to talk is a complex task which involves sounds, meaning, words and grammar. Given the opportunity and encouragement, most children will master the task eventually. Some sounds and words are harder to say than others, and words can come out in a funny order. But if you focus on the errors and constantly criticise, you are likely to discourage the child's willingness to make future attempts. A better way of dealing with this situation is to acknowledge what the child has said, and to model the correct version. For example:

'Yes, it's a big grey elephant'
'Oh dear, it is a big step'

Feedback

Make sure the child knows that he or she is doing well, and that you appreciate the things you are doing together, and what he or she is trying to tell you. Make the child feel worthwhile and valued. Encourage every attempt to communicate.

Summary

What children need most when they are learning language is responsive parents or carers, quick to identify an opportunity for interaction, and sensitive to the language-learning stage that the child has reached. What adults need most is to understand how children learn language, what stages they pass through, and how they can facilitate the language-learning process. Adults cannot 'teach' children language. But they can provide an optimal language-learning environment by observing and responding to all the communicative attempts that children make. They also need to involve the children in increasingly complex joint play activities which enable them to learn about the world and, finally, to talk about it.

Encouraging Play

Play is an important part of each child's development. In the process of learning to play, children go through a variety of stages from very simple exploration of objects to more complex representational or 'pretend' play where they take on a variety of roles. Examples of 'pretend' play include games like 'mothers and fathers' or 'cowboys and Indians'. Through these play activities, children are able to explore and learn about the environment and their place in it. Play is used to help them adjust to new situations, such as the birth of a new baby, and to understand relationships, as in games that involve re-enacting familiar domestic situations.

Over the years of their development, children need to progress through each of the stages of play. However, some children, particularly those experiencing difficulties in other aspects of development, seem to miss a stage in their play or become stuck at a particular level. When this happens, you may need to encourage and help them learn more complex play skills. So it is important that you think about your role in helping children learn to play.

It has been said that play is children's work, but children can very quickly 'switch off' if we approach a play activity as if it is work. Work means effort and doing what someone else wants, whereas play should be something that you do because you want to do it. It should be flexible and, above all, it should be fun. Since many early language skills are acquired through play, you also need to ensure that, at each stage, you encourage play activities that will support the acquisition of these skills.

For very small children, the world must often seem large and forbidding. They need to be near Mum or someone familiar for support and security. They will follow you around as you work, often getting in your way, whining for you to notice them. If you sit down, they will come and beg to be noticed. This is often a good time to stop what you are doing and play for a little while.

If you find it difficult to play, try starting off by just sitting near the child while he or she is playing quietly. If you possibly can, get down on the floor, close to the child. If this feels strange to you, try sitting down with something to do that makes you feel comfortable and at ease, such as a magazine or some other simple activity. When the child is happily playing, look at what he or she is doing. The child will be happy that you are near, showing interest and approval. After a while, the child will approach you, perhaps to show you a toy. You can then comment on what has been happening in the game. Soon, you will be following the child's lead, playing happily together. This will give you both a sense of closeness.

With joint attention established, you are now in a position to guide and extend the child in play. At this stage, children love to be cuddled and your smiles and laughter will also show that you approve. Remember, to stop, watch and listen to the child during the time you spend together.

When you and the child are comfortable sitting together and playing, you can start introducing new toys and actions, and new ways of using familiar toys. For example, you can take turns to feed and bath Teddy, build a bridge for the cars, or throw the ball. These simple turn-taking routines will encourage the child to play with you and develop new play skills. Do not expect the child to follow your every idea, and give encouragement when he or she discovers new ways of doing things, without your help.

As you play, remember to comment on your own and the child's actions. Include appropriate gestures and sounds in the game and encourage the child when these 'performative' sounds are used. These are important forerunners of the words that the child will eventually start to use.

At this stage it is also important that there is a variety of things to play with so that the child can choose what is of interest. These need not be expensive. Blocks, balls, old containers that small objects can be put into, things to roll and shake, cloths that can be used as blankets or to play Peek-a-boo, old plastic and cardboard containers and kitchen utensils are all acceptable to children. It is a good idea to have a box or cupboard where the child can have ready access and is free to explore these toys. New objects can be added from time to time and broken items or those which have lost interest can be removed. Select simple toys that are easy to manipulate and interest the child. This will avoid or lessen the inevitable frustration that comes with a toy that is too difficult or complicated. It will also enable you to build up a positive and happy relationship in which the child wants to learn from you.

Parent Inventory

Today's date: _____ Who is completing the report? _____

Address: _____ Phone: _____

Child's name: _____ Birthdate: _____

Brothers' and sisters' names:_____   _____   _____

                    Ages: _____   _____   _____

Mother's name: _____ Father's name: _____

Phone: _____ Phone: _____

Occupation: _____ Occupation: _____

If English is not the only language spoken in child's home, what other languages are spoken?
_____

Has your child been in a playgroup, preschool, nursery school or class or other early childhood
programme during the past year?   Yes ☐   No ☐   If yes,

Name of centre: _____

Address: _____

Teacher's name: _____ Telephone _____

Who plays best with the child?   _____

Who else spends a good deal of time with the child (relatives, siblings, friends, teachers)?
_____

What are your child's favourite toys? _____

What does your child enjoy doing? _____

What does your child like to eat or drink? _____

Has your child's hearing or sight been tested?   Yes ☐   No ☐

If yes, please give details:

	Date	Results and Comments
Hearing	_____	_____
Sight	_____	_____

Has your child been seen professionally by anyone for speech and language?
Yes ☐   No ☐   If yes,
Who: _____   Where: _____   When: _____
Did this lead to any treatment?   Yes ☐   No ☐   If yes, what, if any, activities were
given to help your child's speech and language? _____
_____

What do you feel are some reasons for your child's speech or language delay? _____
_____
_____

Do you feel your child has any other problems that affect speech or language development?
_____
_____

Would you like your child to improve in any of the following skills? Please tick.

Skill area	Yes (tick)	Comments
eating		
drinking		
toileting		
walking		
using hands		
attending		
listening		
playing		
talking		
understanding speech		
following directions		
behaviour		
getting along with other children		
other (please specify)		

What aspects of your child's development are you most worried about? _____
_____
_____

How well do you think your child will communicate eventually? _____
_____
_____

During the last six months, have these skills changed? Are they more, about the same or less?
Please tick.

Skills	More	About the same	Less	Comments
sounds				
words				
asking questions				
trying to communicate				
understanding speech				
talking to self				

Skills	More	About the same	Less	Comments
talking to others				
playing alone				
playing with others				

If your child talks, does he or she:

Skills	Yes	No	Give example
name people or things			
ask for help, eg 'drink', 'wash dolly'			
ask for information, eg 'what's that?' or 'where's bubba?'			
imitate speech			
call someone			
greet someone			
talk to self			
give information eg 'Daddy home'			

What do you expect your child to do next in his or her communication development?

_____

_____

Are you doing anything special at present to help your child to communicate better? If yes, please give details: _____

_____

_____

What kind of help, if any, do you want for your child at the moment? _____

_____

_____

Is there anything else you would like to tell us about your child? _____

_____

_____

Observation tasks

Play with your child and see what he or she does. Choose a time when you both feel good and are ready to play together. Use toys or books that you know the child enjoys. Follow the child's lead. Talk about what you are both doing. There is no need to complete all sections of the Observation Task in the one session.

Looking together and attending

Use three objects that the child knows such as a soft toy, small car or ball. Show them to the child, one by one. Let the child touch or play with each one after looking at it. Which objects did the child look at and approximately how long (in seconds) did he or she play with each object?

Did the child look at it?

Object	Yes	No	How long (seconds)?
1. _____	_____	_____	_____
2. _____	_____	_____	_____
3. _____	_____	_____	_____

Appropriate play

Play with your child for at least five minutes with three familiar toys or objects. If necessary, show your child how to play with the toys. As you play, watch the way the child plays with the toys. Be sure you select toys or objects that your child has already played with or seen.

Toy or object	What did child do?	Comment
1.		
2.		
3.		

Imitating actions

Using toys and objects that the child is familiar with, such as a car, ball, spoon and cup or a doll, choose some actions that you know the child can do, such as pushing the car, rolling the ball or feeding the doll. Make sure the child is watching as you do each of the actions and encourage the child to imitate you. Say 'Do this' or ' (child's name), do this'. Praise the child if he or she imitates your action.

Action	Yes	Almost	No	Comment
1.				
2.				
3.				

Imitating sounds

Select three sounds you have heard the child make. When your child is watching you, make each of the sounds and encourage imitation. Encourage the child to look at you and say, for example, '(child's name), say ba'. Model each sound no more than three times.

Sounds	Did the child imitate you?			
	Yes	Almost	No	Comment
1.				
2.				
3.				

Imitating words

Show the child three familiar objects that you know the child can say, such as a cup, an apple or a ball. Encourage the child to look at you or the object and imitate you when you label each object. Encourage the child to imitate the name of the object. Say '(child's name), say ball'. Model each word no more than three times.

Word	Yes	Almost	No	Comment
1.				
2.				
3.				

Understanding object labels

Find three objects that are very familiar to the child, such as a soft toy, a hat or a book. Encourage the child to touch, point or in some way show you each object as you name it. Say '(child's name)', show me teddy'. Give the child no more than three opportunities to show you that he or she understands the object labels.

Object label	What did the child do?	Comment
1.		
2.		
3.		

Understanding action words

Find three objects that you know are familiar to your child, such as a car, a soft toy and a teapot and cup. Ask the child to show you what to do with the objects. Say 'Show me how the car goes', 'Show me how teddy walks' and 'Show me how you pour some tea'.

What did you say?	What did child do?	Comment
1.		
2.		
3.		

Following directions

Find three objects that are familiar to the child. Select an action for the child to carry out with each object. Choose actions that you know the child understands and can do. Ask the child to do each action. For example, 'show me how you kiss dolly', 'show me how you put the car in the box', 'show me how you brush hair'.

What did you say?	What did the child do?	Comment
1.		
2.		
3.		

Using language

Play with your child using the same objects you selected to answer the previous questions. Now do the following tasks.

Object labels

Ask the child to name the objects you are playing with.

Object	What did the child say?	Comment
1.		
2.		
3.		

Action words

Ask the child to tell you what is happening when you do something with the toys you are playing with. Say 'what's happening?' while you make the dolly walk, kiss the teddy or drink from the cup.

Action	What did the child say?	Comment
1. _____	_____	_____
2. _____	_____	_____
3. _____	_____	_____

Now make a list of the gestures, sounds and words used by your child while you played together. Write down what the child says on the Communication Record Form.

Communication Record Form

Sounds, Gestures, Words or Phrases

Child's name _____ Date _____

Sound, Gesture Word, Phrase	Date first used	To whom?	What was going on?	What was the child trying to say?	Was this used again often?

Index